Hunter-Gatherers

Archaeological and Evolutionary Theory

INTERDISCIPLINARY CONTRIBUTIONS TO ARCHAEOLOGY

Hunter-Gatherers

Archaeological and Evolutionary Theory

ROBERT L. BETTINGER

University of California, Davis
Davis, California

PLENUM PRESS • NEW YORK AND LONDON

Library of Congress Cataloging-in-Publication Data

Bettinger, Robert L.
    Hunter-gatherers : archaeological and evolutionary theory / Robert
L. Bettinger.
        p.   cm. -- (Interdisciplinary contributions to archaeology)
    Includes bibliographical references and index.
    ISBN 0-306-43650-7
    1. Hunting and gathering societies. 2. Social evolution. 3. Man,
Prehistoric.   I. Title. II. Series.
GN407.3.B48   1991
303.4--dc20   90-25228
                                                                    CIP

10 9 8 7 6 5 4

ISBN 0-306-43650-7

© 1991 Plenum Press, New York
A Division of Plenum Publishing Corporation
233 Spring Street, New York, N.Y. 10013

Printed in the United States of America

Preface

Hunter-gatherers are the quintessential anthropological topic. They constitute the subject matter that, in the last instance, separates anthropology from its sister social science disciplines: psychology, sociology, economics, and political science. In that central position, hunter-gatherers are the acid test to which any reasonably comprehensive anthropological theory must be applied. Several such theories—some narrow, some broad—are examined in light of the hunter-gatherer case in this book. My purpose, then, is that of a review of ideas rather than of a literature. I do not—probably could not—survey all that has been written about hunter-gatherers: Many more works are ignored than considered. That is not because the ones ignored are uninteresting, but because it is my broader purpose to concentrate on certain theoretical contributions to anthropology in which hunter-gatherers figure most prominently.

The book begins with two chapters that deal with the history of anthropological research and theory in relation to hunter-gatherers. The point is not to present a comprehensive or even-handed accounting of developments. Rather, I sketch a history of selected ideas that have determined the manner in which social scientists have viewed, and thus studied, hunter-gatherers. This lays the groundwork for subjects subsequently addressed and establishes two fundamental points. First, the social sciences have always portrayed hunter-gatherers in ways that serve their theories; in short, hunter-gatherer research has always been a theoretical enterprise. Second, these theoretical treatments have generally been either evolutionary or materialist—or both—in perspective.

The remainder of the book explores evolutionary and materialist perspectives in relation to contemporary theoretical contributions to hunter-gatherer studies of two kinds.

The first consists of hunter-gatherer research that is governed by theories of limited sets, that is, those that speak to limited sets of behaviors. By definition it is the job of limited theories to reconcile general principles to particular cases by showing how such cases result from the general principle in the presence of special conditions. The presence of such conditions is both necessary and sufficient to identify a case as belonging to the set for which the theory is intended—such classifications being, thus, theory based. It is, further, the interaction between the general principle and the salient properties of the special, set-defining conditions that accounts for what is observed. Theories of limited sets can serve as either interim steps in the construction of general theories or means of articulating extant general theory (Kuhn 1962:24-34). Either way it is clear that limited theories are no less "theoretical" than theories of general sets—they are simply less general.

By design, limited theories are practical and meant for application in the real world: They are theories that have, in archaeological parlance, direct test implications. I attend particularly to research guided by two limited theories that have dominated hunter-gatherer archaeology and ethnography over the last decade: middle-range theory research (the subject of Chapter 3) and optimal foraging theory (the subject of Chapters 4–5). Sections of these chapters draw upon ideas originally put forward in an earlier work (Bettinger 1987) that appeared in Volume 16 of the *Annual Review of Anthropology*.

The second kind of hunter-gatherer research addressed here is governed by theories of general sets, or general theories. Such theories are constructed of fundamental principles that are meant to apply to widely divergent phenomena and for that reason are often highly abstract and their meaning difficult to grasp. The general theories in question here attempt to account for the elementary logic that underlies human behaviors of all kinds; our interest in them relates to their potential application to hunter-gatherers. Of special importance here are theoretical constructions grounded in two fundamentally different schools of thought: neo-Marxism, including especially structural/French Marxism (the subject of Chapter 6) and neo-Darwinism. Within the latter I distinguish and treat separately evolutionary ecology (the subject of Chapter 7) and more recent theories of cultural transmission (the subject of Chapter 8). With a few exceptions, hunter-gatherer archaeology has in recent times deliberately avoided this sort of general theory. As I will make clear, that is clearly to its detriment.

By way of introduction, lastly, the reader will undoubtedly note that I seem at times to be addressing two rather different audiences, one archaeological, the other anthropological. This is intentional, for as I hope to make clear, hunter-gatherers are today—and have been historically—a common ground upon which converge many disparate subdisciplines within anthropology and, within those subdisciplines, many different points of view. As I hope to make clear further, the development and current state of hunter-gatherer research is such that there is no clear distinction between archaeology and ethnology as regards either theory or subject matter. Indeed, the time has long since past when hunter-gatherer archaeologists could afford to ignore anthropological theory and theorists and the ethnographic record, just as the time is also long past when anthropologists and ethnographers interested in hunter-gatherers could afford to ignore archaeological theory and theorists and the archaeological record.

Acknowledgments

The list of individuals who contributed in fundamental ways to this book is almost endless. My colleague and close friend, Bill Davis, directed my attention to references, listened to my ideas, and read and commented on most of the manuscript for this book. Chapter 6 largely derives from a graduate seminar on Marxism and Anthropology given in the spring of 1986; Davis and I were listed as co-instructors but he was the guiding force. Another close colleague and friend, Peter Richerson, offered similar assistance and likewise read and commented on the entire draft. In the fall of 1988, Robert Boyd and the other participants, in a continuing seminar series in cultural evolution offered by Richerson and me, read and commented on Chapters 1–2. These seminars were supported in part by the Sloan Foundation. Boyd has, in addition, been particularly helpful in contributing comments and advice pertaining to the quantitative modeling of evolutionary processes. Another participant in our cultural evolution seminar, Clyde Wilson, provided helpful comments on the work of his former professor, Leslie White. Dave Meltzer also selflessly agreed to read and comment on Chapters 1–2. His detailed observations, frank criticisms, and helpful suggestions pointing me to sources I had ignored caused me to rewrite both chapters in their entirety and made it possible for me to avoid many foolish errors of fact and logic. Yet one more close colleague and friend, Aram Yengoyan, is another who read and commented on the first two chapters. His ideas about the history of anthropology, especially the work of Morgan and Kroeber, proved quite useful.

Bruce Winterhalder deserves special credit. He read the entire draft—and sent 12 single-spaced pages of comments and observations. This caused me to rethink and rewrite several chapters, most notably 4–5 and 7–8. I am also indebted to Mike Jochim, whose enthusiasm encouraged me to undertake this project, and Eliot Werner, whose support helped me see it through. Several other individuals contributed in more subtle ways to the ideas set down here:

Marty Orans, Tom Beidelman, Don Grayson, Dave Thomas, Jim O'Connell, Dave Madsen, Judy Polanich, Gary Macey, and Mike Delacorte. Thanks also are due to the staff of the Department of Anthropology: Nancy McLaughlin, Sandi Williams, Jane Foster, Debbie Pederson, and Gayle Bacon.

Finally, none of this would have been possible without the constant support and encouragement of my wife Sharon and son Ian. Many precious hours that should have been spent with them were poured into this book.

Contents

Hunter–Gatherers

**Archaeological and
Evolutionary Theory**

Chapter 1

Progressive Social Evolution and Hunter-Gatherers

INTRODUCTION

It is commonly held that early accounts of hunter-gatherers are primarily descriptive and that evolutionary and materialist social theories and explicitly evolutionary and materialist accounts of hunter-gatherers are uniquely mid-twentieth-century inventions. This is simply not so. Hunter-gatherer research has traditionally been undertaken within explicit theoretical frameworks and all but the most recent and doctrinaire interpretations of hunter-gatherers, evolutionary and materialist alike, are constructed out of arguments and assumptions that are hundreds, sometimes thousands, of years old. The first two chapters of this book examine some of the more important of these theories and assumptions and the larger intellectual traditions in which they participated to provide a broader sense of the theoretical and historical context in which modern hunter-gatherer studies are embedded.

The fact of the matter is that whether describing or interpreting, students of hunter-gatherers have historically adopted interpretive perspectives that are comparative, evolutionary, and materialist. That is abundantly clear from the ancient and familiar justification that hunter-gatherers are worth studying because they represent an antique stage of human culture—a living snapshot of human life in its oldest, most primitive state (Sollas 1915:389; Forde 1934:371). Hunter-gatherer research, ethnographic and prehistoric, has traditionally

1

emphasized cultural features that have obvious comparative or evolutionary implications, and hunter-gatherers have frequently and effectively served students of mankind as yardsticks against which the developments of other more culturally evolved and highly accomplished peoples can be compared (Pearce 1988:200, 208). They have been equally instrumental in illustrating the intimate relationships that exist between human societies and the natural environments in which they live.

Hunter-gatherers, however, have contributed more to anthropology than illustration: The theories of anthropology have been shaped in fundamental ways by hunter-gatherers. It was primarily in response to direct encounters with primitive peoples, many of them hunter-gatherers, that anthropology itself arose. Subsequent attempts to understand hunter-gatherer lifeways have directly contributed to the development of many powerful anthropological theories: structural-functionalism, environmental possibilism, structuralism, cultural ecology, and neofunctionalism, to name but a few. It is arguable, indeed, that what distinguishes anthropology from other social sciences is that it has theories of primitives and that anthropology did not and could not emerge as a separate discipline until there were such theories. Note that here I am using the term *primitive* in its traditional sense: to denote an evolutionary stage of development and identify peoples whose technologies, organizations, and cultures are, relatively speaking, "undeveloped"; peoples whose support is dependent on relatively simple tools and strategies—most often lacking benefit of either metal tools or domesticated plants or animals—and whose activities are organized around small local groups that are more or less economically, socially, and politically autonomous. The definition of "primitive" is central to anthropology in that it designates a core subject matter. It remains as true today as in the past that no anthropological theory can lay any credible claim to generality until put to the test against primitive peoples, hunter-gatherers in particular. Hunter-gatherers are not merely a part of anthropology, they are one of its cornerstones. Indeed, some would argue that to the degree that anthropology has lost sight of this basic premise in the last few decades so has the discipline lost its central focus and direction.

It is not stretching the point too far to observe, further, that the intellectual significance of hunter-gatherers has often extended beyond anthropology. It was hunter-gatherers, sometimes imagined, sometimes real, that prompted the philosophical inquiries and provided the subject matter out of which were built some of the more influential theories of adaptation and evolution in other disciplines. It is not hard, thus, to find early examples that illustrate how other fields were informed by observing hunter-gatherers and using them as a basis for comparison with other kinds of groups. Darwin, for instance, employed hunter-gatherers, particularly the Fuegians of South America, in precisely this manner in his classic work on man (Darwin 1871), which appeared during the latter half of the nineteenth century—roughly the time anthropology was emerging as a separate social science. It is possible, of course, that Darwin was simply following the example of Lubbock (1872:viii), who had this kind of developmental and comparative perspective firmly in mind when he advocated that contemporary hunter-gatherers be used as models of early human society; Darwin certainly relied heavily on Lubbock's survey of primitive societies. It is quite evident, however, that from the start Darwin had regarded the human case as central to his evolutionary theory and his field notes show that in the Fuegians he saw a primitive people that in certain respects bridged the gap between modern peoples and their closest animal relatives (Alland 1985:13).

Even Lubbock and Darwin were relative latecomers in this respect. They did not lead, but rather followed, a tradition basic to western thinking in which the comparison between primitives and civilized peoples calls into question the morals, laws, philosophies, and, in some sense, the "naturalness" of the latter and requires that the differences between the two be explained (cf. Burrow 1966:3; e.g., Pearce 1988:3).

Ideas about evolution and environment have often been invoked to explain the behavior of hunter-gatherers, perhaps because these primitives are in the curious position of requiring explanation in both natural and historical terms (i.e., they are part of both natural and cultural history). It would seem so, at least, for ethnographic interpretations of both kinds (evolutionary and environmental) are as old as Western philosophy itself (e.g., Glacken 1967; Burrow 1966:11). In this respect, among all primitive peoples, hunter-gatherers have been most central to the exploration of materialist and evolutionary themes because, on the one hand, they are regarded as ultimately primitive, that is, simple in the extreme, and thus the most susceptible to simple, uncomplicated explanation, and because, on the other, they depart farthest from the behavioral model observers have historically expected humans to assume. In short, hunter-gatherers force the issue of human cultural variability to the fore, where it is prone to be explained in terms that are either evolutionary-historical or materialist-geographical or some combination of the two.

The power of such explanations is suggested by their tenacity: Remarkably few nonevolutionary, nonmaterialist arguments have been able to gain a foothold in hunter-gatherer studies. Indeed, until just a decade ago, only two fundamentally distinct general models of hunter-gatherers—one developmental, the other ecological—could be identified within the whole of anthropological literature. Evolutionary and materialist themes are elementary to both these models but in differing ways and with differing emphasis.

The Developmental Model: Hunter-Gatherers as Primitives

The earlier of the two models was a developmental one solidly rooted in traditional concepts and philosophies that crystallized in theories of social progress, unilinear evolution, and Social Darwinism as anthropology began to establish itself as an independent social science during the second half of the nineteenth century. It portrayed hunter-gatherers as primitives—culturally backward groups capable only of the simplest undertakings. The model derived from the deceptively simple proposition that culture develops from less to more advanced forms and that technology and subsistence are basic to this development. The heart of this model is the concept of progressive social evolution: Individual cultures advance through a well-defined series of stages: band → tribe → chiefdom → state (e.g., Fried 1967; Service 1962), for example, or, alternatively, savagery → barbarism → civilization (Morgan 1877). Whatever specific formulation is used, the stages are organized in such a way that material concerns, for example, the quest for food, are gradually lessened by technical advances, for example, agriculture, and replaced by social, moral, and religious concerns. In this way, developmental models relate evolution to nature by setting the two in opposition. That is, the force of progressive social evolution works against the materialist forces of the natural environment: Culture evolves by the replacement of the natural economy (ecology) with a political economy.

> Human independence of environment culminates in socialry . . . the progressive emancipation from environment signalized in the higher culture-grades measures the conquest of Nature through industrial activity. (McGee 1898:295)

Hunter-gatherers, whose daily lives are preoccupied with subsistence and related material needs, are portrayed as disadvantaged and backward folk, in essence, fossils from an earlier stage of human evolution. Very long ago, Hobbes spelled out the miserable fate to which hunter-gatherers were condemned in the developmental model.

> No culture of the earth; no navigation . . . no account of time; no arts; no letters; no society; and which is worst of all, continual fear, and danger of violent death; and the life of man, solitary, poor, nasty, brutish and short. (Hobbes 1962:100 [original 1651])

There is obvious potential for drawing moral implications from the developmental model as well, for that which is primitive can also been interpreted as "backward" and "retarded" and, thus, in a larger sense "inferior."

> But after making every possible allowance for savages, it must I think be admitted that they are inferior, morally as well as in other respects, to the more civilized races. (Lubbock 1872:572)

> There is a curious tendency observable in students to overlook aboriginal vices and to exaggerate aboriginal virtues. It seems to be forgotten that after all the Indian is a savage, with the characteristics of a savage. (Powell 1891:35-36)

None of these ideas were original to early anthropology. Quite the contrary, they were the very elements of Western philosophy out of which anthropology itself was fashioned.

The Ecological Model: Hunter-Gatherers in Harmony with Environment

Between 1960 and 1970, the developmental model of hunter-gatherers was successfully challenged and replaced by an ecological one (e.g., Lee 1968; Flannery 1968). Unlike its predecessor, the model was distinctly anthropological (and almost exclusively American) in origin. Although it borrowed heavily from biological and ecological theories, the model was produced by anthropologists for anthropologists and was identifiably allied with neofunctionalist theory (e.g., Vayda and Rappaport 1968) and the early (technoenvironmental determinist) version of cultural materialism (e.g., Harris 1968a).[1] Fundamental to this model are the concepts of adaptation and homeostasis. Cultures are portrayed as populations that collectively solve adaptive problems through novel, and often complex, social, technical, political, and religious means. The resulting cultural formation is then regarded as a finely tuned adaptive system that reacts to changes in one component by compensations in another, often seemingly unrelated, component.

This represents a fundamental departure from traditional progressive social evolutionary theory in that subsistence and economy are no longer set apart from, or in opposition to, the more esoteric parts of culture—religion in particular. Quite the opposite, in this model, subsistence and religion are likely to be related in fundamental ways. For instance, a society may insulate itself against periodic local food shortages by instituting obligatory ritual interactions between many local groups having access to different resources.

Whatever specific intrasystemic relationships are inferred, the cultural system as a whole is regarded as being in equilibrium, each part regulating and being regulated by the others. This ecological model reverses the logic of the earlier model of hunter-gatherers as underprivileged and backward. Indeed, because regulation of the local system is made the frame of analytical reference, the concept of primitive, which is inherently comparative, ceases to have any useful meaning. In this view hunter-gatherers are no longer inferior: They are an advantaged and, in their own way, sophisticated folk who made the leap to agriculture only when circumstances beyond their control irrevocably upset their traditional ways of life. To see the difference between the developmental

---

[1] Here and throughout the remainder of the text I distinguish between the early version of cultural materialism (cf. Harris 1968a) and the later version (cf. Harris 1979). Both are concerned with the problem of adaptation, but the latter presents a model of the processes through which adaptation is effected that the former lacks.

and ecological models in this respect, compare the gloomy, developmental characterization of hunter-gatherers by Hobbes, quoted before, with the following ecological characterization of them by Flannery:

> We no longer think of the preceramic plant-collectors as a ragged and scruffy band of nomads; instead, they appear as a practiced and ingenious team of lay botanists who know how to wring the most out of a superficially bleak environment. (Flannery 1968:67)

Discussion

The fundamental differences between progressive social evolutionary and neofunctional-ecological explanatory frameworks that underlie these two different models of hunter-gatherers seem clear enough. Given these differences, it is all the more interesting that members of both camps approach the explanation of hunter-gatherers in virtually identical terms, accepting it as given that material conditions and technoenvironmental context account for most of what hunter-gatherers do. The neofunctionalist, of course, assumes that such explanations suffice universally, regardless of developmental stages or cultural complexity. The progressive social evolutionist, on the other hand, staunchly rejects strict technoenvironmental explanations of behavior in more complex sociopolitical settings (e.g., the state), where such things as ideology and politics must be taken into account, but has no qualms in reducing explanation to technoenvironmental terms for hunter-gatherers. That is, of course, because among the formal divisions recognized in progressive social evolutionary theory, it is only hunter-gatherers whose condition is not explained in terms of some earlier stage: That theory contains no evolutionary account of hunter-gatherers. This is not to say that social evolutionary theorists regard the stage of hunting and gathering as unsusceptible to processual analysis, that is, as an arbitrary construction. Rather they argue that the forces that drive social evolutionary progress are not yet manifest in hunter-gatherers, the corollary being that technoenvironmental context — the force of which lessens during the course of social evolution — is dominant.

This convergence of interpretive frameworks of social evolutionists and ecologists has been the source of much confusion in hunter-gatherer research both past and present. In particular, students of hunter-gatherers have frequently attempted to understand primitive economy and society as adaptations to local circumstances under the tacit assumption that such work cannot fail to have social evolutionary implications. From the evolutionary perspective, however, these efforts are in a sense counterproductive. The more successful students of hunter-gatherers are in showing how technology and environment are reflected in adaptive behavior, the more difficult it is to imagine how evolutionary change might occur without invoking the existence of other kinds of forces or agencies. This is a long-standing problem; even Darwin (1871) faced it: Lacking resort to progressive vitalism, he was unable to see any escape from the black hole of savagery (cf. Alland 1985:21, 176). In point of fact, the venerable and deep-rooted assumption that hunter-gatherers are "adapted" and that the object of hunter-gather research is to uncover the logic of that adaptation is fundamentally at cross-purposes with the study of evolutionary processes capable of producing change.

Social evolutionary theorists have always grasped this potential paradox in hunter-gatherer research. They are quite aware that the recognition of primitives and hunter-gatherers as separate anthropological categories requires an evolutionary perspective and that, by the same token, most evolutionary theories themselves require primitives and hunter-gatherers as a basal stage or category. Just the same, their interest in social evolution necessarily draws attention away from hunter-gatherers and hunter-gatherer adaptations and necessarily introduces elements commonly regarded as foreign to the primitive (e.g., political or enlightened religious motivations).

Hallpike's recent attempt to develop a theory of social evolution solidly in the tradition of progressive social evolutionary theory (Hallpike 1986) illustrates why it is that progressive accounts of evolutionary theory are so often only peripherally concerned with hunter-gatherers.[2] If one assumes, as Hallpike does, that evolution is a directional transformation from primitive to advanced (Hallpike 1986:15-17), it follows that it is principally in the more complex social formations, particularly the state, that the manifestations of evolutionary processes become evident (Hallpike 1986:17). The rudimentary technology and social arrangements of primitive peoples are, by contrast, evolutionarily uninteresting except as a basis for comparison.

For these reasons the case can be made that in anthropology the stronger the interest in cultural evolution, the lesser the interest in hunter-gatherers and ecological-materialist explanation. Conversely, the greater the interest in ecological-materialist explanation, the greater the interest in hunter-gatherers. This observation has far-reaching implications and underscores a point made earlier: Hunter-gatherer research is inextricably embedded in larger theoretical agenda and it is those agenda, not the hunter-gatherers themselves, that dictate the

---

[2]The evolutionary theory developed by Hallpike (1986), however, differs fundamentally from traditional social evolutionary theory in rejecting the assumption that technology and adaptation to the environment become less important as social complexity increases. Thus, Hallpike contends that in the hunter-gatherer case, "demands on functional and adaptive efficiency are very low" and a "wide range" of solutions, social and technical alike, "will all work perfectly well" (Hallpike 1986:141-142). In Hallpike's view, the range of workable possibilities available to hunter-gatherers is almost unlimited, efficiency being irrelevant; Oldowan tools and Australian section systems are cited as cases in point (Hallpike 1986:114, 142).

course of hunter-gatherer research in particular historical cases. It is less clear but equally true, that the theoretical frameworks that dictate the course of hunter-gatherer and other kinds of anthropological research are themselves, in turn, embedded in larger historical contexts. It follows that to understand the history of hunter-gatherer studies requires that attention be paid not only to the research that has been done but also to the broader social and political purposes for which it was done.

Because these points seem so often overlooked by many students of hunter-gatherers it will be useful to pursue their implications in greater detail in reference to the early history of two closely related anthropological traditions — British and American — where the study and approach to hunter-gatherers has historically been rather different: Hunter-gatherer research has been far more important and influential in American anthropology than in British anthropology. The choice of these two traditions of hunter-gatherer research is particularly appropriate to our purpose, because in the British and American cases, the nineteenth-century rise of anthropology as a separate discipline was closely identified with the development and formalization of theories of progressive social evolution. Those theories sought to reconcile the relationship between nature and culture and worked to interpret hunter-gatherers in such terms.

The historical analysis of hunter-gatherer research that follows is divided into three parts spread over this chapter and the next. The first part briefly examines the history and key elements of nineteenth-century Anglo-American social evolutionary theory. Of note here is its historical grounding in political theory and intellectual independence from Darwinian theory. The second part considers the British tradition of social evolutionary theory in terms of its effect on hunter-gatherer research. The case is made that the political context within which British social evolutionary theory developed in the nineteenth century actively discouraged studies in which either the influence of natural environment or understanding of primitive peoples (especially hunter-gatherers) figured in any important way. The third part of this historical discussion, contained in Chapter 2, considers the history of American hunter-gatherer research in terms of both social evolutionary and neofunctional-ecological theory. Here it is argued that, in contrast to the British case, the political and social climate in nineteenth-century America caused social evolutionary theorists to regard nature, environment, and primitive man as fundamental ingredients to their larger explanatory frameworks. In America, this interest in nature, environment, and primitive man ultimately proved more lasting than social evolutionary theory itself and laid the groundwork for neofunctionalism and the ecological model of hunter-gatherers. It is particularly notable that neither that theory nor that model has any significant British counterpart: The best they could offer was Forde (1934) and possibilism.

SOCIAL EVOLUTION AND PRIMITIVE HUNTER-GATHERERS

The developmental model of hunter-gatherers as primitives was firmly anchored in an understanding of cultural evolution as traditionally embraced in British and American anthropology—from Maine (1861), Spencer (1876, 1882, 1896), Tylor (1871), Morgan (1877), and Powell (1885, 1888a), to Service (1962), White (L. White 1959), Fried (1967), and Flannery (1972). As Burrow (1966) and Dunnell (1980:40-41) have observed, this anthropological brand of evolution, which emphasizes the consequences of directional progressive modification of cultural wholes—or "Culture" as a whole—owes little to Darwin. Darwin was more interested in processes than consequences and in populations of individuals than in groups of individuals constituted as cultures. Natural selection was relevant to cultural evolution only in the limited role assigned to it by the Social Darwinists—Spencer (1910b:174-180) and the Spencerists in particular, who regarded it as only one of many important evolutionary processes. Spencer portrayed selection as a force for progress that weeded out inferior cultural forms (later discussions; see also Burrow 1966:219). Thus, in contrast to Darwin, for Spencer the process of selection (i.e., as a mechanism) was less important than the cumulative consequences of the evolutionary process, which was progress toward perfection (e.g., Spencer 1868a, 1870; Peel 1972:xxi-xxiii; Burrow 1966:115, 203, 274-277; see Chapter 9). For Spencer, as for all the other progressive evolutionary social theorists, the history of culture is a journey of transformation from early disorderly primitive stages to later more orderly advanced stages; and as the earliest stage, hunting and gathering is the least progressed, which is to say the most primitive and disorderly.

By implying that Darwinian processes in general, and natural selection in particular, were fundamental to the theories (as distinguished from political philosophies) of Spencer and others of his ilk at the time, the term *Social Darwinism* has undoubtedly been the source of much mischief. Equally culpable is the related notion that, if not derived directly from the theoretical work of Darwin, the flourish of theories of social evolution in Great Britain and the United States during the last third of the nineteenth century was at least inspired by his contributions. As many have pointed out (e.g., Burrow 1966:19-21, 100, 113-116), this is simply not so: Darwinian theory and processes were irrelevant to the evolutionary theories of Maine, Spencer, Tylor, Morgan, and Powell because his concern was not theirs, and theirs not his. Unlike Darwin (cf. Alland 1985:19), these men regarded themselves as social and political theorists. They worked in and on a history of ideas about moral values whose subject was man and man's place in the world (Peel 1972:xxiii-xxiv; Hinsley 1981:285-286; Meadows 1952:73). It was a school of social and political philosophy to which

Darwin contributed little of consequence directly, though he was undoubtedly as affected by it as its major figures. Spencer spelled out the deeper purpose of social evolutionary theory in these terms:

> "Give us a guide," cry men to the philosopher. "We would escape from these miseries in which we are entangled. A better state is ever present in our imaginations, and we yearn after it; but all our efforts to realize it are fruitless. We are weary of perpetual failures; tell us by what rule we may attain our desire." (Spencer 1865:11)

Progressive Social Evolution as Political Theory

The progressive evolutionary schemes advanced by Maine, Spencer, Tylor, Morgan, and Powell were rooted in traditional ideas and philosophies that predate Darwin by many centuries and whose chief concern is with government and politics. Harris (1968a:26-27) tracks this evolutionary heritage to the Roman philosopher Lucretius and, more indirectly, to the earlier writings of the Greek Epicurus. Three concepts seem to have been particularly influential in shaping this heritage: the idea of progress, the idea of environmental influence, and the idea of political economy. Each of these ideas contained important political and social ramifications and, in drawing so heavily upon them, nineteenth-century anthropology clearly indicated its intention to participate in the larger sphere of political philosophy.

Progress

The idea of progress as a natural condition or process is perhaps most properly attributed to what Lovejoy (1964) terms the "Great Chain of Being," which he traces to the "this world/other-world" opposition that pervades the writings of Plato and Aristotle. As initially construed, that concept held the universe to be an atemporal creation filled with an infinite variety of entities that described a natural, and permanently fixed, continuum of lower to progressively higher worldly creations.[3] When later reworked to suit the philosophy of the Enlightenment, the Chain of Being became an active process rather than a static description: Creation was temporalized, and the position of entities, both within the continuum (or chain) and with respect to perfection measured in absolute

---

[3]It was decidedly *not*, as Schrire avers (1984:4), this fixed continuum, or chain, into which eighteenth-century Europe first attempted to fit primitive peoples, however. Rather, by then a growing awareness of logical and moral inconsistencies in the static interpretation of the physical universe (one cause for growing doubt regarding the authority of the Church and clergy in such basic matters as morality and philosophy) led to the reinterpretation of the Chain of Being as a process acting over time.

scale, was mutable and hence subject to progressive improvement (Lovejoy 1964:246).

The Chain of Being was not an empirical exercise, intended merely to describe the world as it was or as it might become. Its deeper purpose was to discover the inner logic of natural order that could then serve as a basis for developing political and moral philosophies of behavior. That the concept of progress was so seminal to development of progressive social evolutionary theories during the eighteenth and nineteenth centuries underscores the fundamental participation of those theories in the larger tradition of political philosophy.

Environmental Influence

Theories of environmental influence made an equally important contribution to the tradition of social evolutionary thought. Glacken (1967:80-114) painstakingly traces theories of this sort to the ancient Greeks, especially to the writings collectively attributed to Hippocrates, and particularly to the treatise *Airs, Waters, and Places*, in which are discussed various influences of the environment on the mental and physical attributes of individuals. Hippocrates was not an environmental determinist. Quite the contrary, as Glacken (1967:87-88) shows, in another essay, "Ancient Medicine," Hippocrates portrayed the environment as a challenge to be overcome by man, for example, by the domestication of plants and animals and by advances in the preparation of food. In this and related works (cf. Glacken 1967:95-96), the Greeks developed the concept that the history of man is away from nature (human behavior governed by nature) and toward civilization (human behavior governed by man).

Because they emphasized the historical rise of humans from a beastlike, natural state to civilization, these ancient theories of environmental influence can be seen to contain the rudiments of protoevolutionary theory.[4] Particularly

---

[4]Some of these evolutionary implications were quite specific. Hippocrates, Bodin, and Montesquieu, for instance, all noted that differences of climate caused peoples of the northern, southern, and temperate regions to assume intellectual qualities reminiscent of the three ages of man (Glacken 1967:440-441): youth, middle age, old age. Such observations contained the rudiments of an evolutionary theory. There was, further, from at least the Middle Ages onward the belief that civilization was moving from, variously, east to west, north to south, south to north, or, for Jefferson in the New World, west to east (cf. Glacken 1967:276-278, 597). Absolute direction here seems to have been less important than simple distance from a central point; in nearly all such theories, cultural development increased and the force of environment decreased as one moved from distant times and places closer to home (cf. Glacken 1967:272, 286, 444). Here, again, are the rudiments of a model of evolution; indeed, many early evolutionary theories were similarly structured, cultures near at hand tending to be portrayed as more advanced than ones far away. As students of the Kulturkreise pointed out, of course, the inverse correlation between distance and development could be explained in other ways.

noteworthy here is the implication that less civilized peoples are more subject to the environment than more civilized ones, which became a central theme in the progressive social evolutionary theories of Spencer, Morgan, Powell, and others. Further, like those nineteenth-century social evolutionary theories, from the time of the Greeks onward, theories of environmental influence were often intended to serve as a basis for political theory. Plato, Aristotle, St. Thomas Aquinas, Machiavelli, Bodin, and Montesquieu, for instance, all regarded an understanding of environmental effects and environmental context as essential to both the development of moral theories of government and colonial rule and a proper interpretation of history (Glacken 1967:92, 274-275, 273-276, 431, 434, 445, 568; see also Burrow 1966:66-67).[5]

Political Economy

Theorists of the Enlightenment formalized many of the evolutionary ideas that were central to theories of environmental influence, most particularly the notion that human progress is measured by the degree of independence from environment. In that sense, the thrust of Enlightenment theory was deliberately antimaterialist or at least nonmaterialist. At first, this assertion seems wrong-headed because it is commonly agreed that modern economic theory began with the Enlightenment, and economy and materialism are inseparable in the minds of many anthropologists. Materialist interpretations of behavior, however, were neither an Enlightenment invention (cf. Roll 1953:20) nor a distinctive theme of Enlightenment inquiry.

Materialism was certainly fundamental to many Enlightenment theories, those of the Scottish utilitarians in particular. Unlike some of their French

---

[5]It is possibly this historical connection with political theory that explains why environmental theories and theorists have so seldom essayed determinist interpretations. As Glacken's history of environmental theories shows, it is the theme of tension between the forces of environment and culture, and the problems this raises regarding the issue of morality, that dominates the historical development of theories of environmental influence. It has been generally appreciated since the time of the Ancients, for instance, that theories of environmental influence are in one sense inherently good and in another inherently bad. They were good in their implied relativism: One cannot judge the culture of another in terms of one's own, the environments being different; Jefferson made such a case for the North American Indian (Hallowell 1960:15; cf. Pearce 1988:93-94). Environmental theories, however, were at the same time inherently dangerous: In their fatalism and determinism they seem to deprive individuals from any real power to change their nature, which was a result of climate (for an analogous argument regarding genetic fatalism, see Chard 1969:73). St. Thomas Aquinas, Bodin, Montesquieu, and countless others less notable considered that contradiction and consistently decided that the effect of environment, although powerful, can be overcome—as modern civilization, government, and technology all show. Precisely the same nature-culture dualism found in these political philosophers would later be seen in the anthropological theories of, among others, Boas, Kroeber, Forde, and Steward.

counterparts (e.g., Comte and Condorcet), who divided their conjectural histories of human progress by ages of reason, the Scots divided theirs by economic stages, from hunting and gathering to civilization. Classical economic theory (e.g., Adam Smith 1776) was forged in these historical expositions, a key issue being the origins and consequences of economic surplus. In part, the Scottish effort was intended to counter the claims of certain French economists (the Physiocrats) who had argued that surplus was the result of the invention of agriculture, that agriculture was the only true source of surplus, and had made this the basis of a theory of a natural economy unalterable by such externalities as politics (Roll 1953:128-137; Gudeman 1986:71-89). As one might expect, given their interest in developmental and evolutionary theory, the Enlightenment utilitarians, Smith in particular, were unsatisfied with static analyses of the sort the Physiocrats proposed, especially because they seemed to preclude a clear understanding of capitalist economies driven by industry rather than agriculture.

In response, they set about to understand human economic behavior in terms of principles that would transcend specific technoenvironmental circumstances by including, among other things, such considerations as political context and the forces of markets and exchange. As part of this, Smith introduced nonmaterialist assumptions regarding the nature of rational choice, strategies, and decisions, as a means for addressing the relationship between economic means and economic goals. The resulting conjectural histories implied that as man progressed, classical economic theory and formalist principles increasingly took precedence over the more basic material concerns: The natural economy (ecology) is replaced by a political economy. Unfortunately, this fundamental Enlightenment contribution – the distinction between ecology on the one hand and economy on the other – so clearly understood by Smith, Mill, and all modern economists, remains today confused in the minds of many anthropologists (cf. Burling 1962; Rosenberg 1980:54).

Social Policy and Progressive Evolutionary Theory

Because nineteenth-century anthropologists saw their theories as contributing to social and political thought, the issues most hotly contested between them were often those that had obvious implications for the conduct of government and the development of social policy. This frequently had the effect of causing what were rather minor (sometimes nonexistent) differences of general theoretical viewpoint to be exaggerated by disputants involved, who were often less interested in theoretical consistency than in making the strongest possible case for a favored social policy. Anthropologists have sometimes looked back on these debates and taken them at face value (i.e., divorced from their political context) and assumed that they reflect the presence of fundamentally different schools of thought within progressive social evolutionary theory. There were differences within social evolutionary theory, to be sure, but on the whole these were minor in comparison to the important ideas most nineteenth-century social evolutionists held in common—the concept of social evolution as the progressive emancipation of man from his environment through the growth of culture.

Spencer and Powell, two particularly prominent and outspoken social evolutionists of the nineteenth century, are cases in point. They seemed to subscribe to divergent and philosophically irreconcilable views regarding the nature of progress and the processes that caused it. The core of their disagreement, however, was not about theory *per se* but rather the implications of theory for contemporary social policy. This often led them to claim they could deduce more from their theories than they actually could without contradicting themselves.

Spencer and Powell

Spencer and the Social Darwinists differed from other social theorists in the progressive tradition (e.g., Tylor, Morgan, and, especially Powell), in their philosophical commitment to monist explanations in which human consciousness and motives were merely reflexes rather than creative forces for change. Spencer insisted that progressive social evolution could be derived from basic physical principles applicable to all natural systems (Spencer 1868a, 1868b, 1910a:501-502). In Spencer's system, it was the direct interaction between an organism and its external environment that produced evolutionary change. As part of this, he made innovative use of natural selection as a mechanism that explained why progress should result as populations grew (Spencer 1852, 1910b:179-180).

> For necessarily, families and races whom this increasing difficulty of getting a living which excess of fertility entails, does not stimulate to improvements in production—that is, to greater mental activity—are on the high road to extinction; and must ultimately be supplanted by those whom the pressure does so stimulate. (Spencer 1852:499-500)

In contrast, Powell joined with his friend, the sociologist and social reformer Lester Ward (e.g., 1903:16; Welling 1888:21-22), in his adamant disavowal that "purposeless" Darwinian processes such as selection could be relevant to understanding social evolution, where change was brought about "decisively" through "purposive action" (Hofstadter 1944:68). For Powell and Ward (and largely also for Tylor and Morgan), human evolution was "telic" or "anthropoteleological," that is, caused by the adjustment of means to ends actively driven by human invention (Kimball 1968:175, 203; Powell 1883).

> The progress of animal evolution has cost the world a hell of misery; and yet there are philosophers, professors of our colleges, and authors of world-renowned books who believe that the law of human evolution, the method by which man may progress in civilization, is the survival of the fittest in the struggle for existence. . . . Man does not compete with plants and animals for existence, for he emancipates himself from that struggle by the invention of arts; and again man does not compete with his fellow-man for existence, for he emancipates himself from the brutal struggle by the invention of institutions. Animal evolution arises out of the struggle for existence; human evolution arises out of the endeavor to secure happiness: it is a conscious effort for improvement in condition. (Powell 1888b:304, 311)

Because, in rejecting a strictly Darwinian interpretation of social evolution, he necessarily rejected the relevance of natural selection in that context, it might appear that Powell had distanced himself as far from Spencer and the Social Darwinists as he had from Darwin. That is not the case, however. Indeed, it would be a mistake to conclude that their disagreement over natural selection by itself constituted a fundamental difference between the evolutionary views of Powell and Spencer, as has occasionally been suggested (cf. Hallowell 1960:55-56; Hofstadter 1944).

In the first place, natural selection was not fundamental to Spencerism (Peel 1972:xxii). Spencer held that the force of natural selection lessened as society progressed. He willingly conceded that in civilized states—the empirical case Powell nearly always used in criticizing Social Darwinism—natural selection was of little or no importance.

> Natural selection, or survival of the fittest, is almost exclusively operative throughout the vegetal world and throughout the lower animal world. . . . But with the ascent to higher types of animals, its effects are in increasing degrees involved with those produced by inheritance of acquired characters; until, in animals of complex structures, inheritance of acquired characters become an important, if not the chief cause of evolution. (Spencer 1898:632)

> Among the civilized human races, the equilibration becomes mainly direct [i.e., by inheritance of acquired characters]: the action of natural selection being limited to the destruction of those who are constitutionally too feeble to live, even with external aid. . . . Natural selection acts freely in the struggle of one society against another; yet among the units of each society, its action is so interfered with that there remains no adequate cause for the acquirement of mental superiority by one race over another, except the inheritance of functionally-produced modifications. (Spencer 1898:553)

Spencer claimed in the abstract to explain all natural systems in the same terms, but when it came down to actual cases, his position was essentially the same as Powell's: The laws that govern animals (natural selection) are not those that govern man and society (inheritance of functionally acquired characters).

Powell was guilty of similar contradictions. He denied in general that natural selection had anything to do with human progress but by deliberately focusing these discussions on more complex societies, Western civilization in particular (e.g., Powell 1888b: 301, 321-323), he seemed to imply, along with Spencer, that selection might be a force to be reckoned with in more primitive contexts. The suspicion was confirmed when, as the director of the Bureau of American Ethnology, he allowed (and undoubtedly encouraged; cf. Hinsley 1981:239-243) publication of an ethnographic account of a hunting and gathering group, the Seri, in which natural selection was used to explain many aspects of behavior and morphology. Not surprisingly, both Powell and the author of the account (W. J. McGee) regarded the Seri as representing the evolutionarily most primitive form of hunter-gatherer in the Americas (Powell 1898:lxvii; McGee 1898:295; see Chapter 2).

> There is a widespread Sonoran tradition that the Seri systematically exterminate weaklings and oldsters; and it is beyond doubt that the tradition has a partial foundation in the elimination of the weak and helpless through the literal race for life in which the bands participate on occasion. A parallel eliminative process is common among many American aborigines; . . . yet it would appear that this merciless mechanism for improving the fit and eliminating the unfit attains unusual, if not unequaled, perfection among the Seri. (McGee 1898:157)

For his part, the sociologist Ward, Powell's friend, was in near-complete agreement with Spencer regarding the role of natural selection as the major force in human evolution prior to the industrial revolution (cf. Hofstadter 1944:75). Ward's own proposal regarding the origin of castes from warfare, for instance, is solidly in the tradition of Social Darwinism and essentially identical to Spencer's and, later, Carniero's account of the origin of complex societies (Spencer 1910b:175-183, 1876:569-576; Carniero 1970).

Beneath all the rhetoric, then, the theories of Powell and Spencer are scarcely distinguishable. Both men were deeply committed to the idea that social progress was a natural evolutionary process and an inevitable one (Kennedy 1978:105; Powell 1888a:97, 99). Both further agreed that social evolution had not yet run its full course, and this is where the problems arose. The differences between them were of degree not kind and centered more on sociology, their philosophies of political morality and social reform in particular, not on their interpretation of the course of human evolution. Powell and Ward took issue with Spencer not over the historical role of natural selection in the course of human evolution but over its future role: Laissez-faire Social Darwinism eschewed social reform as unnatural interference with natural processes (e.g., Spencer 1868c, 1865:348-390). For Spencer, true progress could only result from direct interaction with the environment; being subject to this process, human reasoning (and therefore social policy) could make no independent contribution to social evolution (Kimball 1968:307; Kennedy 1978:45-61). Powell and Ward rejected that argument and held that social reform was inherently no less natural than competition. For them, scientifically guided social policy and social reform were necessary to human progress (Kimball 1968:301, 307).

> Should the philosophy of Spencer . . . become the philosophy of the twentieth century, it would cover civilization with a pall and culture would again stagnate. But science rends that pall, and mankind moves on to a higher destiny. (Powell 1888a:122)

In the last analysis, the difference between the anthropotelesis of Powell and the direct equilibration of Spencer was a matter of voice, human participation in social evolution being active to Powell and passive to Spencer (Kimball 1968:307). Even this difference evaporates if one tries to distinguish the practical implications of these concepts (e.g., to experience a problem and respond to it organizationally can be interpreted as either telesis or direct equilibration). On the other hand, whether social evolution was active or passive was clearly important in the sphere of government and politics. What was at issue between Spencer and Powell was not what had happened in the past or how to interpret primitive society but what would happen in the future and how to interpret modern society.

The social settings Spencer and Powell confronted, however, were remarkably different. It was these differences that charted the divergent courses of hunter-gatherer research in Great Britain and the United States. As we have seen, nineteenth-century social evolutionary theory held that mankind advanced though gradual emancipation from nature. In Spencer's world, it seemed to be most imperative to understand the culmination of that process—man's final separation from the environment. By contrast, in Powell's world it seemed imperative not to overlook the natural linkages that had once existed and still existed between humans and their environment (cf. Chinard 1947:53-54). The consequences for hunter-gatherer research and environmental-ecological explanations of behavior were obvious.

PRIMITIVES, ENVIRONMENT, AND BRITISH SOCIAL EVOLUTION

The industrial world in which British anthropology emerged during the middle nineteenth century was decidedly "unnatural" in the sense that the forces that were deemed most important were principally those of society, politics, and economy (Chinard 1947:53-54). These had little to do with nature and the environment. This had two related implications. First, studies in which the environment and nature figured prominently were of little instructive value with regard to the contemporary problems that social evolutionary theory was seen as addressing. Second, if environment and nature were not important, then studies of primitives, whose actions were governed by these forces, were equally uninstructive.

Theories of Environment

British prejudice against environmental-ecological explanation was undoubtedly colored in part by disdain for classical theories of environmental influence that, owing to their Mediterranean origins, implied the British Isles were too cold and damp to permit advanced cultural development (cf. Glacken 1967:449). This was a minor obstacle, however; the French (among others) had shown how easily one could embrace ancient climatic theories by modifying their specific locational implications (Glacken 1967:435). The British would certainly have done so had not their evolutionary tradition and interest in advanced cultural formations (especially their own) prevented it. The belief of nearly all British social evolutionists (excepting, possibly Spencer) that evolution acted to emancipate man from natural forces and the environment, in combination with their interest in more highly evolved social formations, relegated materialist studies of environment and primitive economy to a minor role.

In short, eighteenth- and nineteenth-century British social scientists interested in evolutionary processes had little use for materialist accounts of behavior not because they found them implausible but because they found them irrelevant. British optimism regarding the inevitability of progress and the perfectibility of man, particularly British man, carried the concomitant belief that the evolutionary process had proceeded sufficiently to guess its outcome.[6] The grounding of social evolutionary theory in political economy required this: For theory to be useful as a moral basis for law and government, the evolutionary destiny of mankind had to be clearly deducible from that theory. This necessarily drew attention to more advanced cultures, in particular to Britain and the civilized West, which in all plausible evolutionary accounts of the human race had not only come out on top but so far ahead the issue clearly had

---

[6]As Burrow (1966:59-63) discusses, carried to its logical conclusion, this implication could be devastating to social evolutionary theory itself. If social progress had reached its conclusion in Britain, then neither the lessons that could be learned from primitives nor the study of social evolutionary processes in general were any longer of instructive value to British political economy. In short, social evolution could make social evolutionary theory obsolete.

never been in doubt. Just as evil was a necessary part of the static Chain of Being (not because anyone was really interested in evil *per se* or wanted it to exist but because it was required in theory to define, by its opposition, that which was good), so were primitive cultures, hunter-gatherers in particular, essential to British progressive social evolutionary theory: They were necessary to define, by opposition, advanced cultures.

It was further the case that, because in all plausible nineteenth-century evolutionary accounts the distinction between primitive and advanced societies was a progression from nature to culture, evolution could be seen as a force working against materialism. In combination with the British interest in civilization, this associated evolutionary processes with culture and separated them from nature. Evolution rendered nature and culture separate and opposed to each other in theory: The farther evolution proceeded the less relevant nature became.

Dunbar in 1780 had put it this way:

> Soil and climate seem to act with a gradation of influence on vegetable, animal and intellectual nature. . . . Man, therefore, by his rank in creation, is more exempted from mechanical dominion than the classes below him. (quoted in Glacken 1967:600)

When eighteenth- and nineteenth-century British scholars ventured theories about the effect of environment on mankind at all they were more likely to be in the tradition of German Romanticism than anything recognizably materialist. For Dunbar, as for Humboldt (cf. Glacken 1967), the effect of nature on man differed qualitatively from its effect on animals. As a consequence of his more delicate and impressionable psyche, man was in some ways more affected by nature than other animals. That effect, however, was spiritual, intellectual, and moral, not material as was exclusively true of animals. Nature affected man more through his intellectual appreciation of a majestic landscape than through his calculations as to its edibility.

British social evolutionary theorists clearly understood the fundamental distinction between their progressive brand of progressive evolution and Darwinian evolution when it came to the matter of order and disorder in relation to environment. These theorists saw social evolution working directionally to civilize man by replacing, variously, natural disorder with cultural order, savage ignorance with civilized knowledge, and primitive material concerns with advanced humanistic ones (e.g., Burrow 1966:93, 212). For them, evolution would at some point remove all human ignorance and impose perfect order and harmony. Material worries would disappear, and, having done its work, evolution would cease to operate, there being no remaining disorder or imperfection (i.e., empirical variety) for it to work upon. Spencer (1852) himself had made exactly this point with reference to the force of population pressure:

And after having caused, as it ultimately must, the due peopling of the globe, and the bringing of all its habitable parts into the highest state of culture--after having brought all processes for the satisfaction of human wants to the greatest perfection--after having, at the same time, developed the intellect into complete competency for its work, and the feelings into complete fitness for social life--after having done all this, we see that the pressure of population, as it gradually finishes its work, must gradually bring itself to an end. . . . In the end, the pressure of population and its accompanying evils will entirely disappear. (Spencer 1852:500, 501)

Darwinian evolution, by contrast, lacks arguments about directionality and final states, in large part because variety (i.e., natural disorder) is not assumed to diminish directionally as a function of process. This is why Darwin was so troubled by the discovery of genes: He thought genetic inheritance might blend and gradually suppress the phenotypical variety (disorder) required for his process of natural selection to operate (Boyd and Richerson 1985:75).

Conjectural Fieldwork

The British disinterest in studies of environmental relationships and primitive societies that could only be understood in environmental terms fit neatly with an established reluctance to engage in first-hand ethnographic research in faraway places (Harris 1968a:169-170). As we have seen, heuristic historical reconstructions, not detailed empirical studies, were the major inspiration and lasting contribution of Enlightenment social scientists (see also Cassirer 1951). Consequently, the idea of real fieldwork remained wholly foreign to the European tradition of social research exemplified by both French (e.g., Turgot, Condorcet, Rousseau) and British (e.g., Hobbes, Locke, Smith, Millar) conjectural historians. This was, of course, partly a matter of practicality: Conjectural fieldwork arose before there was any real possibility of studying primitive peoples first-hand. That there were more fundamental reasons for this neglect is shown by the fact that ethnographic fieldwork subsequently did not keep pace with improving research opportunities. Compare in this regard the philosophical inquiries of Smith, Spencer, and Tylor with the empirical research of their British, German, and French contemporaries in the natural sciences during the same period. Darwin and Humboldt, for example, were routinely traveling to the far corners of the world to observe their subject matter (cf. Burrow 1966:85).[7]

---

[7]Haddon, in 1898-1899, mounted one of the first overseas anthropological expeditions to the Torres Straits. But the way for it had been paved by an earlier expedition the purpose of which had been exclusively natural historical (Burrow 1966:86). The succeeding anthropological expedition was meant to salvage a record of expiring cultures, not to devising theories or put them to the test. As a direct result, in its preoccupation with endless description, Haddon's report is reminiscent of early

Here again, it is their historical connection with political economy that accounts for the distinctive behavior of social evolutionary theorists: The mid-nineteenth-century crisis of political philosophy could not wait for drawn-out empirical studies. With no shortage of plausible theories one could develop in comfort at home, there was simply no need for social scientists to travel abroad and live with primitive peoples to obtain them.

Bringing these disparate lines of evidence together, the early grounding of British anthropology in conjectural history and political economy had at least two important consequences: (1) it deflected attention from primitive peoples and theories of environmental influence and (2) it discouraged first-hand empirical research. Both go a long way toward explaining why it is that hunter-gather studies and anthropological theories that rest on an understanding of ecology and the natural environment have seldom enjoyed strong British followings.

Spencer's Case for the Importance of Environment

Among all the nineteenth-century British social evolutionists, Spencer alone stood to make the case that nature and environment were essential to understanding human behavior and the course of social evolution. For the most part, his arguments fell on deaf ears and, in the end, his whole attempt was rejected.[8]

Spencer, the man, here must be held in part responsible. (Hofstadter 1944:48; Burrow 1966:179-182). Pedantic, personally reclusive, and conceptually intransigent, Spencer was unpopular among many of his English contemporaries, and his theories suffered accordingly. Yet this explanation tends to trivialize the nontrivial—the tradition of British evolutionary thought being anything but trivial. Spencer could not avoid participation in that tradition yet could not succeed in dominating it. Even those among his close circle of highly influential friends (e.g., Huxley) rejected his arguments (cf. Carniero 1967:xlviii; Kennedy 1978:68-69).

---

attempts at empirical research in British sociology most of which, as Burrow (1966:88-90) documents, lost their way in a morass of detail that remained incomprehensible in the absence of a generalizing theory.

[8]Spencer was, of course, far less popular in Britain than America (cf. Burrow 1966; Peel 1972:xxxvi-xxxiv). Even in America, Spencer's influence was much greater outside than within the social sciences, anthropology in particular. Among the lay public, his acceptance was furthered in no small part by his emphasis on individualism and self-sufficiency—ideals that Americans endorsed, and by the popular conviction, particularly among the captains of industry in postbellum America, that success was something that anyone could achieve, the accomplishments of some and the failure of others being explicable in terms of the individuals rather than systems. Spencerism explained in natural terms how it could come to pass that equally free men could be so markedly unequal in wealth (cf. Hofstadter 1944:46).

Paradoxically, Spencer, the radical evolutionist, failed to convince his British audience precisely because early British anthropology was committed to evolutionary rather than materialist-environmental explanations of human progress. It was not his evolution but his materialism—particularly his suggestion that humans could be understood in terms of processes that governed all natural systems—that made Spencer's theories unacceptable (e.g., Spencer 1868a, 1870, 1910a:501, 1852; compare, however, Dunnell 1980).

As were most social evolutionists of his time, Spencer was convinced that he could project the destination of evolutionary progress (e.g., Spencer 1876:569-596). He was, after all, politically motivated and convinced of the correctness of his political theories. This required that the course and final outcome of social evolution be derivable from those theories and that they necessarily imply the advanced achievements of European civilization. From the perspective of progressive evolutionary philosophy, however, in doing this, Spencer seemed to contradict himself in fundamental ways. As we have seen, his monist philosophical commitment to the idea that the same natural principles govern all systems (e.g., 1910a) seemed inconsistent with his argument that direct equilibration (inheritance of functionally acquired characters) dominated human social evolution, whereas natural selection dominated the evolution of lower organisms (see also Carniero 1967:xlvii). More to the point here, his idea of an evolutionary social millennium seemed inherently nonmonist. The driving generative force behind Spencerist evolution is multiplicative causation or the persistence of force (Kennedy 1978:104): Every cause has more than one effect. It is quite clear that this force must weaken as the millennium is approached but would only do so if the final social state has a specific predetermined form. If that is so and if, as Spencer assumed, society is an organic unity perfectly adapted to its environment, then it follows that the components of the environment must also not undergo further change and therefore must also represent specific predetermined forms. But if that is so, then the laws that govern the natural environment are quite clearly not the same as those that govern society because the two give rise to completely different predetermined forms, natural on the one hand and social on the other.

All plausible progressive evolutionary theories were partly contrived in the sense that they were required to predict and legitimize the superior achievements of western civilization (see Burrow 1966:97). Spencer's formulation, however, strained even these generous limits on credulity. His contention that natural principles were applicable to understanding Western civilization narrowed the gap between nature and culture to no useful purpose save that of establishing the superiority of his own political philosophy over those of others whose claims were more modest. The whole enterprise seemed, in short, unacceptably self-serving.

BRITISH HUNTER-GATHERER RESEARCH: ETHNOGRAPHY

It is consistent with the theme developed here that hunter-gatherer research has never enjoyed the great following in Britain that it has in the United States. What recent movement there has been to remedy this neglect seems to have stemmed primarily from an archaeological appetite for ethnographic models that might be applied to the Paleolithic (e.g. Isaac 1968; cf. Schrire 1984). This reflects interest not in hunter-gatherers *per se* but in the most ancient past, that is, in history. It is most telling here that the list of participants in the "Man the Hunter" symposium (Lee and Devore 1968) names but one British anthropologist: J. Woodburn (actually this is an exception tending to prove the rule, because Woodburn's affiliation was with the London School of Economics). Little of this is surprising given an historical tradition in which primitive societies and environmental relationships are of secondary interest.

The relatively minor contribution of primitive peoples to nineteenth-century British theories of social evolution did not mean that such peoples remained mysterious in theory. On the contrary, they had a clear place in theory and were all too predictable and easily interpreted. In contrast to more complex societies, in particular Western society, about which evolutionary debate raged, the hunter-gatherer case was open and shut. Lubbock (1872) developed in great detail the major themes of progressive social evolutionary theory as the British believed they applied to primitive peoples.

According to Lubbock, the first and only concern of hunter-gatherers is with the means of existence. Thus,

> It is impossible not to admire the skill with which they use their weapons and implements, their ingenuity in hunting and fishing and their close powers of observation. (1872:544)

Despite these natural skills, primitives are limited in technical capability (p. 551) and therefore constantly engaged in the pursuit of food and continually in fear of starvation.

> There are, indeed, many who doubt whether happiness is increased by civilization, and who talk of the free and noble savage. But the true savage is neither free nor noble; he is a slave to his own wants, his own passions; imperfectly protected from the weather, he suffers from cold by night and the heat of the sun by day; ignorant of agriculture, living by the chase, and improvident in success, hunger always stares him in the face, and often drives him to the dreadful alternative of cannibalism or death. (p. 595)

It is this obligatory participation in nature that defines the state of savagery and, as a consequence, the differences that are observed to exist between primitive peoples, "follow evidently and directly from the external conditions in which different races are placed" (p. 557).

Concerned only with subsistence, primitives showed none of the mental, moral, and religious traits associated in theory with social evolutionary progress.

> Savages have often been likened to children, and the comparison is not only correct, but also highly instructive. Many naturalists consider that the early condition of the individual indicates that of the race--that the best test of the affinities of a species are the stages through which it passes. So also it is in the case of man; the life of each individual is an epitome of the history of the race, and the gradual development of the child illustrates that of the species. Hence the importance of the similarity between savages and children. Savages, like children, have no steadiness of purpose. (p. 570)

Several lines of evidence suggest these qualities of primitives reflect limited mental abilities. "The savage is like a child who sees and hears only that which is brought directly before him" (p. 598). The Tasmanians, for example, have no means of expressing abstract ideas (p. 451). "The names for numbers are, however, the best, or at least, the most easily applicable test of mental condition among the lower races of man" (p. 574). Here the data are unequivocal: Most savages cannot count past four (pp. 448, 531, 574-575).

As might be expected of peoples standing on the lowest rung of social evolutionary development, primitives show none of the ethical qualities associated with evolutionary progress. There are numerous illustrations. Australian women are regarded as mere property (p. 449). The social position of American Indian women is degraded (p. 519). Indeed, overall, "the harsh, not to say cruel treatment of women, which is almost universal among savages, is one of the deepest stains upon their character" (p. 569). Apparently the same kind of treatment is extended toward neighbors because savages are almost always at war (p. 554). They should not be faulted for this for there is little to suggest primitives can distinguish between right and wrong. Indeed, "some of them can hardly be regarded as responsible beings, and have not attained any notions . . . of moral rectitude" (pp. 566-567). Among the more notable examples: "Australians are governed by a code of rules and set of customs which form one of the most cruel tyrannies that has ever, perhaps, existed on the face of the earth" (p. 450). "The Sichuana language contains no expression for thanks; the Algonquin had no word for love; the Tinne no word for beloved; mercy was with the North American Indians a mistake, and peace an evil" (pp. 564-565). In sum, it can be said that "neither faith, hope, or charity enters into the virtues of a savage" (p. 564).

Worst of all, primitives lack any of the religious sentiments that guide advanced societies and civilizations. "The Eskimo have neither religious or idolatrous worship, nor so much as any ceremonies to be perceived tending towards it" (pp. 511, 515). Neither do the Fuegians (p. 541). Indeed, "many, we might almost say all, of the most savage races are . . . in this condition" (p. 576). This makes sense given the limited conceptual abilities of savages. "How, for instance, can a people who are unable to count their own fingers, possibly raise their mind so far as to admit even the rudiments of religion" (pp. 580-581).

The Priority of Theory

It is easy to challenge Lubbock's analysis of hunter-gatherers as depending too heavily on traveler's accounts that were sometimes unreliable. There is, however, no reason to believe that Lubbock would have viewed things any differently first-hand. Many of his sources were unquestionably good (e.g., Darwin), and everything they reported was fully compatible with the interpretation Lubbock developed (cf. Alland 1985). Progressive social evolutionary theory provided Lubbock and others with an explicit model of what savages ought to look like, and even from the piecemeal data then available it was clear that the fit was perfect—only the fine points of primitive technology remained uncertain (p. 547). Hunter-gatherers offered what was at the time perhaps the surest support for the tenets of British progressive social evolutionary theory. The interesting problems, the ones that had yet to be solved, lay elsewhere, in more complex social settings.

Progressive social evolutionary theory had a host of long-lasting repercussions within British hunter-gatherer ethnography. In the case of Australian Aborigines, it muddled the thinking of a whole generation of anthropologists on the matter of primitive religion. As classic primitives whose concerns in theory should have been purely material, the Australians could not possibly have anything remotely resembling religion (cf. Stanner 1965).[9] Ironically, in the final analysis this did not have the intended effect of deflecting attention away from Australian religion and toward Australian technology and adaptation to environment. Rather, the distortions of Aboriginal ritual behavior contained in accounts colored by these progressive social evolutionary assumptions (and in equally distorted accounts positing aboriginal belief in "High Gods") caused subsequent ethnographic fieldwork in Australia to dwell much more on the study of myth, ritual, and religion than has generally been the case for hunter-gatherers (cf. Yengoyan 1979).

---

[9]A similar evolutionary bias caused Morgan erroneously to deny the presence of complex social formations in Mesoamerica (cf. Hallowell 1960:53; Morgan 1876).

BRITISH HUNTER-GATHERER RESEARCH: ARCHAEOLOGY

For the most part, British prehistory has followed the lead of British social anthropology in relegating hunter-gatherer studies to secondary status—all the while contributing very little to evolutionary theory (cf. Daniel 1950). Hudson (1981) has documented the traditional and overriding concern of British archaeology with history, specifically British and classical history, and the rise of civilization as documented in the great achievements of the Ancients.[10] This was consistent with the tone of progressive theories of social evolution, particularly Spencer's (1876, 1882, 1896), which, by emphasizing the rise of Western civilization, were strongly historical in nature. Joining in the spirit of British social evolutionary theory, British archaeologists have often seemed to place little value on the information to be gained from studying primitive hunter-gatherers.

Remarks by Sir Mortimer Wheeler in the last chapter of his popular text, *Archaeology from the Earth* (Wheeler 1954), help to convey here one conception of hunter-gatherers among British prehistorians and the implications of that conception for the manner in which they have historically conducted research. Wheeler establishes with finality the distance between himself and the contemporary student of hunter-gatherers in his characterization of the aboriginal inhabitants of the now-famous Mesolithic site of Starr Carr, Yorkshire (J. G. D. Clark 1971):

> As squalid a huddle of marsh-ridden food-gatherers as the imagination could well encompass. (Wheeler 1954:231)

His opinion of hunting and gathering as a lifeway in general is no more charitable.

> I am not prepared to admit the Noble Savage within my general definition of the term ["noble"], for the simple reason that he is a savage, suffering from a savage's restricted vision, tangental reasoning and lack of "opportunity." I have in mind something far more complex and comprehensive; something in fact which implies the background of civilization or some approximation to it; where the intelligence has been subjected to the widest possible range

---

[10]The British experience in this respect differs markedly from the one in the United States, where there has seldom been any suggestion of historical connection between archaeologists (or, for that matter, ethnographers) and the cultures they study and where, as a consequence, there has always been a clear separation between the disciplines of anthropology and history. Put another way, British archaeology has tended to deal with a classical past that helps define what the civilized Briton is; American archaeology has tended to deal with a savage past that helps to define what civilized Americans are not (see Chapter 2). Americanist historical archaeology is an exception in this regard—but clearly one that proves the rule.

The History of Americanist Hunter-Gatherer Research

THE EARLY YEARS: 1600–1880

As we have seen, social evolutionary theory rested on the premise that material economy—more particularly subsistence economy—is fundamental to cultural progress and determines its evolutionary trajectory. Hunter-gatherers were conceptually critical to that premise. In opposing culture and nature, progressive evolutionary theory necessarily implied that the behavior of primitive peoples was to be construed in natural rather than cultural terms, that is, as a direct response to nature, technology, and environment. It followed that in its initial stages evolutionary progress was accomplished by replacing the natural hunting and gathering economy with a cultural economy founded on agriculture (see later discussion). As hunter-gatherers known in the nineteenth century showed, without this first step human progress was impossible (cf. Chinard 1947:51; Pearce 1988:66–72, 132). In social evolutionary theory, then, ecology and environment and hunter-gatherer research were inseparable; one could not account for the latter without considering the former.

As we have also seen, the tradition of British social evolutionary theory regarded environment and hunter-gatherers as problems that were essentially solved and required little further attention. Operating within the same theoretical framework, individuals in the United States arrived at a different conclusion: Environment and primitive peoples were poorly understood, and the development of a complete theory of social evolution required more thorough studies of both subjects.

The difference was partly a function of geography. There were in the

United States primitive peoples, many of them hunter-gatherers, that could be studied first-hand. As European naturalists had been able to study plants and animals directly in their drawing rooms, gardens, and estates, so could American anthropologists study their subject matter in their own backyards. Sooner or later, this was bound to foster an intellectual concern for environmental and technological context—topics that remained matters of speculation for European conjectural historians and social evolutionary theorists. It did not hurt that in the case of primitive New World peoples, the study of environmental context was entirely consistent with any version of progressive evolutionary theory to which one might subscribe. As we have seen, the theory of social evolution as progress allowed Powell to join Ward and others in denying the utility of selectionist interpretations as a basis for contemporary social policy without requiring him to abandon them in the special case of primitive hunter-gatherers, where he himself often found them most useful (see also Burrow 1966:226-227).

As Pearce (1988) and Chinard (1947:53-54) point out, the American interest (as opposed to European disinterest) in primitive peoples and natural environment was more than a simple matter of geography and easy accessibility. Between 1600 and 1850, Americans developed a distinctly un-European world view in which they saw themselves in a distinctly un-European national struggle: not against external challenges posed by other nations, ethnic groups, or conquering despots, as was the case in Europe, but rather against internal challenges posed by nature and the environment. To this end, Americans employed the Indian as a symbol of nature and, through that device, a symbol of what contemporary Americans were not and should not be (Pearce 1988:104, 208). Much simplified, Indians were savages; as hunters they were a part of nature and representatives of New World prehistory. Americans were civilized; as agriculturalists they were apart from, and masters over, nature and represented the New World present and future.

Because European world views made little reference to either the environment or primitive peoples (see Chapter 1), European ideas about primitives were comparatively uncomplicated (Pearce 1988:4). Primitives were simply noble to those who used them as a device through which to criticize progress and civilization (as in the primitivism of Rousseau)—and simply ignoble to the defenders of social evolutionary progress and civilization (as in the progressivist antiprimitivism of Charles Dickens, James Mill, and Buffon; see later discussion).

By contrast, because Americans saw Indians as the contradiction of their own multifaceted national character, the American portrayal of the savage Indian character was necessarily multifaceted and in that sense much more sophisticated than its European counterpart (Pearce 1988:103). The philosophy of social evolutionary progress assured Americans it was their manifest destiny to civilize the New World, to replace savagery with civilization. The Indian was, thus, to be pitied as one whose carefree and unfettered way of life was doomed and whose natural rights to the land had to give way to progress and civilization (Pearce 1988:53). Guilt arising from the recognition of this regrettable but inevitable unfolding of social evolutionary progress gradually produced the idea Pearce terms *savagism* (1988:xvii, 76). In it, both savage Indians and civilized Americans were imbued with both noble and ignoble qualities, though of different kinds, and the differences between savage and civilized qualities were seen primarily to reflect differences in material circumstances, that is, technology and environment (Pearce 1988:115, 121, 131). American anthropology arose from early attempts to harness these ideas about primitives, environment, and social evolutionary progress to a workable program of scientific research.

Jefferson on Primitives and the New World Environment

Morgan is often credited with being the first American to attempt a blend of evolution and materialism, but the distinction more properly falls to Thomas Jefferson. His progressive evolutionary interpretation of living native American cultures seems to have been for its time every bit as materialistically sophisticated as Engel's adaptation of Morgan, which Harris (1968a) proffers as the first systematic periodization of prehistory. Jefferson believed that by touring the United States ethnographers could "relive" the essential stages of human evolution.

> Let the philosophic observer commence a journey from the savages of the Rocky Mountains, eastwardly towards our seacoast. These he would observe in the earliest stage of association, living under no law but that of nature, subsisting and covering themselves with the flesh and skin of wild beasts. He would next find those on our frontiers, in the pastoral state, raising domestic animals to supply the defects of hunting. Then succeed our own semi-barbarous citizens the pioneers of advance civilization, and so in his progress he would meet the gradual shades of improving man until he would reach his, as yet, most improved state in our seaport towns. This, in fact, is equivalent to a survey, in time, of the progress of man from the infancy of creation to the present day. (Letter from Thomas Jefferson to William Ludlow, dated 6 September 1824; quoted in Chinard 1947:54)

Given his many and varied intellectual pursuits, Jefferson's interest in the primitive inhabitants of the New World in a sense requires no explanation. His special interest in materialist-ecological interpretations of social evolution, however, did not arise of its own in a vacuum (cf. Glacken 1967:681-682; Chinard 1947:42, 56; Pearce 1988:91-94). He developed and presented these interpretations as alternatives to environmental and evolutionary propositions regarding New World peoples and environments advanced by Old World scholars of the armchair tradition. Here, Jefferson was reacting principally to the evolutionary interpretations of the famous French naturalist Buffon and other antiprimitivists including Roberston, a Scottish social evolutionary philosopher whose work, directly and indirectly, drew extensively on the work of Montesquieu, Buffon, and others influenced by Buffon, including Peter Kalm, Cornelieus de Pauw, and Abbé Raynal, all of whom had written on the subject of the suitability of the New World as a human habitat (Chinard 1947:38, 42-44). Buffon's seminal contributions to evolutionary theory in relation to the mutability of species are well known. His interpretation of New World natural history, however, emphasized environmental rather than evolutionary causes. It was solidly rooted in, and in some ways drew directly from, the older tradition of theories of environmental influence. For Buffon the primitive state, that is, lack of evolutionary change, of the American Indian was due chiefly to the "weakness" of the New World environment and its inhabitants and the recency of their occupation of that environment (Chinard 1947:31). Simply put, the environment discouraged human invention and achievement. Buffon and others inspired by his work, who often took more extreme positions (e.g., Kalm and Raynal; Chinard 1947:30, 33, 37), argued, further, that parallel environmental effects were readily evident in New World animals, particularly in domesticates brought from Europe, which had grown steadily smaller following their introduction.

Jefferson was offended at every turn by these theories and, being a wealthy intellectual and politically influential, was in a position to do something about it. Early on he made it a point to inform Buffon of his erroneous interpretation of the New World environment and its natural and culture inhabitants (Jefferson 1787). Later, as president of the United States, he took the further, and more important, step of gathering—and seeing that others gathered—empirical evidence to evaluate the implications of Buffon's theory. Moved to action by the speculations of Buffon, Robertson, de Pauw, Kalm, Raynal, and others that he was convinced were as baseless in fact as they were often abhorrent in principle, Jefferson emerges as a pivotal figure in the early development of American anthropology (Hallowell 1960:15; Glacken 1967:681-682). His interest in the evolutionary status of native Americans and the influence of environment on their culture and economy are evident in his instructions as to the ethnographic particulars the explorers Lewis and Clark were to observe on their journey to the Pacific coast (Chinard 1947:56; Hallowell 1960).

Jefferson set important precedents for the future of American anthropology, not only in regard to the participation of the government in development and support of that discipline, as Hollowell has observed, but in the environmental and materialist biases he gave that association. From Jefferson and the

Lewis and Clark expedition (cf. Pearce 1988:106-107), we can easily see the path to later government surveys, particularly that of Powell, and through Powell to a governmentally sponsored program of environmental-materialist inquiry regarding the primitive native inhabitants of the United States. Intellectually, however, the road to Powell lead through Lewis Henry Morgan.

Morgan

Two decades before Powell, Morgan had the opportunity to observe first-hand a comparatively primitive people (Pearce 1988: 130-131), the Iroquois, and it seems reasonable to think that the tangibility of his subject matter lent his evolutionary theories a more contextual and materialist perspective than they would have otherwise had (cf. Bohannan 1965:x, xvi-xvii). It is telling in this regard that in criticizing the Spanish accounts of Aztec royalty, Morgan observed that they lacked "the realism of Indian life" (Morgan 1881:274). Morgan does not emerge as an important fieldworker, to be sure. He had, nevertheless, considerably more experience with primitive peoples than either Spencer or Tylor, which makes his materialism more understandable. It is perhaps this sense of first-hand familiarity with the American Indian that caused Morgan to choose so prosaic a subject as houses and houselife for a volume in which material and evolutionary themes were intertwined.

> To a very great extent communism in living was a necessary result of the condition of the Indian tribes. It entered into their plan of life and determined the character of their houses. In effect it was a union of effort to procure subsistence, which was the vital and commanding concern of life. . . . It is made reasonably plain, I think, from the facts stated, that in the Upper Status of savagery, and also in the Lower Status of barbarism, the Indian household was formed of a number of families of gentile kin; that they practiced communism in living in the household, and that this principle found expression in their house architecture and predetermined its character. (Morgan 1881:63, 139)

Harris (1968a:213-216) notwithstanding, materialism was a fundamental element of the progressive evolutionary theories of Morgan, though to a lesser degree than it was for Spencer.

> The progress of mankind from their primitive condition to civilization has been marked and eventful. Each great stage of progress is connected, more or less directly, with some important invention or discovery which materially influenced human progress, and inaugurated an improved condition. (Morgan 1881:xxv)

Unlike Tylor, Morgan was at least willing to hazard an explicit formulation of the relationship between specific technological innovations and the course of evolution. It can hardly be denied, in any event, that Marx was attracted to Morgan because of the materialism in his unilinear evolution (e.g., his reliance on technological developments that define stages of progress; Morgan 1877:9; Hobsbawm 1964:24-25; cf. Harris 1968a:213-214).[1]

ENVIRONMENT AND ECOLOGY IN EARLY AMERICAN ANTHROPOLOGY: 1880-1920

From Morgan it is only a small step to the beginnings of American anthropology as a formal discipline, where the prominence of the environmental-materialist perspective is clearly evident. It is well known, to be sure, that Boas inaugurated his career with a study of the relationship between culture and geography among the Eskimo of Baffin Island (Boas 1888) and, having done this much, never again explored such relationships seriously. Yet many of his equally distinguished contemporaries did just that, for Boas by no means spoke for early American anthropology as a whole; indeed, at the time he was a rather minor figure (cf. Buettner-Janusch 1957; Meltzer 1983). The funding for early American anthropology was largely provided by the government, and it was in Washington, specifically within the Smithsonian Institution, where the power lay. There, under the leadership of Powell, the scientists at the National Museum and the Bureau of Ethnology undertook penetrating studies of environment and technology without wandering through the sterile morass of extreme environmental determinism as later set down by those such as Huntington (1945, 1963) and Semple (1911).

The institutional support for such ethnographic studies looms large indeed when one surveys just the list of important ethnobotanical contributions made by individuals in federal service (e.g., Palmer 1871, 1874, 1878; cf. Bye 1972; Coville 1892; Dutcher 1893; Chestnut 1902). With the formal employment of O. T. Mason by the National Museum in 1884, governmental support for environmental and materialist research broadened to include the problem of primitive technology, a subject theretofore largely uninvestigated.

As we have seen, the direction in which Powell took Washington anthropology was partly the result of a long-standing tradition of governmental research that began with Jefferson and Lewis and Clark. Powell did not join in that tradition for the sake of mere science. He championed the study of nature

---

[1]Although their theories shared much in common, (i.e., conflict), Spencer's support for individualism and capitalism prevented Marx from turning there for a theory of primitives: Morgan was the logical alternative.

and man and the study of primitive man in relation to nature as part of an overarching theory of progressive social evolution intended as a blueprint for social policy.

Powell and Social Progress

The world that Powell and Morgan confronted was remarkably different from the one in which Jefferson had first sought to gain an understanding of the relationship between nature and primitive mankind. By the close of the nineteenth century, America was no longer the wild continent the Pilgrims had encountered. Joined by the railroad and telegraph and the subject of ambitious and intense federally sponsored surveys, little remained that could be called truly unexplored or remote. Timber, mining, and agricultural interests and the western press of settlement threatened quickly to gobble up what little of the pristine environment then remained intact. As Hinsley (1981) has pointed out, this profoundly affected the way Powell and other Americans saw themselves and how they saw the future.

As we have seen, unlike Great Britain and the rest of Europe, America has always seen itself as a nation born in the wilderness and firmly rooted in that wilderness heritage (Chinard 1947:53-54). By the end of the nineteenth century, however, the wilderness itself was quickly fading and with it the natural setting of the American self-image. The social evolutionary theories of both Morgan and Powell spoke to this issue. To a far greater degree than Morgan, however, Powell sought to reanchor Western civilization through a social evolutionary theory that ultimately led back to the natural environment.

As they had been to Jefferson, the American Indian was essential to the social evolutionary theories of Powell because as primitives they had always been regarded as part of the natural landscape. The impending loss of the wilderness was, to a great degree, paralleled by the imminent demise of aboriginal America and its "wild" hunter-gatherers (e.g., Pearce 1988:163, 208). In many ways, late nineteenth-century Americans saw in the "Indian problem" the elements of their own dilemma: peoples increasingly disenfranchised from their wilderness heritage and natural context. The chief difference lay in the fact that, through enlightened (i.e., scientifically guided) social policy, civilization could do something about the problem; primitives had neither the means nor the intellect to do so.

The Museum Connection

As Hinsley (1981:83-83) and others have observed, museums of natural history were places where these problems could be confronted intellectually and where a sense of natural order could be restored for nineteenth-century Americans.

Joseph Henry, first secretary of the Smithsonian Institution, made this a theme
of his address at the dedication of the American Museum of Natural History.

> [The American Museum of Natural History] is to be a temple of nature in
> which the productions of the inorganic and organic world, together with
> the remnants of the past ages of the human family are to be collected,
> classified, and properly exhibited. It is to be . . . an attractive exhibit which
> shall arrest the attention of the most unobserving of those who, having been
> confined all their lives to the city, have come to consider edifices of brick
> and of stone as the most prominent objects of the physical world. (Joseph
> Henry [1874], quoted in Hellman 1968:24-25)

Primitive peoples provided the essential linchpin for this natural order. As
Margaret Mead (1960) has pointed out, the image of primitive peoples as part of
nature was fostered very early on in America by museums of natural history. By
placing the art and technology of North American Indians in halls adjacent to
those containing biological and geological specimens, "the tradition was established by which anthropology . . . became part of natural history [in accord with
progressive social evolutionary theory]. . . . Man was shown to be a part of
nature . . . Man in nature and man transcending nature." (Mead 1960:10-11).
Himself convinced that the study of the sciences was an essential ingredient of
anthropological training, Powell was fully sympathetic to this idea and played a
key role in developing that theme (cf. Buettner-Janusch 1957; Hinsley 1981:162).
Through the museum context, the early roots of mankind in nature could be
demonstrated to the public in such a way that they would understand their own
evolutionary relationship to nature.[2]

Otis T. Mason was a leading figure in this early museum research. As made
clear by their titles (e.g., "Technogeography, or the Relation of the Earth to the
Industries of Mankind"), his works were guided by a creative (rather than
strongly deterministic) theory of materialism (Mason 1894, 1895, 1905;
Buettner-Janusch 1957). A prominent founding member of the Anthropological
Society of Washington (progenitor of the American Anthropological Association) and notable contributor to its journal, the *American Anthropologist*, as well
as to the Smithsonian Institution and U.S. National Museum *Annual Reports*,
Mason undoubtedly deserves credit as the architect of the materialist approach
we know today as technoenvironmental determinism (cf. Harris 1968a). Wissler
(1914:449) was quick to credit the contributions of Mason in relation to his own
work on natural and cultural areas. Kroeber, too, was fully aware of the
importance of Mason's works, including (Harris to the contrary: 1968a:374) the

---

[2]Given the important role museums played in developing progressive social evolutionary theory, it
is difficult to credit the claim of Collier and Tschopik (1954:771) that museum men in the period
from 1890 to 1920 were "empirical, strongly historical, and anti-evolutionary."

one entitled "Influence of Environment on Human Industries or Arts" (Mason 1895), in which was introduced the concept of the environmentally defined "culture area."

It is of more than passing significance that Mason seems to have taken for granted that archaeology and ethnology shared a common purpose (cf. De Laguna 1960:94). Within the Smithsonian Institution, that had been assumed from the very beginning (Hallowell 1960:31). This, undoubtedly, reflected the American idea of savagism in which contemporary Indians, addicted to a hunting lifeway, were portrayed as part of American prehistory (Pearce 1988:192-195): The subject matters of New World ethnology and archaeology were thus one and the same. This shared museum heritage (in which both Mason and Powell were important figures; cf. Buettner-Janusch 1957:319-321) and the consequent mutual interest of both disciplines in studies of material culture—a necessary aspect of museology and a central explanatory theme in savagism—seems best to account for the close relationship that has historically existed between American archaeology and cultural anthropology. In short, it is arguable that the distinctive alliance of these disciplines in the United States is due more to the idea of savagism and the museum tradition of technoenvironmental materialism it inspired than to governmental involvement in the Moundbuilder problem (cf. Willey and Sabloff 1980:79). Indeed, the latter must be seen not as a cause of the American archaeological/ethnological alliance but rather as a response to the same forces that produced it.[3]

Technogeography and Social Evolution

In Mason's technogeography, the interaction between nature and technology caused primitive peoples to follow parallel but historically distinct lines of development resulting in the formation of culture areas, or *oikoumene* (Mason 1894:148-153). That line of reasoning, however, seemed contradictory in its implications to the millennial unity of civilized mankind envisioned in the progressive social evolutionary theories of Powell and others (1885, 1888a; Morgan 1877, Kimball [cf. Ward] 1968:197, 224, 302; McGee 1899:439, 446-447; Hinsley [cf. Holmes] 1981:288; Spencer held a similar view [cf. 1865:476-484]). To bring his views into line with those theories, Mason argued that the "centrifugal" technoenvironmental forces that led to cultural differentiation in

---

[3]One cannot avoid drawing the further conclusion that it is the early grounding of technoenvironmental materialism in museums, rather than institutions of higher education, that explains the subsequent decline of materialist theory and rise of Boasian particularism in American anthropology. As Bureau director and museologist, respectively, Powell and Mason produced no real students. Boas, on the other hand, produced them by the score: Kroeber, Mead, Benedict, Lowie, Sapir, Speck, Herskovits, and so on.

primitives were superseded in the more advanced stages of civilization by "centripetal" political, technical, and intellectual forces that would in the end (i.e., under Western civilization) unite the world as a single culture area (Mason 1894:153).

In this respect, Mason's technogeographical version of world-systems theory is a particularly good example of how an overriding interest in social evolution and its effects tends to diminish the importance of technoenvironmental explanation and the instructive value of primitive peoples. In Mason's scheme, the most powerful force was intellect, and the people who used that power to the fullest were destined to inherit the earth. Outside the National Museum, Powell exhibited these philosophical tendencies to a far greater degree. As Powell's interest in social evolution and its potential for application in social policy grew, his interest in studies of environment and primitive peoples lessened. Most of his later work dealt with social evolutionary theory and metaphysical philosophy (Darrah 1951:350-384); preoccupied with these, he never finished his manuscript on the Numic-speaking hunter-gatherers of the Great Basin, the aboriginal group with which he was most familiar. Thus, as had been the case with the interpretation of the American Indian through the idea of savagism (cf. Pearce 1988: 232), it appeared more and more that Powell's interest in anthropology had less to do with understanding primitive man than in understanding Western civilization.

Further, as his commitment to his own social evolutionary theory grew, Powell grew more willing to stretch empirical cases to match predictions, particularly when it came to hunter-gatherers. As had been the case with Spencer (Kimball 1968:296; Kennedy 1978:15-16), Powell and one or two of his more devoted staff members increasingly found ethnographic facts about primitive peoples interesting only insofar as they could be used to support a theory the truth of which was not in question (Meadows 1952:99). A comparatively minor and easily forgiven example was Powell's attempt to demonstrate that Numic hunter-gatherers were zootheistic because, being in a state of savagery, they depended on plants and animals for subsistence (Fowler and Fowler 1971:21). Subordinate McGee's effort to please Powell by hammering the Seri into the mold of Powellian social evolutionary theory was far more bold—and wholly unforgivable (cf. Hinsley 1981:239-245).

McGee's Seri Ethnography

During the course of a 1894 Bureau of American Ethnology collecting excursion to the Southwest, W. J. McGee, a geologist-turned-ethnologist working under the direction of Powell, heard lurid accounts of a warlike people called the Seri and decided they merited the immediate scientific attention of the bureau. Over the course of two different field expeditions to coastal Sonora, Mexico, in that year and the next (1895), McGee managed to spend only "about a week" interviewing perhaps 60 Seri (McGee 1898:13; but see Hinsley 1981:239). On the basis of this and the historical sources at his disposal, McGee published a 343 page ethnography. Though less openly chauvinist, his account of the Seri is remarkably compatible with the spirit of Lubbock's survey of primitives.

As Powell (1898:lxv-lxvii) noted in introducing the monograph, the point that emerges most clearly with the Seri is that their "activities . . . reflect environment with exceptional closeness." Representing the "lowest recognized phase of savagery" (McGee 1898:294), the Seri are profoundly affected by natural selection.

> The lowly Seri are actually, albeit unconsciously, carrying out a meaningful experiment in stirpiculture—an experiment whose methods and results are equally valuable to students. (p. 163)

The harshness of "Seriland" is clearly reflected in Seri physique and ingrained habits and especially evident in their excessively migratory behavior (pedestrian habit), inability to make or use complex tools (lack of tool sense), and distrust of aliens (race sense; p. 156).

> A striking correspondence between Seri physique and Seri habitat is revealed in the pedal development, with the attendant development of muscle and bone, lung capacity, and heart power, together with other faculties involved in the pedestrian habit. (p. 157)

> The Seri, male and female, young and old, may be described as notably deep-chested and clean-limbed quick-steppers, or as human thorough-breds.(p. 138)

Exacerbated in part by an unspoken primitive superstition preventing them from camping near water, "the tribesmen and their families are perpetual fugitives (their movements being too erratic and aimless to put them in the class of nomads)" (pp. 181, 221).

Unfortunately, although physically well adapted, the Seri remain severely limited in their technical abilities.

> A trait of the Seri . . . is habitual use of hands and teeth in lieu of the implements characteristic of even the most lowly culture found among most primitive tribes. (p. 152)

> The Seri may be described with reasonable accuracy as a knifeless folk. (p. 152)

> Conformably with their striking independence of knives, the Seri are conspicuously unskillful in all mechanical operations involving the use of tools. (p. 153)

The Seri are practically without flaked or chipped implements, . . . they eshew and discard stones edged by fracture whether naturally or through use. (p. 248)

[Natural stones] come into use as implements through chance demands met by hasty selection from the abundant material . . . the great majority of the objects so employed are discarded after a use or two. (pp. 248-249)

[On the whole], Seri industries are significant as (1) local, (2) fortuitous, (3) primitive, (4) autochthonous; and these features combine to illumine a noteworthy stage in primitive thought. (p. 267)

The Seri are positively animal-like in their hostility to outsiders.

The race-sense of the Seri may be regarded as the product of long-continued stripicultural processes, initially shaped by environment, yet developed to unusual degree by somatico-social habits, kept alive largely through continuous environmental interaction. (p. 163)

The Seri can no more control the involuntary snarl and growl at the approach of the alien than can the hunting-dog at sight or smell of the timber-wolf. (p. 155)

Even at first sight the painted devices [female face-painting] bring to mind the directive markings of lower animals . . . and in view of the implacably militant habit of the Seri it would seem evident that the[se] artificial devices are, at least in their primary aspect, analogous to the natural markings [of animals]. (p. 167)

With respect to social organization, "the clan organization of the Seri conforms closely with that characteristic of savagery everywhere" (p. 274). As the theories of Morgan and Powell predict, "the most noticeable social fact revealed about Seri rancherias is the prominence of the females" (p. 269).

The tribe is made up of clans defined by consanguinity reckoned only in the female line. (p. 168)

The social unit is the maternal clan, organized in theory and faith in homage of a beast-god. (p. 274)

Mortuary ceremonies attain their highest development in connection with females, the recognized blood-bearers and legislators of the tribe. (p. 287)

In keeping with Morgan's explanation for the presence of matrilineality in savagery, among the Seri "there is some question as to the clear recognition of paternity" (p. 272).

On the whole, as primitive hunter-gatherers had been generally to Lubbock, to McGee and Powell, the case of the Seri was open and shut.

> Esthetic activities afford a means of measuring developmental status or the relative positions in terms of the development of races and tribes. . . . On applying these principles to the Seri tribe, in the light of their meager industrial motives and still poorer esthetic motives, it would appear that they stand well at the bottom of the scale. (McGee 1898:179; see also Powell 1898:lxv-lxvii)

It scarcely requires comment that McGee erred on many points: the Seri were not matrilineal (and may actually have been patrilineal; Bowen 1983:245) nor were burial practices strongly marked by sex (Bowen 1976:48). They often camped near water (Bowen 1976:23-24), and they made and used chipped stone tools of many kinds (Bowen 1976:85-86).

Of course, in one sense, it is not particularly surprising that McGee's facts were often wrong and sometimes self-contradictory (e.g., compare McGee 1898:115, with McGee 1898:150); given the limited time McGee spent in the field and the haste with which the analysis was done, that was unavoidable. Given the immense importance Powell and his associates placed on social evolutionary theory, it is perhaps not even surprising that McGee was so willing to stretch facts. What is surprising is that the facts he chose to stretch, particularly in characterizing the Seri as innately hostile and warlike, seemed blatantly to contradict Powell's own early vision of primitive peoples as essentially peaceful (1888a:102; 1891:39). In many ways, that contradiction epitomized the degree to which Powell, as social evolutionist, had finally come to care so little about hunter-gatherers.

The Seri of McGee's time were undeniably warlike—no doubt about that. There was also no doubt that this reflected a long history of bloody contact with land-grabbing, racist (i.e., civilized) Westerners—including, most prominently, the very same land baron that hosted McGee's visit (Bowen 1983:232-234; McGee 1898:109-117). Yet to draw that conclusion would have implied that the impending social evolutionary millennium unification of mankind in which the primitive centrifugal forces of technology and environment would be overcome by civilized intellect was going to be something less than Powell had cracked it up to be. Rather than face that, McGee and Powell chose to ignore all the historical facts they had amassed and argued that the Seri were evolutionarily isolated because they were warlike! Clearly, to these social evolutionary theorists neither the Seri, nor hunter-gatherers in general, mattered much any more.

After Powell

Despite their excesses, the estimable efforts of Powell, Mason, McGee, and others established the environmental- materialist perspective as a force to be reckoned with in anthropology long after the more extreme claims for environ mental determinism, especially the more chauvinistic ones, fell into disfavor after the turn of the century.

> Men, though singularly specialized in regard to the brain, are but animals subject to the same stimuli, to which they react, particularly when living in a primitive state of cultural development, in essentially the same way. (A. H. Clark 1912:23)

Had environmental explanations been as ineffectual then as is commonly supposed, it is unlikely that Sapir would have felt compelled to begin his classic essay on language and environment by rejecting the assumption that attributed "many elements of human culture to the influence of the environment in which the sharers of that culture are placed," an assumption he clearly took to be both common and widespread (Sapir 1912). Indeed, that the essay was considered important at the time or is so held today and that Sapir felt it necessary to take issue explicitly with the view of "some . . . taking the extreme position of reducing practically all manifestations of human life and thought to environmental influences" (Sapir 1912:226) speaks directly to the prominence of the materialist bias in anthropology in the United States during the first decades of the twentieth century.

Even those who rejected environmental interpretations of most human institutions followed Powell, Mason, and McGee in accepting their value in the hunter-gatherer case.

> It is in its beginnings . . . that culture leans most heavily on environment. (Dixon 1928:12-13)

Because primitive culture is limited culture, this view was also that of the so-called "cultural possibilists" (e.g., Kroeber 1939; Wissler 1926; Forde 1934). It was also the position of the cultural ecologists (Steward 1938:1; cf. Vayda and Rappaport 1968) and others like them (e.g., Speck 1915), who saw more than just limitations when it came to understanding the relationship between material conditions and organizational responses. Indeed, the folk with whom Powell worked most closely, the Numic-speaking peoples of the American West, were and still are regarded as among the most primitive human culture could produce and therefore the most susceptible to environmental explanation. As Steward observed in his landmark work on these groups via the method of cultural ecology:

> Greatest success should attend analyses of societies which evince a less complicated history, whose structure is simpler in content and form, and whose institutions were most extensively patterned by subsistence activities. Such societies usually exist among the simple hunter-gatherers. (Steward 1938:1)

It is interesting to note that as Steward's attention shifted to cultural evolution (e.g., Steward 1955), he became increasingly less interested in the effect of environment and technology on hunter-gatherer adaptation. Indeed, as David Thomas (1983a) has shown, there is a tendency in Steward's later writings to gloss over adaptive variability among Great Basin hunter-gatherers in order to make them fit the mold of an evolutionary level (stage) of sociocultural integration. The case, thus, is very much like that of Powell. Steward found it necessary to downplay hunter-gatherers and materialist explanations in order to produce an evolutionary account of culture change, emphasizing once more the natural conflict between models of hunter-gatherers, which emphasize adaptation and stability, and models of cultural evolution, which emphasize change.

MATERIALISM AND EVOLUTION IN AMERICAN ARCHAEOLOGY: 1920–1960

The Pecos Classification

American archaeology was an active participant in, or at least consumer of, the materialist tradition in anthropology by at least the 1920s. Although its materialist and evolutionary underpinnings have generally been overlooked, the Pecos classification of southwestern prehistory (Kidder 1927) scarcely conceals the fundamental influence of these concepts on Kidder and the other participants in that seminal archaeological conference. At the time, all known archaeological manifestations in the Southwest were potentially attributable to one of either two kinds of agricultural peoples: the earlier pit-house dwelling Basketmaker or later apartment dwelling Pueblo. Taken at face value, the evidence seemed directly to contradict the unilineal evolutionary assumption that agriculture represented a developed rather than basal stage of social evolution. Indeed, as we have seen, in such theories agriculture is the evolutionary innovation needed to set social progress in motion. This seemed to preclude the possibility of a basal southwestern culture founded on agriculture. With that theoretical inconsistency clearly in mind, Kidder and the conference participants added to the known prehistoric cultures of the Southwest a purely hypothetical one, Basketmaker I, which they characterized in general terms as a nomadic hunter-gatherer phase. The creation of this hypothetical stage, for which evidence was later found and classified by Jennings (1978:97) and others (Cordell 1984:55) as the southwestern manifestation of the Desert Archaic, established in theory that agriculture was the basis for all the distinctive traits one typically associates with the cultures of the American Southwest, for example, settled village life and ceramics, and which at the same time distinguish it from the marginal hunting and gathering cultures of the Northern Periphery (i.e., the Great Basin).

Jennings (1957) would later take the basic assumptions of the Pecos sequence in an entirely different direction. Persuaded that environment presented an insurmountable obstacle to evolutionary progress in the Great Basin, he argued that there the kind of hunter-gatherer adaptation that characterized basal southwestern prehistory (i.e., Basketmaker I) had persisted with little change from 10,000 years ago to the ethnographic present. He later expanded this view to the North American continent generally, arguing that, north of Mexico, all developmental advances beyond the Archaic Stage of hunting and gathering could only be explained in terms of exotic influences (Jennings 1968: 182).

The Midwestern Taxonomic System

The archaeological classification system developed in the American heartland scarcely a decade after Pecos, known as the Midwestern Taxonomic System (McKern 1939), codified precisely the same materialist perspectives that had been evident in the Pecos classification. The Midwestern Taxonomic System grouped cultural entities through a hierarchy of successively more general levels, beginning with a relatively large number of units, termed *foci*, defined by many and highly specific attributes, and ending with a few units, termed *bases*, defined by a small number of the most general and basic traits. The materialist underpinnings of this system can be made no clearer than by noting that, as Morgan's stages, the bases of the midwestern system were invariably defined by economy, the principal distinction between bases resting on the presence of agriculture. In short, for Midwestern archaeologists, economy underwrote culture—and agriculture underwrote the development of all the more advanced cultures and culture traits.

SUMMARY

If we acknowledge the debt owed by contemporary materialist theories of all sorts to Steward (e.g., 1936; cf. Bettinger 1980), and, in turn, the debt owed by Steward to Kroeber and Wissler (cf. Harris 1968a:338-340), and, successively, theirs to Mason, and Mason's to Jefferson and, indirectly, Buffon, then, as we have already seen with theories of progressive evolution, it is no trick at all to trace materialist interpretations of hunter-gatherer behavior far beyond the beginnings of anthropology to the time of the ancients. The heritage can scarcely be denied.

That materialist theory is closely connected historically with hunter-gatherer studies is perhaps not so surprising after all, however. It is, for instance, a distinctly materialist perspective that permits a mode of subsistence, that is, hunting and gathering, to be identified as a stage of cultural evolution. Further that evolutionary theory and materialist theory should have become linked in the hunter-gatherer case is, as we have shown, altogether logical, given the nature of these theories. In these accounts, hunter-gatherers were unable to control production of their supply of food and thus wholly dependent on nature, which, for the Social Darwinists at least, was not just an unreliable provider but, as an agent of selection, an active opponent.

Insecure in this most basic requirement of life, hunter- gatherers were constantly foraging for food. This left little time to explore inventions that might have materially improved their quality of life or to devote to more contemplative pastimes, art for example. Hunter-gatherer culture was therefore impoverished and primitive in every phase and aspect, from technology to religion. As witnessed by events in the European Paleolithic, evolving sophistication in technology and behavior eventually brought marginal gains in these respects. All the same, the model told that after the discovery of fire and ability to make basic tools, agriculture—which ended the worldwide dominance of hunting and gathering—was the first significant human invention, the first truly progressive step in human culture.

Note that it is not at issue here whether any of the hunter-gatherers that were characterized in this way were actually primitive as advertised; as we have seen in the cases of conjectural history, the natural histories of Buffon and de Pauw, and the biased early treatment of aboriginal Australian religion, until the mid-twentieth century most characterizations of hunter-gatherers derived less from critical ethnographic or archaeological observation than from preconceptions—more charitably, hypotheses; their basis was in evolutionary or materialist theory rather than fieldwork.

In these early evolutionary formulations, the agricultural revolution represented progress. The details of the process attracted relatively little attention. The ultimate domination of agriculture was not in doubt (certainly all empirical evidence spoke to this effect). The major questions had to do with the point at which the invention itself would finally take shape as an idea to be acted upon and how long thereafter its spread would require. Put another way, the agricultural revolution was material with respect to conditions (i.e., in the need to establish a reliable food supply) but mental in origin, its source lying in the idea that a planted seed will grow and produce food (MacNeish 1964). For the archaeologist, questions about agriculture centered not so much on origins and causes as on the timing of the invention and its diffusion as an idea.

RESEARCH AFTER 1960:
HUNTER-GATHERERS AS ECOLOGISTS

The concept of "hunter-gatherer primitives" remained viable until about the mid 1960s when it had to face some facts. The most telling of these were generated by the ethnographic research done in the early 1960s by Lee (1968, 1969) among the !Kung San of the Kalahari and by others among a variety of other groups, mostly in Africa and Australia. This material first reached the attention of the general anthropological community by means of a Wenner-Gren symposium entitled "Man the Hunter," held in April 1966 in Chicago (Lee and DeVore 1968) The impetus for this symposium was an earlier one entitled "Origin of Man." As so many times before, the implication here was clearly that hunter-gatherers should be studied for the light they might shed on the evolutionary transition from animal to human.

The resurgence of ethnographic research of the mid-1960s exposed basic flaws in the existing model of "hunter-gatherer primitives." Virtually none of its predictions was confirmed: Hunter-gatherers seemed not to die young nor constantly to wage war against nature and starvation. According to Lee (1969), they ate well, lived long lives, and had plenty of spare time. Even more damning—at least to progressive evolutionary theory—hunter-gatherers seemed to work less and yet eat better than agriculturalists living in the same environments (Woodburn 1968). They were, in fact, the very picture of affluence.

It is, in retrospect, surprising that the idea of hunter-gatherers affluence took hold as quickly as it did, for the empirical data offered in its support were certainly not overwhelming. Two circumstances help to make this radical change of view somewhat more understandable. First, the progressive evolutionary interpretation of hunter-gatherers as limited by their primitive technology greatly restricted the potential for understanding these systems as they actually worked. Traditional developmental models centered on the question of what *could* be rather than what actually was; to deal with the latter required a change to a perspective in which hunter-gatherer systems were taken at face value as systems that worked rather than as systems destined to fail and be replaced by a better ones.

Second, the 1960s was a period of marked social unrest and upheaval arising in part from a pervasive disillusionment with technology, the politics of industry and industrial states, and the callous treatment of the natural environment at the hands of technology and industry. By contrast, the same elements— technology, industrialism, and the subduing of the environment—were viewed as advances in progressive evolutionary social theory. The social rejection of these concepts had an unmistakable effect on the anthropological interpretation of hunter-gatherers at the time, as frequent attempts to compare hunter-gatherers favorably against Western industrial society clearly showed (Sahlins

1968:85-89; Lee 1969; for a similar interpretation regarding the impact of social views on neofunctionalism, see Friedman 1979).

Whether or not the data it furnished justified the view of hunter-gatherer affluence, by establishing that the invention of agriculture might not have advanced the human condition on all fronts—and particularly with respect to nutrition and energetic efficiency (but see Harris 1971:204-206) where its superiority had always been assumed to lie—the ethnographic research of the 1960s doomed the developmental model of hunter-gatherers as primitives. At least two phenomena were now left unexplained: (1) the basis for hunter-gatherer behavior (backwardness and ignorance of helpful innovations no longer applied), and (2) the origins of agriculture (improvement in subsistence and quality of life no longer worked).

To fill this gap, hunter-gatherer specialists turned to contemporary anthropological theory, specifically to the school of "new ecologists" (Murphy 1970) and neofunctionalist theory (e.g., Vayda and Rappaport 1968) and the closely allied technoenvironmental determinist interpretations of cultural materialism (e.g., Harris 1968a; cf. Orlove 1980). Not coincidentally, these theories repeated certain key themes common to nearly all previous hunter-gatherer research, most importantly a stated interest in cultural evolution (Harris 1968a; Vayda 1968:viii-ix; Vayda and Rappaport 1968:496) and an unshakable bias in favor of materialist explanations that only a few (e.g., Sahlins 1968) were willing to abandon.

To be sure, this newer hunter-gatherer model was more than just neofunctionalist theory. The early writings of Steward (1936, 1937, 1938)— which had established the benefits of an ecological approach to hunter-gatherers grounded in a solid understanding of local environments—were particularly influential (cf. Damas 1969:4; Lee and DeVore 1968:412) despite criticism of those early works by leading neofunctionalists (e.g., Vayda and Rappaport 1968; see later discussion). Those who sought theoretical advice outside the discipline found contemporary work in ecology particularly helpful (e.g., Wynne-Edwards 1962, Odum 1959; Lack 1954). These ecological theories seemed to lose something in anthropological translation, however; the biologists were interested in physical populations that could be sampled and censused, the anthropologists in more ethereal cultural "systems" (Peoples 1982).

A (arguably *the*) principal issue upon which the older interpretation of hunter-gatherers as primitives and this newer ecological one differ is essentially that which seemed to (but actually did not) separate Spencer from other progressive theorists, namely the monist concept that the same kinds of laws apply to all natural systems, human and nonhuman alike. As we have seen, the progressive evolutionary view of hunter-gatherers as primitives (including Spencer's) was necessarily antithetical to such an interpretation: Progress took place by the replacement of material forces with social, religious, and symbolic ones (or, for Spencer, by the analogous replacement of natural selection with functionally acquired heritable modifications). This suggests the presence of two fundamentally different kinds of forces (e.g., material/physical vs. intellectual-/spiritual) one applying to animals, the other exclusively to humans. Kroeber in his possibilist distinction between natural influences and cultural "geist" and Steward (though in lesser degree) in his separation of "culture core" and "culture noncore" can be seen as firmly committed to this kind of dualism. Undoubtedly both inherited their interest in nonmaterialist forces directly from Boas and through him indirectly from the German Romantic School of economic history, which, as led by Gustav Schmoler in the 1880s (cf. Davis 1978), was preoccupied with unique and irreducible aspects of culture. Particularly notable here is that Schmoler and the Romantics were at that time locked in debate with the Austrian School of marginal value theorists, led by Karl Menger, who advocated explanations arising from formal economics. For Steward and Kroeber (and arguably even Boas), culture was divided along exactly the lines that divided the Romantics and Marginalists: One part of culture was explicable with reference to environment, technology, and economy (the core), the other was inexplicable in any other terms except its own (the noncore). The latter concerned Boas almost exclusively, Kroeber predominantly, though not exclusively (e.g., 1939), and Steward only secondarily: His chief interest was with the first component that was interpretable in utilitarian and economic terms. Unlike Weber, neither Kroeber nor Steward resolved the relationship between their utilitarian and romantic interests; Boas resolved the potential conflict simply by ignoring the material sphere. The ecological model of hunter-gatherers took the opposite view to greater extremes: It did not merely ignore the romantic, historical, and nonmaterial, it denied them altogether.

In the monist ecological interpretation that emerged, hunter-gatherer behavior was no longer of superstition and ignorance: It was of rationality and adaptation; these peoples made camp, hunted, gathered, celebrated, and mated—always with one eye on an "adaptive ledger," the balance from which determined their chances for survival.

Group selection also played a role, and most versions of the hunter-gatherer ecologist model included some reliance on what my colleague William Davis terms *methodological collectivism*: the idea that human behavior originates and is justified at the level of the group, social system, or culture rather than at the level of the individual (see Chapter 7). The third key element of this model, another contribution of the "new ecology" and very closely related to its concept of adaptation was homeostasis (Vayda and Rappaport 1968:495), the idea that consciously or unconsciously all human behaviors had an underlying logic—that of sustaining the group in which they were found over the long haul, that is, over evolutionarily meaningful intervals.

The Archaeological Connection

American archaeology took an active part in the development of these concepts, particularly as they related to hunter-gatherers. At the time, the discipline was badly divided internally regarding the larger scientific goals of archaeology and the relationship of these to social anthropology. Lewis Binford (1962, 1968a) and a handful of notable others (e.g., Flannery 1968; Hill 1968; Longacre 1968) led a growing number of dissidents who criticized the research of "traditional" archaeology and archaeologists as unduly preoccupied with description and culture chronology and contributing little to the understanding of culture process. They argued that, for a social science, archaeology was unacceptably undisciplined and unscientific (Spaulding 1968; for an earlier expression of the same view, see Kluckhohn 1940). That could only be rectified by developing an analytical framework built around the development and testing of lawlike propositions regarding the regularities of human behavior—in short, by doing anthropology. That amounted to a redefinition of anthropology by archaeologists because behaviors not susceptible to understanding through such lawlike propositions were, by definition, outside the realm of anthropology. The movement came to be termed the "new archaeology" (cf. Caldwell 1959; Flannery 1967).

The tenets of the new archaeology were compatible with neofunctionalist theory in many critical respects. As did neofunctionalism, the new archaeology held that cultures had to be understood as dynamic systems: Cultures were systems with subsystems. That implied that social and political systems, the center of all serious anthropological theories, affected, and were affected by, such material systems as technology and the environment. That further implied that important social and political processes produced tangible, that is, material, consequences that could be observed through careful archaeological fieldwork guided by deductively derived hypotheses. The spatial distribution of stylized ceramics or the degree of association between design motifs on sherds, for instance, could be used as a basis for inferring prehistoric postmarital residence patterns (cf. Longacre 1970; Hill 1970; Deetz 1965). In addition, the new archaeology followed Leslie White (1959) in adding to this systemic approach the definition of culture as an extrasomatic means of adaptation (Binford 1968b:323; Flannery 1972). This meant that, in the last instance, any kind of human behavior could be understood and explained only in relation to its contribution to an adaptive system. That was, of course, exactly what the neofunctionalists were saying.

The Old Copper Complex

A 1962 paper entitled "Archaeology as Anthropology" (Binford 1962) documents the break of the new archaeology from progressive evolutionary theory and its alignment with neofunctionalism. At issue was the culture history of hammered-copper technology in the Upper Great Lakes archaeological manifestation known as the Old Copper complex. This was sometimes cited as a case of cultural "devolution" because it ran contrary to sequence of metal use expected in progressive evolutionary theory where more efficient forms replace ones less efficient (e.g., as Childe [1935] postulates for the Old World, where the use of metal tools increases economic efficiency and encourages the division of labor, paving the way for other advances that lead to urbanization). In the Old Copper complex, the utilitarian use of copper for points and knives during the Archaic Period gives way to predominantly nonutilitarian use in the subsequent Early and Middle Woodland periods.

Binford took up the Old Copper complex problem as a basis for demonstrating the benefits of interpreting culture as a system composed of subsystems and thereby refuting the idea that the archaeological record was unidimensional and reducible to interpretation from a single perspective. He argued that although the Archaic copper points and knives might be utilitarian in form, their actual function was as nonutilitarian grave goods for individuals who had achieved high status as hunters in an egalitarian social system. In this systemic perspective, the copper points and knives were part of the social, rather than technological, subsystem and therefore "sociotechnic" rather than "technomic" in function. A shift to a ranked social system in which inherited (ascribed) status rivaled individual achievement in determining social position was said to explain the shift to nonutilitarian hammered-copper objects in Woodland times.

In terms of the contrasts between progressive evolutionary theory and neofunctional theory, Binford's interpretation of the Old Copper complex is notable in three respects. First, whereas in progressive evolutionary theory materialist concerns and technology dominate the lives of hunter-gatherers to the exclusion of social concerns, here it is argued that such a view distorts correct interpretation of the Old Copper complex, Archaic hammered-copper points and knives being part of the sociopolitical system. Second, although technology and social organization are interpreted as representing different subsystems, as in all neofunctionalist theories, there is no clear partition between the two: Technology is reflected in social organization, social organization in technology. And third, despite these systemic interconnections between social organization and technology, it is clearly technology, more specifically, subsistence, that dominates and gives social organization its form—at least this is true for the Archaic hunter-gatherers around which the discussion revolved.

The Old Copper complex was interesting but it was only a special case. The new archaeology very quickly became involved in developing and applying models with explicitly systemic, ecological and neofunctional elements that could be used in understanding hunter-gatherer lifeways in more general terms (e.g., Binford 1968b; Flannery 1968; Thomas 1972). A particularly memorable example was Flannery's cybernetic analysis of preagricultural cultural systems in the Tehuacan Valley of Mexico. There, Flannery argued, seasonally restricted availability of key resources and simple aboriginal exploitative decision rules that resolved scheduling conflicts when more than one resource was available had produced a stable (homeostatic) and unspecialized adaptation insulated against both natural disaster and cultural and social innovations that might lead to more complex adaptive forms.

Through such studies, the ecological model of hunter-gatherers, neofunctional theory, and the new archaeology grew up together sharing the same theoretical predilections: adaptation and homeostasis, evolution, materialism, and methodological collectivism.

Discussion

Though it was both more satisfying and plausible than the developmental and evolutionary alternative, which it had replaced, the ecological model of hunter-gatherers was hardly much better when it came to matching field observation with general theory; in fact, it proved extremely difficult to operationalize (cf. Flannery 1973). Its emphasis on "systems" hampered efforts to specify what the basic units of study were, and, hence, the loci of relevant cultural behaviors and levels of cultural selection and evolution (Murphy 1970:164-165). Neither did it specify how one might go about identifying "adaptive" behaviors. In short, it was not always clear (1) who or what was acting; (2) to what purpose; or (3) how hypotheses might be tested.

This confusion was made all the worse by the tendency of neofunctionalists to seize on celebrated oddities of culture—scapulimancy (Moore 1965) or the potlatch (Piddocke 1965) and through long and weakly verified causal chains deduce how these might in some sense be construed as adaptive. Because most behaviors have at least some potentially beneficial effects, it was difficult to devise methods by which one might be able to identify "maladaptive" behaviors except after the fact—that is, societies that do not survive have maladaptive behaviors. As we shall see elsewhere (cf. Chapters 7, 8, and 9), the manner in which any general theory of culture deals with maladaptive behaviors is particularly revealing of its inner mechanics and potential for operationalization.

It will be useful here briefly to relate Piddocke's analysis of the potlatch of the southern Kwakiutl as representative of the neofunctional perspective that replaced those earlier interpretations in which hunter-gatherers were portrayed as primitives. The task is made easier by the care with which the argument is constructed by Piddocke and by the detailed and very insightful review analysis of that construction by Orans (1975), to which the reader is referred for a more intensive consideration of the general form of neofunctional arguments.

The Kwakiutl Potlatch in Neofunctional Perspective

The Northwest Coast potlatch was a cycle of feasts hosted by the local kinship group (*numaym*) to celebrate various important social events, particularly *rites de passage*. Invited guests, usually from other numaym or tribes, were feasted and gifted by the host, who generally augmented his stores with those donated for the purpose by other numaym members and borrowed from others outside the numaym. The potlatch cycle was driven by obligations: If they were not to lose face, invited guests were obligated to accept gifts given by the host, which further obligated them to reciprocate with a future potlatch in which a slightly greater quantity of goods was distributed. Those who potlatched gained prestige commensurate with what they gave away. Refusal of a gift outright sealed one's inferior social position, and failure to reciprocate with a potlatch of similar scale signaled inferior economic and social power and standing and, hence, prestige. It was, thus, not only possible but in some sense probable that two individuals competing for social status might compete in a reciprocal series of potlatches of ever-increasing size. The potential for such excesses seemed born out in ethnographic accounts of the potlatch, in some of which goods and chattels were not only given away but actually destroyed in huge quantities, usually by casting them on the potlatch fire.

The neofunctional challenge was to make rational sense of the potlatch, which, when taken at face value, seemed so grandly irrational and materially counterproductive. It was, after all, the sacrifice potlatch of the Kwakiutl that captured for Benedict the ecstatic Dionysian excesses to which those peoples—indeed apparently all native Americans except the Pueblo—were prone (Benedict 1959:163-180). To the neofunctionalist, of course, this was no explanation at all: It reduced explanation of human behavior to the shadowy workings of the human psyche, while ignoring material conditions that seemed at least equally germane.

Not surprisingly, Piddocke neglects Benedict's interpretation altogether. He is more concerned with a less extravagant and eminently level-headed interpretation arising from theories of environmental possibilism (cf. Codere 1950). In the possibilist account, the potlatch is explained by arguing that such economic excesses are altogether expectable (which is not to say determined or even anticipated in the form observed) by the natural productivity of the Northwest Coast environment.[4] Yet possibilism offered no explanation of the potlatch *per se*: it did not explain why the potlatch did occur—only that it was not precluded from occurring—which seemed self-evident.

---

[4]Benedict (1959:157, 174) apparently accepted this position, too, seeming to imply that the Northwest Coast environment permitted a more extreme expression of competitive traits than was possible elsewhere.

To Piddocke, however, the possibilist interpretation is not merely wrong, it is wrong-headed: To accept it as even half right prevented the possibility of a true explanation of the potlatch. The potlatch is not an idiosyncratic culture pattern *permitted* by a "fantastic surplus economy" but rather a sophisticated adaptation *required* to counteract severe periodic local food shortages. In the course of this explanation, the showy destruction and sacrifice of the potlatch, which had so captured the imagination of students of the Northwest Coast, is dismissed as a Contact Period response occasioned by the disastrous historical decline in native population in combination with the appearance of Euroamerican goods and technology, which raised the quantity of material goods owned per capita while deflating their real value (see also Codere 1950; Belshaw 1965:20-29).

Piddocke's neofunctional alternative emphasized the function of the potlatch in maintaining over the long run an even distribution of resources among a people who had grown to the natural limits of their environment, in which as a consequence resources were always somewhere in short supply. Proximately motivated by prestige, potlatches were given by those enjoying momentary surpluses of edible resources, who distributed them among invited guests or used them to purchase goods, which were also distributed at the potlatch. By reallocating unequally distributed resources among groups who acted alternately as recipients and hosts, the potlatch benefited those for whom resources were momentarily scarce and in this way maintained a long-term equilibrium between population and resources at a level higher than would have otherwise been possible.

The altruistic and methodological collectivist (i.e., group selectionist) elements of this argument are clear because Piddocke, following E. S. Curtis (1915:143-144) against Codere (1950), argued that those who potlatched could never hope to recoup what they gave away; therefore it followed that rich numaym supported poor numaym. The benefit, thus, was to some group larger than the one defined by actual descent (the numaym).

The homeostatic or equilibrating elements of the model are equally clear because the potlatch counters short-term deviations of wealth or prestige: Groups with resources potlatch them to gain prestige, which makes them worthy future guests at potlatches where those gifts will be reciprocated; groups without resources can exchange hard goods to get them from groups that have surpluses, who will, in short order, return them and additional resources as potlatch gifts.

At least two things, however, are not clear. First, what, exactly, is the operational potlatch unit, that is, which is the unit benefited by the subsistence function of the potlatch? It must not be the numaym itself because potlatching is between numaym and, as we have said, Piddocke implies that the potlatch caused poor numaym to be supported by rich numaym. It may even be that the benefiting unit transcended the southern Kwakiutl, because potlatching was often between tribes and, without other evidence, one assumes intertribal potlatching might have supported poor tribes at the expense of rich ones. If this is so, it is not unreasonable to ask whether at the margins the Kwakiutl were not vulnerable to those having different values regarding the potlatch and prestige and who, not being bound by Kwakiutl restraint in such matters, might be able to turn it to their advantage. Of course, any rich Kwakiutl numaym willing to cheat on its obligations could easily thrive and dominate such a system—and one wonders whether and why some rich and powerful numaym did not attempt such domination, Kwakiutl society being so given to the need for social domination. This is perhaps the most telling objection commonly advanced by both microeconomists and sociobiologists against neofunctionalist interpretations.

It is equally unclear that beneficial redistribution resources is the function of the potlatch, if by function we refer to the properties of the potlatch that explain its presence among the Kwakiutl. As Orans notes, the connection inferred between the potlatch and demographic equilibrium is sufficiently indirect that it is as reasonable to assert the potlatch was dysfunctional as it is to assert it was functional. And if the argument is construed as meaning only that some redistribution of goods was an effect of the potlatch, that is hardly a surprise because even in popular vernacular the term *potlatch* has long referred to an occasion for gifting and feeding quests. The question is not whether some redistribution took place but whether that redistribution accounts for the potlatch.

The matter of origins cannot be avoided here even though most neofunctionalists claimed it was unrelated to their own concerns. It is worth distinguishing here, as does Orans (following Kluckhohn 1944), between the adjustive and adaptive properties of behavior. Adjustive behaviors are those that respond to some real or perceived stimuli: Drinking whiskey and building campfires are both adjustive responses to feeling cold. Adaptive behaviors, on the other hand, are those that result in increased probability of survival irrespective of motivation: Building a campfire is an adaptive response to the cold; drinking whiskey usually is not. Owing to the resulting low ratio of surface to volume, large body size is likewise adaptive to cold, though from the perspective of the individual it cannot be construed as adjustive in the same sense as building a fire or drinking whiskey. The neofunctionalist claim was generally that, as with the relationship between large body size and cold, the behaviors in which they were interested were adaptive, not adjustive. Indeed, it was central to their argument that the relationship between a behavior and its latent function remain unrecognized by the actors and in this way insulated from the conscious manipulation of rational, self-interested individuals in the hands of whom it might quickly be subverted and take on more exploitative forms akin to those that might be predicted by a sociobiologist (cf. Bean 1972:86-87; Moore 1965; Rappaport 1968:236-237, 1977). Given this, in the case at hand it is worth asking where the idea of the potlatch itself originated if not in response to the need for resource redistribution. The answer would seem to be in the quest for prestige, because everyone who has studied the potlatch perceives prestige to be its primary motivation (cf. Orans 1975:315).

The question now comes down to this: Is the potlatch explained by its adjustive properties (need for prestige) or adaptive properties (need for redistribution)? The neofunctionalists claim that the function of potlatch is adaptive is no longer easily verified because the presence of the potlatch alone can be explained with reference to the quest for prestige, that is, as an adjustive behavior. Even if the potlatch had no positive adaptive value, it might still be present provided the quest for prestige were sufficiently strong. Worse yet, as a consequence of this connection with prestige, the potlatch can be construed to have had at least some counterproductive subsistence effects: for example, by raising the price of food, by the preferential potlatching with high-prestige numaym (who were less often in need that poor numaym), and so on. In the absence of any firm evidence suggesting the potlatch actually had any of the benefits inferred for it, the case for the subsistence function of the potlatch boils down to a series of unverified speculations. The more direct explanation of the potlatch by prestige, which requires fewer assumptions and is supported by empirical data, is clearly preferable at this point (Orans, however, suggests some strategies by which the neofunctional case might be made stronger).

The Troubles of Neofunctionalism

Whether the topic was potlatch, scapulimancy, or ritual cycles, the fundamental difficulty of neofunctional interpretation remained the same. Without an empirically verifiable theoretical basis for projecting how hunter-gatherers "ought" to act to be adaptive required one to make a fatal leap of faith: You had to assume that the group chosen for study was acting properly to begin with. Once over this philosophical hurdle, the problem for the anthropologist was to show in what way this was so. As I have pointed out elsewhere (Bettinger 1980), this required the additional assumption, generally implicit, that the observed pattern was the only "right" one under the circumstances. Absent this, one could only take the possibilist stance that a given behavior was one of many equally workable ones, which meant that its specific form might have little to do with adaptation directly. The more modest claim that a behavior "worked" but was not necessarily the "best" (e.g., Vayda 1968:x) amounted to nothing more than descriptive tautology. Worse yet, it seemed to contradict the basic neofunctionalist premise. If a workable but suboptimal behavior acted to maintain system homeostasis, it would have been working against the evolutionary forces said to be the source of developmental progress – the same forces that permitted the anthropologist his or her assumption that cultures acted adaptively.

Given the advantage of hindsight, it is arguable that the major advantage of this ecological model over the "hunter-gatherers primitives" model it replaced was its effective challenge to the notion that hunter-gatherers were simply economically deprived and developmentally inferior representatives of an evolutionary stage. But in the last analysis, the ecological model was unsuccessful in constructing a useful theory of human adaptation and maladaptations (e.g., Bean 1972:7-8, 183-190) much less one that could easily be coupled to a theory of macroevolutionary transition and change.

Hunter-Gatherer Homeostasis in Archaeological Perspective: The Problem of Agricultural Origins

Quite apart from its operational shortcomings, the fact that neofunctionalism set so much emphasis on the concept of homeostasis made it extremely difficult to formulate a credible evolutionary interpretation of hunter-gatherers. Behavior tailored for homeostasis and an adaptive status quo seemed an unlikely source of culture change. In archaeology, doctrinaire prejudice against explanations that relied upon historical events (Spaulding 1968) and external causation (Binford 1962) eliminated what seemed to be the only other forces likely to foster disequilibrium and change. This made it all the more difficult to envision how that most important of human achievements, agriculture, could ever have gotten started in the first place. By assuming that preagricultural hunter-gatherer systems were homeostatic and that hunter-gatherers themselves were adaptively rational seemed to preclude any incentive to adopt a novel mode of subsistence that required more work and produced less in return.

The new archaeologists (Binford 1968b; Flannery 1969) produced an ingenious solution to this problem by referring to the same phenomenon that had earlier inspired Spencer, Darwin, Wallace, and, more indirectly, Marx, all via the work of Malthus (1803), namely population growth (see Harris 1968a:114, 223). The scenario ran something like this: At the close of the Pleistocene, hunter-gatherers exploiting newly opened and very rich environmental niches settled down, grew at unprecedented rates, and, to maintain safe population sizes locally, "budded- off" their excess numbers into adjacent marginal environments, the hilly flanks of the Near East, for example. Here they contacted refugee populations spreading from other centers of growth and in these zones of contact eventually overtaxed local resources and were forced to augment wild foods with those artificially propagated. This explanation advanced the case of neofunctionalism by showing how one might explain regional evolutionary culture change as resulting from cultural behaviors the function of which was to maintain homeostasis within individual systems (see also Rappaport 1984:415).

In matter of fact, there was very little difference between Piddocke's explanation of the potlatch and Binford's explanation of agriculture.

As so often in the past, Dunnell (1980:46-47) is once again right on the mark here when he observes that for all its modern tone and ethnographic and ecological sophistication this account differed little from earlier progressive evolutionary explanations: It attended to an evolutionary sequence and stages in the sequence, ignoring the evolutionary processes underlying that sequence and its stages. And like standard progressive evolutionary explanation, this account was transformational: Forces of change were sought within systems (causing its reorganization and transformation) rather than on natural selection acting on individuals or systems that were initially variable as in Darwinian evolution. That archaeology was, during the 1960s and 1970s, so preoccupied with the transition from hunting and gathering to agriculture speaks clearly to the kind of evolutionary explanation with which it felt most comfortable; it was not the kind of evolution Darwin was talking about.

CONCLUSION

In summarizing what we have so far, it is particularly noteworthy, first, that by the late 1970s hunter-gatherer research was neither more conceptual nor more theoretical than it had ever been; neither was it any more materialist, evolutionary, or comparative. It had become, however, increasingly sophisticated in its approach to the environment and man-land relationships. In this respect it was demonstrably different (and arguably more advanced) than research conducted under the earlier "hunter-gatherer primitives" model.

On a less positive note, within the larger field of hunter-gatherer research, archaeologists were having nearly as much trouble matching the newer ecological model against fact as they had previously using older theories and models. It is arguable, indeed, that as archaeology had moved away from culture chronology and history, the match between theory and fact had actually grown worse. It was one thing to develop a chronological sequence of projectile point shapes or bead types: Such things could be measured, classified, and dated more or less objectively and without reference to theory. It was quite another thing to develop and test a model in which "population pressure" causes readaptation; after all, what does "population pressure" look like and how does one measure it (cf. Thomas 1986; Cohen 1977; Cohen and Armelagos 1984)? In sum, making anthropology central to archaeology put a great deal of pressure on archaeologists, who were now expected to learn anthropological theory and make it work on material remains, something that anthropologists themselves had neither taken the time nor felt constrained to do (cf. Campbell 1968:18-19).

Confusions and contractions in neofunctionalist and cultural materialist theories further compounded the problem. On the one hand, neofunctionalism emphasized stability, as in its ideas about homeostasis and ideal culture stages within which this homeostasis presumably obtained; on the other hand, cultural materialism emphasized change, as in the interest shown in cultural evolution (e.g., Harris 1968a) and in particular the preoccupation of hunter-gatherer specialists with agricultural origins (e.g., Wilke *et al.* 1972). Even so, the basic concepts of homeostasis and system maintenance were easily accommodated within a larger and increasingly popular theoretical framework stressing transformational systemic change and progressive evolution by ideal stages (cf. Willey and Sabloff 1980:Figure 120); more than anything else, this would seem to explain the speed and ease with which neofunctionalism took hold in hunter-gatherer archaeology as the new archaeology replaced the old archaeology.

Given such conceptual indeterminacies at the level of general theory, it is in some respects easy to understand why, among all the possible arenas into which hunter-gatherer archaeologists might have channeled their efforts during the late 1970s and early 1980s, the enterprise deemed most worthy of attention was that of developing better links between theory and data through theories of limited sets. As hinted earlier, in addition to circumstances peculiar to hunter-gatherer archaeology proper, this responded to a growing awareness among new archaeologists that the testing of general theory required more informed arguments regarding just what archaeological data were all about (Schiffer 1972; Schiffer and Rathje 1973; Cowgill 1975). For the moment at least, hunter-gatherer archaeologists were willing to overlook flaws in their general theory and to forsake the study of higher level processes to accomplish this. As we shall see in Chapter 3, the choice was beneficial in some respects, detrimental in others.

Chapter 3

Middle-Range Theory and Hunter-Gatherers

INTRODUCTION

Contemporary hunter-gatherer archaeology is preoccupied with theories of limited sets. It will be recalled that such theories are called upon to articulate the principles of general theories. This they do by relating the general principle to particular cases and showing how such cases result from that principle in the presence of special conditions. In this sense, limited theories are theories about special cases that coincide with expectations of general theory. The limited theories that presently dominate hunter-gatherer archaeology began as attempts to articulate the neofunctional general theory (or paradigm) out of which the ecological model of hunter-gatherers was constructed during the "man-the-hunter" era. In broad terms, that paradigm implied that hunter-gatherer societies had to be explained as functioning adaptive systems. As attractive and promising as the idea seemed, it was not altogether clear what it actually meant.[1]

There are at least two different ways to resolve problems of this sort. One is through what my mentor, Marty Orans, used to call the "verifiability theory of meaning." This holds that the meaning of such abstract concepts as *adaptation* can be clarified by building many different kinds of models that apply the concept to different kinds of specific cases; the meaning of the concept and its

---

[1]The informal discussions contained in the *Man the Hunter* volume provide many important historical insights regarding initial attempts to operationalize the neofunctional concept of "adaptation." In one, entitled, "Does Hunting Bring Happiness?", the discussants consider the use of the aboriginal state of mind, that is, happiness, as a possible index of adaptedness (cf. Lee and Devore 1968:89-92).

essential explanatory properties emerge as more models are developed for many different circumstances. In the case of hunter-gatherer adaptation, such models would certainly be expected minimally to include technology and subsistence and settlement patterns (cf. Kuhn 1962:25). That was the operational strategy of middle-range theorists.

A more explicitly theoretical alternative to paradigm articulation is through a process sometimes termed *unpacking*. Here such complex and ambiguous theoretical concepts as adaptation are reduced to first principles for a narrow, but particularly important, range of phenomena (cf. Kuhn 1962:28). This produces a more elegant, formal, and explicit theoretical construct in which the units related by the theory and those relationships themselves are defined precisely. That was the heuristic strategy of optimal foraging theorists.

Middle-range theorists and optimal foraging theorists were both routinely forced to come to grips with fundamental principles and to develop testable models to illustrate them. Middle-range theorists, however, were more concerned with getting results directly useful in interpreting the archaeological record, the optimal foraging theorists with building elegant explanations. Accordingly, the models of middle-range theory are more realistic, those of optimal foraging theory more heuristic. Its with middle-range theory that this chapter is concerned.

The Tradition of Middle-Range Research in Archaeology

If we accept the general definition of middle-range research as an enterprise devoted to the assigning of meaning to empirical observations about the archaeological record, it is clear that, under one guise or another, archaeologists have always done that sort of thing (cf. Thomas 1986; Grayson 1986). That is most certainly what V. Gordon Childe was attempting when he argued that European archaeological assemblages could be interpreted as the products of societies. And it is scarcely conceivable that Max Uhle or Nels Nelson would have observed patterned assemblage variability in the intricately stratified deposits of the Emeryville shellmound without some overarching notion, however primitive, that the archaeological record contained information about time and culture change and that they could interpret its meaning in these terms.

Contemporary middle-range theory participates in this traditional archaeological endeavor of assigning meaning to the archaeological record. Within this tradition, however, it is clearly distinguishable for the emphasis it places on understanding the forces directly responsible for the formation of the archaeological record itself: how the stuff of living cultures actually comes to form an archaeological record. The roots of present inquiry are manifold, but the strongest lead directly from the interest in behavioral models and hypothesis testing that dominated the new archaeology. As will be recalled from the previous chapter, the new archaeology held that because cultures were integrated systems, behavioral variability in one part of the system, say social organization, was likely to be coupled with variability in another part, say in the production of ceramics. At the time, the important implication was that the organizational properties of prehistoric societies, traditionally held to be beyond the range of archaeologists, could be studied archaeologically through carefully deduced arguments relating behaviors of various sorts to expected archaeological consequences.

As Binford (1983a) details, in very short order this approach encountered fundamental problems: As archaeologists began to develop detailed arguments about the material consequences of behavior, it quickly became clear that they did not know what they were talking about. Take for instance, the seemingly innocent argument advanced by Hill (1970) and Longacre (1970). They had deduced that among southwestern Pueblo dwellers, if females made pottery and were instructed in that art by females in the same family, then ceramic variability within matrilines would be less than ceramic variability between matrilines. They further reasoned that this might be reflected archaeologically by the presence of spatially discrete clusters of stylized ceramic sherds reflecting the location of matrilines within prehistoric pueblos. It was quickly pointed out that it was entirely unclear whether in those prehistoric cases only females had made pottery, whether females had learned to make pottery from related females, or whether the deposition of ceramics was likely to be spatially coterminous with the location of matrilines (cf. Plog 1978).

What was worse, anthropology, ethnography in particular, had little to say in such matters. Most ethnographers were traditionally, and remain today, far too concerned with deciding whether the groups they were studying were patrilocal or neolocal or what their dominant mode of production was to stop and ask whether such patterns were reflected in materials that might be of relevance to the interpretation of the archaeological record. It soon grew apparent to archaeologists that such arguments about the formation of the archaeological record would have to be developed from the ground up by archaeologists without the help of social anthropology.

The related fields of "behavioral archaeology" (e.g., Schiffer 1972, 1976) and "ethnoarchaeology" (Campbell 1968; Gould 1978; Kramer 1979) developed directly in response to this situation. The information generated in these areas over the last few years is staggering. The special area dominated by archaeologists interested in hunter-gatherers that has come to be known as middle-range theory (Schiffer 1976; Binford 1981; Thomas 1983b), however, emerged in a central role. Its prominence extends beyond contemporary hunter-gatherer archaeology to hunter-gatherer research generally.

Defining Middle-Range Theory in Archaeology

Just about everyone agrees that middle-range theory concerns itself with inter-preting the archaeological record. Beyond that it is difficult to find any real consensus regarding a workable definition of the approach. Indeed, for an approach so widely accepted and discussed, the idea of "middle-range theory" remains surprisingly problematic. This confusion is reflected in the recent literature. According to Binford, middle-range theory addresses "a) how we get from contemporary facts to statements about the past, and b) how we convert the observationally static facts of the archaeological record to statements of dynamics" (1977a:6). For Thomas (1979:398), its job "is to bridge the gap between the known, observable archaeological contexts and the unknown, unobservable systemic context . . . mid-range theory is necessary to provide relevance and meaning to the archaeological objects". Likewise it "seeks in-variant linkages between the archaeological record to the behavior that pro-duced it" (Thomas 1986:12). For Grayson (1986), it is research that emphasizes the study of extant systems as a means of understanding past behavior. For Raab and Goodyear (1984), who introduced the term (Goodyear, Raab, and Klinger 1978) as a borrowing from sociology and the works of Merton (1968), "middle-range theory is seen as providing a logical link between relatively low-order empirical generalizations and comparatively high-order theories" (Raab and Goodyear 1984:257).

Whether these interpretations differ in any substantial way depends on how one views recent middle-range research dealing with hunter-gatherers, particularly the part most heavily influenced by the writing and ethnographic research of Lewis Binford, whose work in this area inspired its current popular-ity. The underlying framework for much of this research is found in Binford's (1980) analytical classification of hunter-gatherer systems. This is an elegantly constructed model in which availability of natural resources is seen to dictate differing combinations of social, economic, and settlement organization. To-gether these combinations describe a continuum of subsistence-settlement systems (cf. Struever 1968) with highly mobile foragers at one end and highly sedentary collectors at the other.

FORAGERS AND COLLECTORS

In the simplest of terms, Binford explains the difference between foragers and collectors with reference to variability in the quantity and seasonal distribution of resources at their disposal. He argues that in environments that are produc-tive and at the same time spatially and temporally homogeneous (usually tropical), there are no seasons of relative shortage and hence no intrinsic need to store or save resources beyond those needed for immediate consumption. Under these conditions, the organization of subsistence and settlement is extremely simple and highly redundant across time and space. Where these conditions do not pertain, for example, where there are seasonal shortfalls in resources, the organization of hunter-gatherer subsistence and settlement become increasingly more complex as adaptations to these challenges.

To make this model operational at all requires an objective measure of resource productivity, for which Binford uses *effective temperature* or ET (Bailey 1960)

$$ET = \frac{8T + 14\,AR}{AR + 8} = \frac{18\,WM - 10\,CM}{WM - CM + 8} \tag{3.1}$$

where

> T is mean annual temperature in degrees Centigrade
>
> AR is the annual range in temperature between the average temperatures in degrees Centigrade of the coldest and warmest months
>
> WM is the average temperature in degrees Centigrade of the warmest month
>
> CM is the average temperature in degrees Centigrade of the coldest month

Effective temperature (ET) transforms mean annual temperature and annual range in temperature to filter out seasonal fluctuations in warmth, producing in their place a single measure of the available warmth in an environment (effective temperature) in terms of its equivalent in an aseasonal environment. Thus, an environment with an ET of 15 sustains warmth equivalent to that available in an environment in which the temperature is an unvarying 15 degrees Centigrade year-round, that is, with a mean annual temperature of 15 and an annual range in temperature of 0.

The logical connection between ET and environmental productivity, which is required for Binford's purpose, is both simple and direct: By design (Bailey 1960:3), ET expresses temperature at the beginning and end of the period over which temperatures exceed ET, during which vegetation will thrive, *and* the duration of that period. In short, as ET increases, so do temperatures during the season of plant growth and the length of that season. For any environment, accordingly, ET measures plant productivity directly and, therefore, animal productivity indirectly. More indirectly yet, ET also measures seasonality in the special sense that environments with low ET have long winters and those with high ET short winters. We can put this in more concrete terms by noting that environments where ET is greater than 18 lack a definable winter and that environments where ET is less than 10 lack a definable summer.

The relationship between environmental productivity and seasonality, as measured by ET, and the degree of organization in hunter-gatherer settlement systems, as measured by the forager-collector continuum, is perhaps most easily explained with reference to cases representing environments with extremely high and extremely low values of ET, which are in this model associated with foragers and collectors, respectively.

Foragers

Where ET is high, between 25 and 21, and resources are therefore abundant and more or less continuously available throughout the year, hunter-gatherers tend to follow the distinctive hunter-gatherer pattern first described by Lee for the !Kung San of the Kalahari (1969) and shortly thereafter by Gould (1969) for aboriginal groups of the Western Desert of Australia. In both instances, the annual round (i.e., the pattern of annual movements across the landscape) lacks qualitatively different seasonal phases and comprises instead a series of similar cycles. In each cycle, the local group establishes and maintains residence at a central base camp while exploiting the resources available within a two-hour walk around it (see Vita-Finzi and Higgs 1970; Roper 1979). When the resources within this zone, termed *site exploitation area* or (incorrectly) *site catchment*, are exhausted the base camp is moved to a new location, and the cycle just described is repeated. As there is comparatively little seasonal and spatial variability in resources in qualitative terms, these base camps frequently contain the same kinds of things. They differ principally in size, depending on the number of occupants and length of occupation, which in turn depends on the productivity of local environments within which they are located (see Yellen 1977). In such a system, a *foraging* system, the population is said to "map" onto resources, moving its residential base to accommodate easy access for individuals. Given the nature of the environments in which foragers live, this residential mobility alone is sufficient to ensure that there is no incongruity (mismatch) between the distribution of natural resources and the distribution of the population.

Binford (cf. Table 3.1) defines two settlement types generated by forager systems: *residential bases* and *locations*. The residential base (termed *base camp* previously) is the hub of extractive activities, the place from which task groups depart to obtain food and raw materials and to which they subsequently return. It is also the place where most processing, manufacturing, and other activities of maintenance are done. Locations, on the other hand, are the places where extractive activities occur: kill and butchering sites, places of plant procurement, and the like.

The high residential mobility and low differentiation of activities by

Table 3.1. Ideal Characteristics of Foragers and Collectors[a]

	Forager	Collector
Environment	Aseasonal	Seasonal
	Even	Patchy
Settlements	Residential base	Residential base
	Location	Location
		Field camp
		Station
		Caches
Mobility	Residential	Logistical
Technology	Generalized	Specialized
	Expedient	Curated
Pattern of exploitation	Low intake	Bulk intake
Hunting	Encounter	Intercept

[a]After Binford 1978a, 1978b, 1979, 1980.

season that together characterize forager subsistence-settlement systems carry some rather important implications for the archaeological record. For one thing, as residential mobility increases, so does the quality of contextual relationships between given activities and the archaeological residues resulting from those activities. That is, if we think of archaeological assemblages as collections of refuse reflecting the suite of activities carried out over discrete periods of time, it is clear that as the period of accumulation decreases, the probability of functional associations between any two items in that collection increases as does the probability that the activities represented by the collection are functionally related to the location in which it occurs. It follows that groups frequently on the move, foragers in particular, are more likely to deposit refuse reflecting functionally associated tasks and tasks specific to particular locations than are groups more sedentary in orientation: Their assemblages accumulate over longer periods and, owing to the greater depletion of local resources, represent activities occurring over a larger area, often great distances from the residential base. In short, the strength of functional relationships within assemblages and between assemblages and locations, which is commonly termed *grain-size*, will vary between highly mobile forager systems, where assemblages are relatively homogeneous and grain-size is relatively fine, and more highly localized groups, where assemblages are relatively heterogeneous and grain-size is relatively course.

Collectors

As one might reasonably expect, where *ET* (hence environmental productivity) is low and resources are unevenly distributed across space (e.g., in different life zones or biotic communities) and through time (i.e., seasonally), the regional settlement strategies of hunter-gatherers are markedly different from those just described. In particular, as environmental productivity declines and fluctuates more markedly with respect to season, hunter-gatherers confront periods of increasingly long and severe resource shortfall (e.g., winter on the North American Plains, say in Lincoln, Nebraska, where $ET = 10.9$). Put another way, as ET decreases there is an increasing mismatch, or incongruity, between the temporal distribution of a population, which is relatively stable from season to season within a region, and the temporal distribution of its resources, which shows pronounced seasonal fluctuations. These *temporal incongruities* between the distributions of populations and their resources require some sort of compensatory cultural response. Minimally, resources must be stored to extend artificially their temporal availability (and hence, temporal utility). Storage, in turn, means that some resources, generally those available in great abundance for short periods at certain times of the year (e.g., salmon, caribou), must be obtained in bulk, that is, beyond current needs, and preserved for later use. Both resource storage and resource acquisition in bulk demand advance planning and some rather sophisticated organizational tactics.

Hunter-gatherers who rely upon resource storage pay a very definite cost in loss of flexibility within their settlement systems. In particular, although storage solves *temporal incongruities* in the distribution of resources relative to population, it creates *spatial incongruities* between the two. That is so because places where resources are stored act increasingly to anchor populations and thus inhibit their ability to shift residence to match the distribution of resources as these shift seasonally. Put briefly, storage freezes populations at spots of accumulation. The annual movements of many ethnographic groups in the Great Basin, for instance, were tethered to local piñon groves that furnished the principal source of stored winter food (e.g., Steward 1938:82, 232-233).

In such instances, spatial heterogeneity or patchiness in the natural distribution of resources (e.g., between biotic communities or at different points within a river system) may cause further incongruities between these resources and populations that would exploit them. Such disjunctive distributions of resources defy any easy resolution of the spatial mismatches between populations and resources by means of residential movement because travel toward one resource is often travel away from another of equal importance available at the same time. That resources must be stored in increasingly large quantities to offset seasonal shortfalls as ET decreases accentuates these spatial incongruities.

From the forgoing, it should not be concluded that temporal incongruities arise only as unintended consequences of resource storage or that their connection to environmental productivity (ET) is only indirect through such behaviors. Quite the contrary, ET takes a far more direct and active role in causing temporal incongruities within hunter-gatherer systems in the following way: All other things being equal, we would expect the severity of spatial incongruities to increase as ET decreases because then subsistence patterns ought to become more catholic, that is, reliant on a broader range of resources. And as the resources upon which one depends increase, there is increasing potential for disjunctive distributions among them.

Collector system behaviors respond directly to these circumstances. As we have observed, that resources are stored is the most obvious response. As we have also observed, storage is attended by particular strategies of exploitation geared toward the procurement of specific resources in bulk during short periods and often by groups rather than individuals. This is facilitated by a technology organized such that, like food, equipment is *cached* (Binford 1980; Thomas 1983b), much of it being of use for only limited periods and only in specific places. The Netsilik Eskimo kayak, used in the summer and stored out of harm's way the rest of the time, exemplifies such behavior (Balicki 1970:30-31). Equipment of this sort has been termed *curated*, that is, it is saved in anticipation of future use. This is in opposition to tools that are *expedient*, that is, that are made in direct response to an immediate need and that once having served that need are discarded. More generally, it is useful to think of collector subsistence-settlement technologies as a whole as "curated technologies" in the sense that much of the gear used by collectors is made and subsequently set aside and saved with reference to future needs of very specific kinds (Binford 1979). This clearly results from the discrete seasonal phasing that distinguishes collector systems from forager systems. Unlike that of the forager, the annual round of the collector alternates periods of relative inactivity, or downtime (as in winter), with periods of intensive hunting and gathering. Curated technologies accommodate this rhythm: Gear is made and repaired during the offseason, when there is little else to do, and is thus ready later as needed, when resource acquisition demands undivided attention.

Two additional features of collector subsistence technologies, specialization and efficiency, are also understandable with reference to seasonal restrictions on the resources available to collectors. Simply put, collectors must obtain staple foods in bulk for storage during short periods. All other things being equal, this demands greater technological sophistication than is required of foragers, who have no need to engage in storage and, thus, can satisfy their daily needs with a fairly limited set of tools and implements suitable for use over a broad range of conditions. By contrast, the requisite exploitative efficiency of collector technologies must be achieved through the development of an extensive array of sophisticated gear that is highly specialized in function and often difficult to make (Torrence 1983; but see Bamforth 1986). Once made, such gear is carefully saved and put to use only under the narrow range of circumstances for which it was expressly designed.

The organization of procurement in collector systems is likewise distinctive from that of foragers in that the relationship between population and resources is more clearly structured and predictable (and less flexible): Task groups move from centrally located residential bases to obtain specific kinds of resources and return with what they hunt/gather. The forager responds to temporal and spatial resource shortage by residential movement. The collector responds to seasonal resource shortages (temporal incongruities) by storage and to locational mismatches (spatial incongruities) between populations and resources by logistical mobilization, moving specialized task groups to given locations, and by more exhaustive exploitation of resources, often in bulk, by means of more highly specialized tactics and technology.

In combination, the temporal and spatial variability that typifies collector systems is reflected archaeologically by greater variability within sites (reflecting the diversity of activity), and greater variability between sites of different kinds, reflecting seasonal variation and the logistical organization of procurement. In addition to the two settlement types (residential bases and locations) generated by foragers, collectors also generate *field camps* (base camps for task groups, *caches* for resources and equipment, and *stations* for gathering information regarding resources).

On the other hand, reliance on logistical mobility and curated technologies in collector (as opposed to forager) systems reduces the contextual integrity of the association of particular activities at residential bases. That is, in contrast to the fine-grained patterning that characterizes forager systems in which, owing to residential mobility, archaeological assemblages represent short-term foraging bouts; in collector systems many different and entirely unrelated activities occur at the same location. Binford sees all of these differences as having direct consequences for interpreting the archaeological record (1980:17).

Great Basin Foragers and Collectors

Thomas (1983b:24-39) has used the forager-collector model to describe variability in the subsistence-settlement systems of three ethnographic hunter-gatherer groups in the Great Basin: the Owens Valley Paiute and Reese River and Kawich Mountain Shoshone. Although they shared essentially the same technology, the settlement patterns of these three groups differed markedly. Located in an area lacking permanent streams, the Kawich Mountain Shoshone camped near springs or high in the mountains where winter snow could provide water. Throughout the spring and summer, they lived in small family groups that moved frequently to take advantage of limited patches of edible roots and seeds. Hunters and gatherers worked out of the same residential base, returning to it each night. Though highly variable in location from year to year, the fall-winter residential base was more permanent, each family anchoring itself at a single piñon woodland camp, which served as a base for both hunting and gathering. In all these respects, the Kawich Mountain Shoshone conform to the patterns expected of foragers.

The Reese River Shoshone exhibited essentially the same pattern of summer mobility observed for the Kawich Shoshone—small family groups moving from short-term camp to short-term camp in the lowlands. Fall, winter, and spring residence, however, tended to be more regularly fixed in location, families occupying the same general area within the piñon woodland often enough to warrant claiming exclusive ownership of it. In these respects, the Reese River occupy an intermediate position on the forager-collector continuum: Their summer pose conforms with that of foragers; their spring-fall-winter pose with that of collectors.

The Owens Valley Paiute are easily classified as collectors. For most of the year, from spring through early fall, they maintained permanent residential bases on the valley floor out of which both gathering and hunting were conducted and in which resources were stored for winter use. During the late fall, they moved from these permanent residential bases and established temporary residential bases (or field camps) to harvest piñon nuts. Bumper crops sometimes caused these "temporary" residential bases to be occupied throughout the winter. Generally, however, they were occupied only until the harvest was complete, after which groups returned to their valley floor villages.

As one might expect, the importance of stored resources has much to do with the differences in settlement pattern that characterize these three Great Basin groups. The spring-summer mobility of the Kawich Mountain and Reese River Shoshone precluded the possibility of accumulating large centralized caches of food for winter use. For that, both groups were forced to rely on the fall piñon crop, which was notoriously unreliable. To the Kawich, this meant that individual families seldom wintered in the same place two years running, which discouraged any tendency toward territorial claims or permanent social attachments beyond the nuclear family (see also Steward 1938). Piñon stands that were either more reliable or more extensive than those available to the Kawich, allowed the Reese River Shoshone to reoccupy the same winter camps annually and to remain in those camps for longer periods in the spring, during which some seeds and roots could be set aside for use in the coming winter. Even so, complete failure of the local piñon crop often caused the Reese River Shoshone to vacate their traditional winter camps in favor or other locations where piñon was available.

In Owens Valley, on the other hand, the centralization of spring and summer habitation at valley-floor villages permitted the caching of roots and seeds in sufficient quantity in those seasons to last the winter. Thus, even in the event of total failure of the piñon crop, these groups remained in the same villages and suffered little hardship. The piñon crop was harvested when it was available and, if sufficiently abundant, sometimes caused families or whole villages to winter in the piñon woodland.

In this sense, piñon produced quite different effects on the settlement patterns of these three ethnographic groups. For the Kawich and Reese River Shoshone, the storage of piñon provided the only "pull" toward centralization and stability in settlement pattern. Conversely, for the Owens Valley Paiute, the piñon harvest provided a "pull" of opposite kind: When available, it temporarily drew them away from their permanent villages and lowland food caches.

As Thomas (1983b:38-39) observes, the analysis of ethnographic Great Basin settlement patterns in terms of the forager-collector continuum provides many important insights but also reveals some equally important problems with respect to the model. In particular, ethnographic Great Basin hunter-gatherers run the gamut from forager to collector in the absence of any accompanying variation in technology or overriding differences of climate, both of which are anticipated in the forager-collector model. Binford (1980:17) hints at one possible explanation for the differences in settlement variability, noting that by restricting residential mobility, population pressure might require increased reliance on logistical mobility and, thus, movement toward collectorlike strategies. This agrees with the observed variability in the three Great Basin cases in question here: Population densities are lowest for the Kawich, highest for Owens Valley, and intermediate for Reese River. In these cases, then, it may be that population density rather than climatic variability accounts for the differences in settlement strategy. If that is so, of course, one is led to ask whether population pressure is not contributing in important ways to the variability in hunter-gatherer settlement and storage patterns Binford chooses to explain in terms of climate (e.g., Binford 1980:Table 2, Figure 4).

On the other hand, even if it is population that accounts for the observed variability in ethnographic Great Basin settlement patterns, it is unclear why this variability is not paralleled by concomitant kinds of differences in technology (e.g., curated vs. expedient) the forager-collector model leads us to expect. Part of the problem here would seem to lie in Binford's argument that, like shorter growing seasons and patchy resource distributions, increase in population pressure should decrease residential mobility on the one hand and increase logistical mobility on the other. This does not follow. In theory, groups whose residential mobility is restricted by surrounding populations ought to be similarly restricted in their logistical mobility. That was certainly the case in Owens Valley (Bettinger 1989:344). In combination with the difficulty pedestrian hunter-gatherers encounter when trying to transport resources (e.g., Madsen and Kirkman 1988:602), such restrictions make it unlikely that hunter-gather groups respond to increasing population pressure and restrictions on residential mobility by means of increased reliance on logistical mobility in the sense Binford implies. This is probably why, despite their differences in settlement pattern, the Kawich Mountain, Reese River, and Owens Valley peoples shared essentially the same exploitative technology and exhibited roughly the same degree of reliance on logistical mobility, a pattern that holds true for ethnographic Great Basin peoples generally (cf. Bettinger 1989:346-347).

Whatever its flaws, the forager-collector model stands as one of the most important recent theoretical contributions to our understanding of hunter-gatherer behavior. In terms of the future, it is important that the model be regarded as a source of hypotheses that can be tested rather than simply accepted as fixed framework into which archaeological and ethnographic hunter-gatherers can be conveniently compartmentalized as either collectors or foragers. In short, this is a provisional scheme, the implications of which have yet to be worked out in any detail, particularly with regard to study of variability within regions, where it must compete with other, equally appealing alternative models (see Chapter 4).

THE PROCESSES OF SITE FORMATION

The forager-collector model does not by any means exhaust the range of contemporary middle-range research. Substantial effort is currently being expended in a variety of studies that more directly address the tangible materials commonly encountered in archaeological sites. These studies aim to discover the forces that produce the archaeological record itself (commonly termed *site formation processes*) and to use this understanding to "decode" the meaning of that record. In short, at issue here, are the processes that cause particular kinds of (dynamic) behaviors to produce distinct and identifiable archaeological "structures" or (static) signatures (cf. Grayson 1986; Thomas 1986). Research commonly held to exemplify this branch of inquiry would include attempts to operationally define settlement types (residential bases, field camps, etc.; e.g., Thomas 1983b), to distinguish cultural from noncultural faunal assemblages (Binford 1981), and to identify basically different "elementary structures" likely to be found in the archaeological record. In each instance, the goal is to understand the organizational properties that affect hunter-gatherer systems and to use that understanding to interpret the archaeological record (Binford 1979).

Some of the best known of these studies deal with faunal remains – bones. Here, once again, it is Binford who has led the way in developing and applying useful models.

Nunamiut Butchering

Disillusioned after persistent attempts to "decode" the European Mousterian without a relevant model of the behaviors that produced those sites and

assemblages, Binford, in 1969, received funding to undertake an ethnoarchaeological study of the Nunamiut Eskimo of central northern Alaska (Binford
1983a:100; 1978a). Critical to this research was an analysis of Nunamiut
procurement and processing of large mammals. This was important for at least
two reasons. First, meat, specifically caribou meat, constituted the bulk of the
food annually consumed by the Nunamiut. A study of the means by which game
animals were taken, processed, and consumed would thus capture the essential
basis of Nunamuit subsistence and settlement. Second, and equally important,
the remains of large mammals preserve relatively well in archaeological contexts.
This implied that what was learned from the Nunamiut could be applied to
archaeological contexts, particularly the Mousterian sites Binford had found so
frustrating to interpret. This potential for archaeological application was greatly
enhanced because, unlike stone tools, bones occur in easily identified shapes and
in fixed proportions. These features substantially reduce the uncertainties of
archaeological analysis because one knows that for every caribou cranium found
there was once a matching pelvis, two femurs, 26 ribs, and so on.

Working on the assumption that what mattered to Nunamiut butchers
was how best to use the caribou they had taken, Binford set about calculating
the economic utility of the body parts represented by different bones. He argued
that this could be calculated according to the by-weight proportion of attached
meat, marrow, and grease represented by each skeletal element. In this way, and
taking into account skeletal conformations lending themselves to particular
kinds of butchering procedures, Binford produced a scale (termed the modified
general utility index, or MGUI) for individual bones (Binford 1978a:72-74;
Metcalfe and Jones [1988] have since calculated a simpler but equivalent
formulation). Comparison with experiments conducted on domestic sheep
suggested that these values might serve as a basic approximation for calculating
utility indices for most large vertebrates (Binford 1978a:74; cf. Thomas and
Meyer 1983).

Binford then proceeded to examine Nunamiut butchering practices in
light of the circumstances under which individual animals were butchered (e.g.,
time of year, resource demand, distance from camp, etc.) and the consequences
of that butchering in terms of the bones that were left at the butchering location
and those that were transported elsewhere. He showed that, depending on these
circumstances, the Nunamiut use caribou body parts differentially according to
their utility (1978a:81). In general, when demand for meat is relatively low, or
distances between the kill and base camp are large or difficult to negotiate,
Nunamiut butchers selectively cull the best parts, leaving the parts of lower
utility behind. This he termed the *gourmet strategy*. Conversely, when demand is
high or the distance between the kill and the place of intended consumption is
low, nearly all of the important parts are carried away and only those parts with

virtually no utility are left behind. This is termed the *bulk strategy* (Binford 1978a:81).

Binford (1978a:81) also pointed out that each butchering event would naturally produce two different assemblages: one at the location to which the body parts were transported and another at the butchering location itself. The assemblage of bones at the location of storage or consumption would be rich in high utility parts, that is, skeletal elements would be represented in frequencies directly proportional to their utility as measured by MGUI. Conversely, the assemblage of bones at the butchering locality would represent the reverse; such assemblages would be rich in elements representing low utility parts, that is, the frequency of individual skeletal elements would be inversely proportional to the utility of the body parts they represent. The latter pattern is termed a *reverse utility curve*.

The Scavenging Hypothesis

Binford's zooarchaeological model of utility is an exceptionally powerful archaeological tool (at least potentially) because it employs a general understanding of economic behavior in a way that can be used to anticipate, and thus explain, variability in prehistoric faunal assemblages regardless of age. Binford has been quick to take advantage of this to improve understanding of hominid behavior in the early Pleistocene (e.g., 1981). Most notably, he has used the approach to challenge traditional interpretations that portray hunting as a principal factor contributing to the initial development of hominid characteristics (cf. Washburn and Lancaster 1968:293-294; Isaac 1978; Isaac and Crader 1981). In that view early hominid males hunted large animals and carried them back to base camps, where they were shared with females and children. This is held to have led to the early formation of human social bonds, sexual division of labor, and the development of a centralized settlement system.

Detailed comparison of the faunal assemblages found at early African hominid sites and those produced by contemporary nonhuman African predators (e.g., hyena, lion, leopard) led Binford to conclude that something different was going on (1981:294). In particular, he found little difference in the range of skeletal elements represented at these two kinds of locations, both of which were dominated by remains of body parts with little attached meat and, thus, of very low utility. More significantly, at the early hominid sites, the elements showing evidence of human modification were almost invariably those which were useful primarily as sources of marrow. He suggested that this pattern could be most easily explained by arguing that early hominids did not hunt and transport game back to base camps but had merely scavenged small tidbits of marrow from nonhuman predator kills from which all the choice portions had already been removed and consumed by the predators themselves. Contrary to the traditional view, this would seem to imply that hunting and meat consumption played a relatively minor role in shaping early Pleistocene hominid behavior. On the basis of a more extensive analysis, Binford (1985) has more recently generalized that argument to suggest that hunting of medium and large mammals emerged as important human activity only on the eve of the appearance of fully modern man (i.e., *Homo sapiens*).

Late Prehistoric Mountain Sheep Kills in the Great Basin

The same approach Binford used to study the formation of early hominid faunal assemblages has proven equally instructive in much more recent contexts. Thomas and Meyer, for example, have used Binford's model of utility to account for late prehistoric faunal remains from Gatecliff Shelter, central Nevada (Thomas and Meyer 1983). Horizon 2 at that site produced a dense concentration of bones subsequently identified as representing the remains of approximately 24 mountain sheep (*Ovis canadensis*). It is believed that these 24 individuals were taken between late winter and early spring in the course of a single communal hunt.

Despite the unusual stratigraphic integrity of the component in which they were found, the 8,396 mountain sheep bones that were recovered from Horizon 2 represent only a small fraction of the total skeletal assemblage that would be generated by 24 individuals. At least two obvious explanations might account for this fractional representation. First, it might be that the 24 sheep were killed and processed at a distant kill site and the better parts brought to Gatecliff for consumption or storage. That would suggest the site was in use at the time as a residential base or meat cache. Second, it might be that the kill was made very close to Gatecliff, following which the carcasses were dragged to the site whole and butchered to facilitate the efficient transport of meat and related products to a residential base some distance away. That would suggest use of Gatecliff as a field camp. Analysis by means of utility curves comparing element frequency against utility of corresponding body part offered a relatively straightforward solution to the problem.

Following the procedures advocated by Binford (1978a), Thomas and Meyer (1983) showed that the frequency of individual skeletal elements of mountain sheep in Horizon 2 was inversely proportion to their economic utility (measured by MGUI). That is, skeletal elements representing body parts of high utility were much less common than those with relatively low utility. From this, they inferred that the Horizon 2 mountain sheep were killed and butchered at Gatecliff and that all but the lowest utility parts (with bones attached) were transported elsewhere. On this basis, and from other evidence, it is argued that the Horizon 2 component represents a field camp (cf. Binford 1980:10) occupied for a short period by hunters operating some distance from their residential home base (Thomas 1983c:529).

THE MYTH OF MIDDLE-RANGE THEORY

Having reviewed some examples of contemporary middle-range research both theoretical and applied, we are in a position to consider the confusion regarding the nature and definition of middle-range theory mentioned at the beginning of this chapter. There is general agreement that the forager-collector continuum proposed by Binford is theory and, moreover, that it is "middle-range theory" in the sense of Merton (cf. Raab and Goodyear 1984): It begins from the general assumption that, *ceteris paribus*, environment is a—perhaps *the*—strong force in the shaping of hunter-gatherer adaptations and proceeds to an explanation of the organization of technology and archaeological consequences thereof. One gathers from the literature that whether it is "middle-range theory" in the sense generally attributed to Binford (cf. Raab and Goodyear 1984; Thomas 1986) is quite another matter. Herein lies the aforementioned confusion regarding the "true" character of middle-range research.

In current archaeological usage, middle-range research is most often equated with the analysis of site formation processes as exemplified by Binford's study of Nunamiut butchering and early hominid scavenging. Raab and Goodyear fault this current emphasis on site formation, arguing that "middle-range theory" ought be more broadly conceived. That is wholly immaterial. Processes of site formation are eminently subject to theoretical investigation. It is difficult to see in what way such work departs from the ideal Mertonian bridging of theory and fact or, indeed, from any workable approach that involves theory. A theory is a set of systematically connected propositions, empirically verified or potentially verifiable, about the underlying principles that govern relationships within some set of phenomena (cf. Rudner 1966); in this sense, current interest in site formation certainly qualifies as a theoretical endeavor. Whether it is less general and therefore lower in level than Binford's propositions about foragers and collectors and whether this would qualify it as "lower-range" theory or merely "lower- middle-range" theory cannot be evaluated without invoking additional, more value-laden, stipulations regarding the number of phenomena governed and hierarchical relationships between those phenomena.

Of perhaps greater relevance here, current studies of site formation are so intimately intertwined with more abstract notions about foragers and collectors that the two are effectively inseparable—opposing sides of the same coin, as it were. It is thinkable, indeed, that archaeologists value the forager/collector

dichotomy for its obvious and direct implications for interpreting the archaeological record (i.e., its implications for site formation) at least as much as they do
for its contribution to anthropological theory. Binford, of course, is very clear
on this point. His disagreement with Yellen about the reality of "activity areas"
in the archaeological record—a classic problem of site formation—turns on
his interpretations of the structured quality of collector systems in comparison to
the relatively unstructured quality of forager systems such as typify the !Kung
San studied by Yellen (Binford 1978b:359-360). Likewise, his discussion regarding the gear carried by Nunamiut snowmobilers is not simple description
(cf. Binford 1977b, 1979) but seeks regularities along lines he anticipates would
separate collectors and foragers.

Current efforts in zooarchaeology (Binford 1978a, 1981), which fall even
more clearly under the heading of what Raab and Goodyear see as studies of site
formation, show similar theoretical inspiration. Here, as we have seen, patterns
of Nunamiut butchering are explained in terms of larger considerations, in
particular the interplay between resource supply and resource demand. In this
way Binford attacks the "traditional" wisdom that butchering is a cultural rather
than economic activity—his interest evidently being to show the superiority of a
materialist perspective on the archaeological record. Thus, it is variability in
technoeconomic circumstances, not culture or mental templates, that dictate
animal dismemberment (Binford 1978a:452-458).

Likewise, when Binford attempts to distinguish culturally generated
faunal assemblages from naturally (carnivore)-generated ones, it is not merely an
inductive exercise in which a series of assemblages of each kind are objectively
compared; indeed, Binford is emphatic on the point that middle-range (i.e., site
formation) theory does not consist of empirical generalizations, inductive arguments, or ethnographic analogies (1978b:358). It proceeds hand in glove with
some rather general assumptions about the factors that govern human butchering (i.e., what human butchers are up to) and the faunal patterns reflecting
these factors; it is only these patterns that make human faunal assemblages
understandable at all and thus separable from natural faunal assemblages. That
Binford's treatise on foragers and collectors begins (1980:4-5) and closes
(1980:17-19) with discussions regarding the processes that shape archaeological
sites should dispel any lingering doubts about whether theories of site formation
qualify as theories of middle range.

It may help to clarify matters further by disposing the widespread idea that
middle-range research necessarily uses observations about the present to understand the past. Recent studies of the relationship between archaeological
assemblage size and assemblage diversity are a case in point (Jones, Grayson, and
Beck 1983; Thomas 1983c:425-428). Assemblage diversity has frequently been
regarded as an archaeological signature helpful in identifying different kinds of
settlements. This seems intuitively obvious: Multiactivity base camps should

exhibit a broader range of artifact categories than specialized activity temporary camps (e.g., temporary hunting camps). As Jones, Grayson, and Beck (1983) have pointed out, however, there is an intrinsic correlation between assemblage diversity and assemblage size: Small assemblages tend to be limited in diversity, and large assemblages tend to be broad in diversity. Because this is so, archaeological assemblages that differ markedly with respect to the range of artifact categories they contain cannot be assumed to reflect fundamentally different kinds of settlements unless it can be shown that this difference is not simply a function of the sizes of their assemblages. This is an important observation and has many important implications. Further, it easily qualifies as an example of middle-range research that deals with the processes responsible for the formation of the archaeological record (cf. Thomas 1986). Clearly, however, its inspiration had nothing whatever to do with the observation of the present dynamic systems.

The mistake that seems to have been made here is in believing that because middle-range theory links dynamic systems (cultural and noncultural) to the static archaeological record; the development of middle-range theory requires first-hand observation of dynamic (and therefore contemporary and living) systems (Binford 1983a:23). As Binford (1968a:13) himself once noted, this would necessarily condemn us to remain ignorant of any dynamic process that for whatever reason might not be operant at observable levels among contemporary systems; this might prove quite troublesome for Binford in particular, because he seems unwilling to entertain the idea that nonaboriginal societies are capable of furnishing useful clues about past dynamics (cf. 1983b:392).

In emphasizing the necessity of directly observing dynamic systems, middle-range theorists seem to imply that it is the contemporary systems *per se* that are important, which they are not: It is the processes and principles that govern dynamic systems, both past and present, that are important. First-hand observation of contemporary systems may help us to think about principles and processes, but the principles and processes necessarily transcend individual cases, however instructive these cases might be. It is, after all, this transcendent quality that gives special value to principles and processes when uniformitarian assumptions are made about the world. The case can perhaps best be put this way: Would Binford's arguments regarding butchering be any more or less compelling were it to turn out that the Nunamiut never existed? Do analyses that apply the principles of butchering Binford has articulated (e.g., Thomas and Meyer 1983) depend on the logic of Binford's reasoning or the accuracy of his factual observations? In short, would we rather Binford be a good thinker or a good observer? For any logical positivist, of course, to whom the merits of an hypothesis are necessarily independent of its origin, this is no question at all (Hempel 1965): Binford the thinker is to be preferred. In short, we should pay more attention to Binford's logic than to the factual origin of that logic. The data Binford presents lend credibility to his hypotheses, to be sure. Nevertheless it is the potential explanatory power of those hypotheses beyond the special case of the Nunamiut that really matters.

In the last analysis it would seem that the current confusion surrounding definition of "middle-range archaeological theory" reflects basic flaws in the concept itself. If it is worth anything at all, a scientific theory must at least pretend to address a specific body of fact—either those in hand or potentially obtainable. The real or anticipated patterning of these facts are in fact the "signatures" through which the principles of interest express themselves via the phenomena that constitute the limited set. On these grounds I see no qualitative, that is, epistemological, difference between what have been called mid-range theory (*sensu* Thomas), middle-range theory (*sensu* Merton and Goodyear and Raab), and theories of the processes governing site formation (*sensu* Binford). Moreover, no lower order of theoretical endeavor is conceivable. Indeed, if we limit ourselves to scientific enterprises, middle-range theory is a misnomer: Anything lesser in scale ceases to be theory at all.

The forgoing is not meant to deny that there *is* something new and innovative about the manner in which hunter-gatherer archaeology is being conducted today. We are certainly attending to the matters of verification and meaning more explicitly. Yet this is not our first experience with the problem of archaeological verification nor with how we assign meaning to the archaeological record. The current confusion seems to have arisen in the belief that contemporary efforts to apply Binford's forager-collector model to the real world is anything more or less than the latest attempt to do hunter-gatherer archaeology under the umbrella of a consistent theoretical framework (cf. Grayson 1986). As we observed earlier, this revisionism is surely at least in part a legacy from the 1960s— the era of the new archaeology and the man the hunter symposium. It then became apparent that (1) archaeologists had only rudimentary understanding of their data as anthropological and behavioral (as opposed to purely archaeological) phenomena; (2) these data might have some bearing on our understanding of hunter-gatherers and their place in cultural evolution; and (3) research could be done more profitably by recognizing the relationships between theory and data. Yet this must not obscure what should be obvious, specifically, that what is new about contemporary middle-range research is the innovative theorizing of Binford not the matching of theory and fact—which has always been with us (e.g., Steward and Setzler 1938).

It would serve us well to remember, finally, that for all the exciting avenues of investigation it promises, the "new middle-range theory" attends to limited sets of phenomena that at more abstract levels of analysis are governed by different principles—those that are the subject of theories of general sets. This means that to be fully operational, archaeology must give at least much consideration to the linkage between theories of general and limited sets as it does to the linkage between theories of limited sets and empirical patterns. The current version of middle-range theory in archaeology seems to emphasize the latter at the expense of the former.

To forget that theories of limited sets are ultimately derivatives of theories of general sets makes it all too easy to believe that the phenomena we seek to study are true and real, that is, that they are objectively defined. In its search for invariant signatures of behavior—archaeological truths of the "if and only if" kind (cf. Grayson 1986; Thomas 1986)—it would seem that middle-range theory and research has fallen prey to just this trap. Binford (1983a:213) to the contrary, that several alternative explanations are capable of accounting for shifts in diet during the terminal Pleistocene is most assuredly not symptomatic of faulty middle-range theory nor will improvements in middle-range theory eliminate such situations. This reflects nothing more than that both true and false hypotheses/theories can have true implications (cf. Salmon 1976). Thus, as Kuhn (1962) points out, although we regard them to be incorrect in theory, both Ptolemaic astronomy and Newtonian physics remain in service today because they can be used to predict accurately a variety of phenomena: They are false theories that have true implications.

This problem will not go away with the introduction of middle-range theory. Consider, for example, recent middle-range attempts to account for the faunal remains from Gatecliff Shelter. As previously discussed, there Thomas and Meyer (1983) argued that faunal assemblage could be explained with reference to Binford's modified general utility index, which suggested that butchering had occurred at the spot after which the higher utility body parts had been transported elsewhere. Following the lead of Lyman (1985), Grayson (1988) subsequently undertook another kind of middle-range analysis of the Horizon 2 mountain sheep remains. Lyman and Grayson were both concerned that another site formation process might account for the pattern Thomas and Meyer had attributed to butchering and transport. Specifically, they argued that bone destruction might be responsible for the pattern. This is especially troublesome because there happens to be an inverse correlation between the bone density and economic utility. Accordingly, it might well be that the scarcity of skeletal elements representing high utility body parts might only reflect the greater susceptibility of those elements to destruction by carnivores or, less likely, humans. We are thus confronted with two different and equally powerful middle-range models of site formation that seem to produce exactly the same implications. Clearly, both cannot be true. In this case, Grayson argued that because the positive correlation between element frequency and element density was higher than the inverse correlation between element frequency and economic utility, bone destruction rather than human transport was the likely explanation for the composition of the Horizon 2 mountain sheep assemblage. Not surprisingly, Thomas thinks otherwise (personal communication).

Whether the problem is late Pleistocene diet change or Gatecliff mountain sheep, to claim that good middle-range theory will eliminate cases of predictive indeterminacy is clearly wrong. It merely underscores the depth of misunderstanding surrounding the nature of middle-range research, the intimate linkages between theories of general sets and theories of limited sets, and the relationship of both to the scientific enterprise. These relationships are more openly recognized and dealt with in another thriving area of hunter-gatherer research directed by a theory of what would seem to be (but which in reality is not) an altogether different limited set: optimal foraging theory. That is the subject of Chapter 4.

Chapter 4

Hunter-Gatherers as Optimal Foragers

As detailed in the preceding chapters, students of hunter-gatherers have historically chosen to present and interpret their subject matter in materialist perspective. The current interest in optimal foraging theory is a logical extension of this tradition. Such research is viewed by many as an alternative to middle-range theory that is both more solidly grounded in formal theory and more directly related to the basic materialist concerns of subsistence and settlement that have traditionally dominated anthropological treatments of hunter-gatherers. At the moment, optimal foraging theory seems to command a stronger following than middle-range theory among ethnographers whereas among archaeologists the reverse is true. Apart from certain historical quirks of fate having to do, largely, with the personalities involved, the basis for these preferences is not altogether clear. In theory, at least, neither approach confers undue interpretive or methodological advantage where the matter of research context alone is concerned: The range of potential ethnographic and archaeological applications for both optimal foraging theory and what is called middle-range theory are virtually unlimited.

THE MODELS OF OPTIMAL FORAGING

Optimal foraging theory came to anthropology via biology (e.g., MacArthur and Pianka 1966). It might just as easily have been borrowed from economics in which its principal tenets constitute one part of microeconomics, specifically the part that attends to the rational decision making of individuals under a set of

83

specified conditions that include limited resources and unlimited needs; the remaining part of microeconomic theory—or *theory of the firm* as it is sometimes termed—concerns various larger economic formations (e.g., free market and monopoly) and their effects on the range of choices available to consumers.

The anthropological version of optimal foraging theory asserts that in certain arenas, human decisions are made to maximize the net *rate* of energy gain. These arenas include choices of diet (unconstrained and constrained dietary breadth), foraging location (patch choice), foraging time, foraging group size, and settlement location. Only the first three have been explored in any detail in the human case, and even this characterization has meaning only in a relative sense because the field itself is still quite young. Because our intent here is as much to discuss the theory as its application, before discussing specific instances of anthropological and archaeological research that have been guided by optimal foraging theory, it will be worthwhile to review the rudimentary mechanics of the most common versions of the models governing diet breadth, patch choice, foraging time, and central place foraging. We begin with the basic model of diet breadth, which is simplest conceptually and the one that has been most frequently applied in hunter-gatherer research.

The Diet Breadth Model

In the basic model of diet breadth, foragers confront an array of items that may vary with respect to their (1) abundance; (2) amount of energy produced per item; (3) amount of energy needed to acquire the energy from each; and (4) amount of time needed to acquire that energy once the item is selected. We term this a *diet breadth model*, of course, because the items and their utilities are dietary or nutritional, that is, kinds of food or prey and their energetic content. The structure of the model, however, is easily generalized to fit any number of other situations involving rational choices in which utility can be judged in a single dimension. As we shall see momentarily, for example, the patch choice model is merely a special case of the same general model from which the diet breadth model is derived.

With respect to the diet breadth model specifically, however, the problem for the economy-minded forager is to select the combination of food types that maximizes his net energy intake per unit of foraging time, that is, the amount of energy captured less the amount of energy expended during the period spent foraging. It is assumed that (1) barring exceptional circumstances, the amount of time and energy needed to extract energy from a given item of a given kind and the amount of energy it produces in return are fixed; (2) decisions made are evaluated in terms of momentary return rates, that is, alternatives resulting in higher momentary return rates are chosen over those that result in lower momentary return rates; and (3) preferences for food types are qualitative and complete rather than partial: An item is either in the optimal set or it is not.

To solve a problem of this kind, we first ask what would be rational in the best of all possible worlds. Because we have assumed that costs and benefits are fixed, the only possible room for variation is in the relative abundance of items of each kind. The best (and simplest) case is where all kinds of all items are infinitely abundant – which is to say that they are so abundant that one has no need to search for them at all. How we choose among the various items would in this special instance turn exclusively on the net rate of energy intake per unit of extraction time for each kind of item available. Here, the logical choice is to select only the kind of item yielding the highest rate of return per unit of extraction time. This would give the highest possible overall net rate of energy intake under this best of all possible circumstances. In other words, where no search time is charged, only the time and energy needed to extract energy from the item in question, the logical choice is to select only the kind of item yielding the highest net return per unit of extraction time. This gives us the highest possible energy intake under these best of all possible circumstances.

It is instructive, however, also to ask what would be our best option if given these same circumstance we were for some reason required to exploit at least two kinds of items rather than merely the one giving the highest rate of return per unit of extraction time – say because of scarcity of the most preferred item. The answer, clearly, is that we should select the combination that includes the kind of item yielding the highest rate of return per unit of extraction time and the kind yielding the second highest rate of return: All other resources have lower rates of return and thus any combination including them would result in a momentary rate of return lower than that resulting from the combination of the highest and second highest kinds. Extending this line of reasoning to include all the kinds of items under consideration gives us a ranking of items ranging from those we would most prefer to exploit to those we would least prefer to exploit, this ranking being determined by the net energy produced per unit of extraction time for each item. This ranking is quite important for, as we shall see, no rational forager will pass over a more preferred item to exploit one less preferred, which is another way of saying the use of a low-ranked resource necessarily implies the use of all higher-ranked resources when they are available.

In the real world, of course, nothing is infinitely abundant: All resources must be sought out prior to their exploitation. This means that our momentary rate of energy return must include time (and perhaps energy) spent searching for items to exploit (again, food types). This requires that we reevaluate our selection of resources because the resource that we would most prefer to exploit (because its rate of energy return once found is highest) may be so rarely encountered that to seek it exclusively would result in a very low rate of return.

Consider, then, a forager selectively seeking only the most highly ranked resource available; the overall rate of return for this can be calculated by ascertaining the amount of time and energy it takes to find this resource and extract its energy and the amount of energy this generates. Suppose, however, that in the course of the search, the forager fortuitously encounters an item ranking second only to the one initially sought. Whether the forager halts the search for the first ranked resource to exploit the second ranked one will depend on whether the rate of return for the latter activity, which at this point includes only the time and energy that would be expended in extraction, is greater than the anticipated rate of return when searching *and* extracting energy from only the first ranked resource. This captures the sense of what is meant by the term *contingency model*: The forager confronts a contingency and decides between two courses of action on the basis of rates of energetic return applicable at the very moment the decision is made. The example further illustrates why the choice to use a given resource is independent of its abundance and depends exclusively on its cost and returns of its exploitation *once it is found (i.e., excluding the search phase)* relative to overall rate of return when only resources of higher rank are being sought and exploited (i.e., counting both search and handling phases).

A little further reflection is sufficient to expose the flaw in our initial intuition that, owing to the decrease in search time, we might sometimes increase our overall rate of energetic return by exploiting an item the return rate for which is lower than the return rate for exploiting all higher ranked items, provided the resource added were sufficiently abundant to offset its lower energetic return. To see the fallacy in this requires only that we examine the limiting best case in which this new resource is infinitely abundant. This would mean that the overall rate of return would become the return rate for exploiting that resource exclusive of search time, which, of course, would be lower than the overall rate of return before that resource was added.

The quantitative expression of the diet breadth contingency decision is as follows (cf. Schoener 1974):

$$\frac{e_x}{t_x} > \frac{\sum_{diet} p_i e_i - C_s T_s}{\sum_{diet} p_i t_i + T_s} \tag{4.1}$$

The quantity to the left of the inequality is the rate of energy return for a food type being considered for inclusion in the diet where

e_x is its net energetic yield
t_x is the amount of time needed to extract that energy, often termed *handling time*

The quantity to the right of the inequality is the rate of energy return for a diet that includes all foods types with higher rates of return than the one to the left of the inequality where

p_i is the proportion of the ith food type in the environment

e_i is the usable energetic yield per item of the ith food type

t_i is the time expended per item in extracting energy from the ith food type, that is, per item handling time

C_s is energetic cost per unit of time expended in searching all items up to and including the ith food type

T_s is the time expended in searching for all items up to and including the ith food type

As in our example, we include search time when calculating rate of return for the diet but not when calculating rate of return for the resource being considered for inclusion in that diet. In practice, items are added to the diet in order of decreasing rank (i.e., net rate of return) so long as the inequality favors the item being considered. When this inequality reverses, optimality has been reached, and the diet should exclude the item responsible for the reversal and all lower ranked items.

These quantities and relationships are depicted graphically for an hypothetical set of resources in Figure 4.1. Here, search time decreases and handling time (i.e., time expended in extracting energy once an item is located) increases as increasingly lower ranked items are added to the diet. The changing amount of time expended overall per unit of net energy intake is plotted as a function of shifting search and processing times as items are added to the diet in order of decreasing rank (i.e., highest to lowest). The nadir of this curve marks the diet breadth producing optimal rate of energetic return (i.e., the lowest overall expenditure of time to acquire a unit of net energy); greater or lesser selectivity in diet will produce rates that are suboptimal.

Two counterintuitive implications of the diet breadth model deserve special mention. First, as Equation 4.1 makes clear, the abundance of a resource has no bearing on whether it is included in the optimal diet; that depends entirely upon the abundance of all more highly ranked resources relative to their energetic yield. Second, as resource abundance declines, search time increases, and the breadth of diet increases in compensation. Under no circumstance is any resource that is in the diet to begin with dropped from the diet as food grows scarcer nor is any resource dropped simply because it has become scarcer.

The Patch Choice Model

Just as resources are not infinitely abundant in time in the real world, which is the subject of the diet breadth model, neither are they infinitely and uniformly abundant through space, and this is the subject of the patch choice model. In many ways decisions that must be made about places in which to forage resemble those that must be made about items of diet—so much so that the patch choice model can be regarded as a special case of the basic model of diet

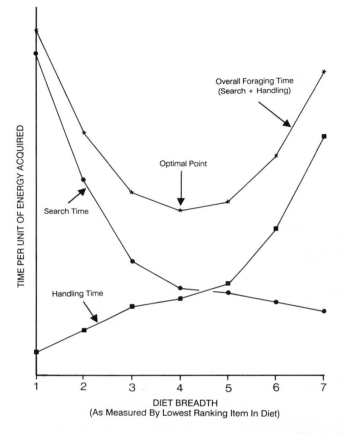

Figure 4.1. Graphical solution of diet breadth problem (after MacArthur and Pianka 1966). Items of diet are initially ranked according to net energetic intake per unit of handling time so that handling time increases with increasing diet breadth. Items are added to the diet so long as the decrease in search time is greater than increase in handling time. Here, addition of the fifth item is suboptimal because it increases handling time more than it decreases search time.

breadth. More precisely we can think of decisions about patch choice as a special kind of breadth model in which the items are patches that contain resources rather than the kind in which the items are the resources themselves, as in the diet breadth model. As is in the diet model, however, the relevant utility is energy, as are the relevant costs. And, as in the breadth model, optimality is evaluated in terms of rate, that is, in addition to energy, time is a critical characteristic of all possible choices among patches.

The forager confronts an array of patches that differ with respect to the energy they contain and the time needed to extract that energy. As in the diet breadth model, patch types are ranked from highest to lowest, in this case according to net rate of energy intake per unit of foraging time (the sum of all search and handling time in the patch). The highest ranked patch type will produce the best return per unit of foraging time, obviously, but if it is rare, which is to say, if patches of that kind are widely spaced, time spent in travel between them may cause overall rate of energetic return (i.e., net energy relative to travel and foraging time) to be suboptimal. As in the diet breadth model, patch types are added to the foraging itinerary in order of decreasing rate of energetic return on foraging time up to but excluding the patch type for which the rate of energetic return per unit of foraging time is less than the overall rate of return for traveling to and foraging in all higher ranked patch types. The quantitative expression of the patch choice decision is identical to the one given for the diet breadth model in Inequality 4.1, except that meanings of certain terms are changed.

The quantity to the left of the inequality is the rate of energy return for patch type being considered for inclusion in foraging itinerary where

e_x is its net energetic yield

t_x is the amount of search and pursuit/processing time needed to extract that energy

The quantity to the right of the inequality is the rate of energy return for the foraging itinerary that includes all patch types with higher rates of return than the one to the left of the inequality where

p_i is the proportion of the ith patch type in the environment

e_i is the usable energetic yield per patch of the ith patch type

t_i is the time per item expended foraging (searching and pursuing prey) in the ith patch type

C_s is energetic cost per unit of time expended in foraging in all patches up to and including the ith patch type

T_s is the time expended in traveling between patches of all types up to and including the ith type

The implications of this model are in many respects analogous to those in the model of diet. As in the case of diet breadth, a decrease in overall food abundance may cause a patch initially excluded from the foraging itinerary to be included. Thus if resource abundance drops uniformly over all types of foraging patches, then the range of patches used may increase because the wise forager then becomes less selective, that is, less willing to travel to preferred patches while passing over others less productive on the way. More intensive use of many kinds of patches in a small geographical area is, thus, a logical response to diminishing resource availability.

In contrast to the diet breadth model where depletion cannot result in greater selectivity (i.e., cause an item formerly in the diet to be dropped), differential depletion of the resources in patch types can easily cause a patch initially included in a foraging itinerary to be excluded: Increasing use of the patch simply drops the rate of return to unacceptable levels. In a further departure from the diet breadth model, in the patch choice model an increase or decrease in resource abundance is ambiguous in its implied effect on the overall foraging itinerary because both search and foraging time are affected, as shown in Figure 4.2. For example, increasing resource abundance overall decreases amount of time spent foraging per calorie in all patches, which implies that patch selectivity should lessen. However, because increasing resource abundance makes all patches more productive, it also decreases the proportion of time spent traveling between patches relative to time spent foraging within them, which implies that patch selectivity should increase. In short, increasing overall resource abundance causes both travel time and foraging time to decrease, so it is unclear whether patch choice should expand, contract, or remain unchanged.

Differences between kinds of foragers reduce this ambiguity somewhat. Foragers that spend proportionally more time in pursuit and processing than in search behave more predictably in this respect: They show more uniformly restricted patch use where resources are abundant and more uniformly ex-panded patch use where resources are scarce. In Figure 4.2, for instance, rate of energy intake per unit of foraging time is unaffected by a 50% increase in prey abundance for a forager who spends no time searching. For the forager who originally spent as much time during search as after search, on the other hand, the same 50% increase in prey abundance has a noticeable effect on rate of energy intake within the patch. For such a forager, increasing abundance of prey encourages increasing patch selectivity (as a consequence of the effect on rate of energy intake per unit of travel time) and at the same time decreasing patch selectivity (as a consequence of the increasing rate of energy intake per unit of foraging time). Under these circumstances, we would expect the forager who spends no time in search to become more selective in the use of patches than the forager who initially spent as much time in search as in pursuit.

Foraging Time: The Marginal Value Theorem

As we have seen, the models of diet breadth and foraging itinerary (patch choice) tell us where to eat and, once there, what to eat. But they do not tell us how long to stay in a place while eating. In theory, of course, the amount of time spent in a patch should depend on the quantity and quality of resources it contains and the rate at which these are depleted. The overall abundance of

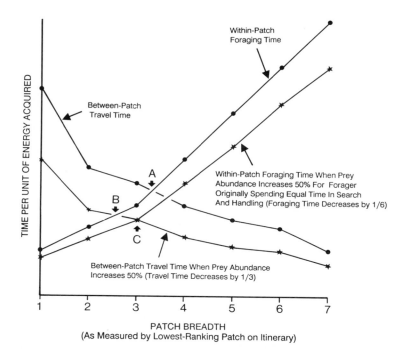

Figure 4.2. Graphical solution to patch choice problem (after MacArthur and Pianka 1966). Patches are initially ranked according to net energetic intake per unit of foraging time so that within-patch foraging time increases with decreasing patch selectivity. Patches are added to foraging itinerary so long as decrease in between-patch travel time is greater than the increase in within-patch foraging time. Point "A" is optimal under original conditions. When prey abundance increases by 50%, between-patch travel time decreases by one-third because there is more prey in each patch. This prey increase has no effect on the within-patch energy intake rate of a forager that originally spent (and continues to spend) no time in search, whose new optimum is at point "B." However, for a forager originally spending as much time in search as in handling, a 50% increase in prey abundance decreases search time by one-third and, thus, within-patch foraging time by one-sixth. The new optimal point for this forager is at point "C."

resources within the environment presumably is involved here as well. This problem is the subject of a somewhat different model, developed by (Charnov 1976) and termed by him the marginal value theorem. Just how the model works is most easily understood with reference to its graphic solution as presented in Figure 4.3. That figure plots, for a given patch, total energy intake (Y axis) as a function of time spent within the patch (X axis). Also shown is the rate of energetic intake for the environment as a whole (i.e., overall energy intake relative to time expended on travel between patches in the itinerary, on foraging within patches, and on handling items in the diet). The curve of the rate of

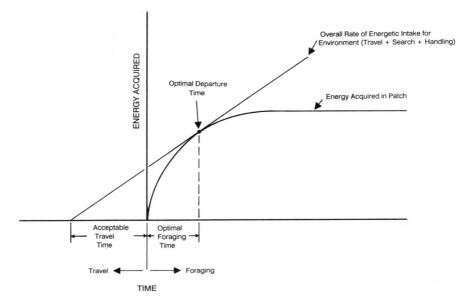

Figure 4.3. Graphical solution to patch departure problem (after Charnov 1976). Line representing overall rate of net energetic intake for environment is drawn tangent to asymptotic curve representing cumulative energy acquired as within-patch foraging time increases. The intersection of the environment line and patch curve indicates optimal departure time. Proceeding from the origin to the left, "T" marks the maximum acceptable amount of time that should have been spent traveling to the patch.

energy intake within the patch is steep initially to represent the rapid rate at which abundant prey are taken before the patch is depleted. As resources within the patch become increasingly rare, however, the rate of energy intake, and hence, the slope of the curve, declines until it eventually becomes asymptotic. After this point, the forager has no prospects for acquiring further energy locally and should leave. The question is whether the forager should eat every last scrap of food in a patch or abandon it at some specific point when it is only partially depleted.

The solution to this problem turns out to be very simple. When the rate of return within the patch drops to the overall rate obtainable in the environment as a whole (i.e., energy relative to all the relevant travel, search, and handling times for all its patches), the forager should move on. Graphically this solution is obtained by drawing a tangent to the patch curve, a line the slope of which is equivalent to the overall environmental rate of energy intake. The intersection of the curve and the tangent marks the point in time (i.e., on the X axis) at which the forager should leave and seek a new patch. Incidentally, the intersection of the tangent and the X axis delimits the maximum amount of time the forager should have spent in travel to this particular patch (see later discussion).

In the marginal value theorem, then, the contingency is one in which the rate of return on foraging time begins to decay from the moment resources begin to be extracted from the patch. When, after some period, this rate equals the rate that can be expected in the long run when moving from patch to patch within the environment the optimal "cutoff" has been reached, and the forager should move.

Central Place Foraging

Central place foraging models (Orians and Pearson 1979) contain a spatial dimension that is lacking in the others we have reviewed so far. In these analyses, foraging is modeled as a trip with a given point of departure and return. During this trip foraging takes place in patches the expected energetic return from which can be described in terms of a monotonic, nondecreasing curve plotting expected intake as a function of time when prey equal to or greater than a specific size are taken.

This is illustrated in Figure 4.4 (cf. Orians and Pearson 1979:Figure 1), where energy is plotted on the Y axis and time is plotted on the X axis: Round-trip travel time between central place and patch is to the left of the origin, foraging time is to the right. To simplify matters in this example, search accounts for all foraging time (i.e., there is no handling time), and only one prey item is taken each trip. The two curves shown relate time and energy in different ways for the patch. The lower curve (termed here an expected time curve) plots for prey of different sizes (i.e., containing different amounts of net energy, C_i,) the amount of time, S_i, that will lapse before encountering prey of a size greater than or equal to C_i. The upper curve (termed here an expected energy curve) plots an amount of energy, C'_i, the forager can expect to accumulate during the expected foraging interval, S_i, by taking any item of prey encountered whose size (net energetic content) is greater than or equal to C_i. That is, directly above any point, S_i, C_i, on the lower (expected time) curve, there is on the upper (expected energy) curve a corresponding point, S_i, C'_i, indicating the net energy the forager will most likely acquire each trip by selectively targeting prey greater than or equal to C_i.

For a patch characterized by the expected time and energy curves shown in Figure 4.4, a line drawn from a point to the left of the origin on the X axis that represents the distance in time, T_i, to and from the hypothetical central place *and* tangent to the expected energy curve will define the optimal solution to the central place foraging problem. This line intersects the Y axis at an energetic "cutoff" point marking the minimal prey size, Ci, that ought to be taken given

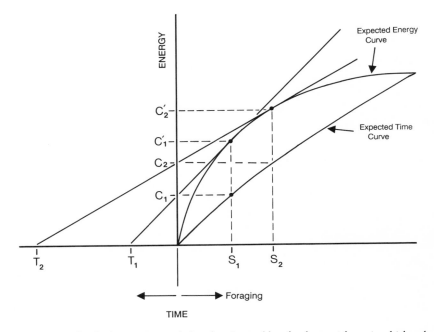

Figure 4.4. Graphical solution to central place foraging problem for the special case in which only search contributes to foraging time (after Orians and Pearson 1979). The lower curve (expected time) plots the amount of search time, S_i, required to encounter prey greater than or equal to a given size (i.e., energy content), C_i. For the same foraging (search) intervals, the upper curve (expected energy) plots the amount of energy, C_i', a forager can expect to obtain when harvesting prey as large or larger than C_i. As shown, increasing central place to patch round-trip time from T_1 to T_2 increases optimal within patch foraging (search) time from S_1 to S_2, minimal prey size from C_1 to C_2, and expected energy intake from C_1' to C_2'.

the energetic content of the patch and the round-trip distance between the patch and the central place. By definition, the intersection of the curve and this tangent indicates for these conditions the expected amount of time it will take to encounter and secure an acceptable item of prey (i.e., greater than or equal to the recommended size, C_i, and the expected size of that prey, C_i'. As shown in Figure 4.4, as round-trip travel time between the patch and the central place increases, time spent within a patch, minimum acceptable prey size, and expected prey size should all increase concomitantly (as shown, if $T_2 > T_1$, then $S_2 > S_1$, $C_2 > C_1$, and $C_2' > C_1'$). By the same token, as shown in Figure 4.5, when distance between central place and patch is held constant, within-patch foraging time decreases, whereas minimum acceptable prey size and expected prey size both increase, with increasing within-patch resource abundance, here indicated by different within-patch expected energy curves (cf. Orians and Pearson 1979:Figure 6).

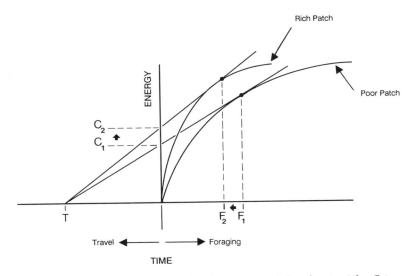

Figure 4.5. Effect of within-patch resource abundance in central place foraging (after Orians and Pearson 1979). Increasing abundance increases minimum prey threshold and decreases within-patch foraging time.

Figure 4.6 illustrates the effect of round-trip travel time on the central place foraging model when there are two kinds of prey that differ in terms of net energetic content and amount of handling time required per unit of net energy (after Orians and Pearson 1979:Figure 4). In this case, C_1 and C_2 are the net energetic contents of prey 1 and prey 2, respectively, and C_u is the mean per item net energetic content when both are taken as encountered. Similarly, S_1 and S_2, H_1 and H_2, and F_1 and F_2 are the handling times, search times, and the total within-patch foraging times (search plus handling) for prey 1 and prey 2, respectively, and F_u is the mean per item within patch foraging time (search plus handling) when both prey 1 and 2 are taken as encountered.

For the conditions illustrated, a line passing through the points F_1,C_1 (the overall within-patch rate of net energetic return when exploiting only prey 1) and H_2,C_2 (the within-patch rate of net energetic return that results from handling—but not searching for—prey 2) defines a critical threshold, T_1, to the left of the origin on the X axis. With respect to this patch, for central places with travel times below this threshold (graphically, nearer the origin), only prey 1 should be taken. A second line drawn between the points F_2,C_2 (the overall within-patch rate of energetic return when exploiting only prey 2) and H_1,C_1 (the within-patch rate of net energetic return that results from handling—but not searching for—prey 1) defines a second critical travel time threshold, T_2. For central places at or beyond (graphically, to the left of) this point, only prey 2 should be taken from the patch. For central places with travel times greater than

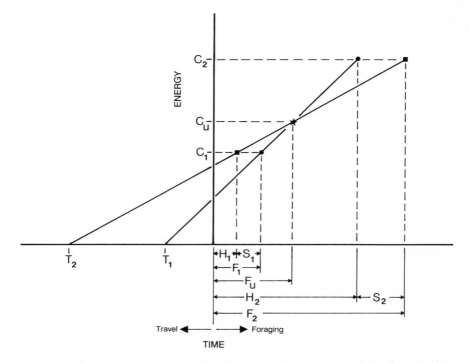

Figure 4.6. Effect of travel time relative to handling time and prey size in central place foraging (after Orians and Pearson 1979). Given the conditions indicated, only prey 1 should be taken for central places closer to patch than T_1 (because $C_1/T_1 + H_1 + S_1 > C_2/T_1 + H_2$), and only prey 2 should be taken for central places farther than T_2 ($C_2/T_2 + H_2 + S_2 > C_1/T_2 + H_1$). Between T_1 and T_2, both types of prey should be taken, yielding a rate of energetic intake during foraging of C_u/F_u.

or equal to T_1 and less than or equal to T_2, both prey 1 and 2 should be taken as encountered. In that case, the intersection of the two threshold-defining lines indicates the within-patch rate of net energetic intake, F_u, C_u, associated with the 2-prey policy.

Figure 4.6 makes it clear that in central place foraging, choices about prey types are contingent upon the energy content of each prey relative to both travel and handling time. That is, in contrast to the simple diet breadth model, where ranking is determined by the ratio of energy to handling time, in central place foraging, ranking is by the ratio of energy to travel *and* handling times. It follows that where travel times are low, handling time is more important. This is why in our example prey 2 is ignored for travel times less than T_1: Its ratio of energy to handling time is less than the ratio of energy to search plus handling for prey 1 and travel time is not large enough to affect this advantage. On the other hand, where travel times are large, handling time grows relatively less important, and for very large travel times, handling time becomes almost insignificant. In such cases, the most salient variable is package size. This is why in our example prey 1 is ignored for central places with travel times greater than T_2: Above this threshold, travel time is large enough to destroy all the advantages prey 1 enjoys as a consequence of its lower rate of handling time. Thus, one very important implication of this model is that the ranking of items of diet will vary as a function of distance to central place: Low-ranking items in patches near at hand may be high-ranking items in patches far away.

Figure 4.7 (cf. Orians and Pearson 1979:Figure 10) models a case in which there are, at different distances from the central place, three patches with different resource characteristics as illustrated by their different expected energy curves. These round-trip travel distances are represented by displacement of the patch curve to the right of the origin, the greater the distance the greater the displacement. It is clear from this presentation that the forager should exploit prey of size C or greater only from patch II. If the forager encounters prey on the way to the patch, that is, before T_2, that prey should be taken if at that moment, the ratio of its size to round-trip travel time to the central place is greater than the slope of the line drawn from the origin tangent to the curve for patch II. This corresponds to the shaded area shown in Figure 4.7.

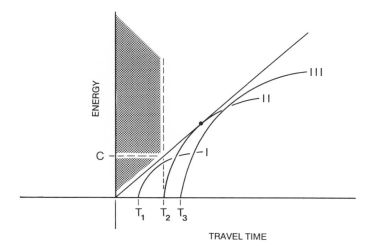

Figure 4.7. Effect of travel time on patch choice and diet breadth in central place foraging (after Orians and Pearson 1979). Here, where three patches (I, II, and III) occur at varying round-trip distances (T_1, T_2, and T_3) from the central place, the forager takes only prey of size C or greater from patch II. The shaded area corresponds to the circumstances (ratio of prey size to travel time) under which prey encountered on the way to the patch should be taken: These result in rates of energetic intake greater than or equal to those expected when traveling to and foraging within patch II.

APPLICATIONS OF OPTIMAL FORAGING THEORY

Relatively little known to anthropology in 1980 (cf. Bettinger 1980), optimal foraging theory has since gained rapid and widespread acceptance and currently competes on an even footing with middle-range theory/research in terms of popularity. It fully deserves this attention; its utility has been convincingly demonstrated in many insightful field studies of contemporary hunter-gatherer behavior. A few of these are reviewed next (see also Borgerhoff-Mulder 1988).

The Aché of Paraguay

Hawkes, Hill, and O'Connell (1982) have employed optimal foraging theory to great advantage in their interpretation of Aché subsistence behavior and in the course of this dispel many common myths about hunter-gatherer foraging. They show, for instance, that tropical rainforests are not necessarily marginal for hunter-gatherers, as is commonly held (cf. Meggers 1971; Lathrap 1968). Neither is it the case that tropical hunter-gatherer diets are invariably dominated by plants. Most important, they show that the standard portrayal of hunting as high risk, high yield and gathering as low risk, low yield (Lee 1968:40) is far too simple a view to understand empirical cases.

For the Aché, the uncertainties associated with hunting are vastly outweighed by the net caloric returns per foraging hour: Excluding search time, hunters net between 65,000 and 6,000 calories per foraging hour; gatherers seldom (if ever) exceed 5,000. Given this and the abundance of available game, it is hardly surprising that that the Aché eat well. Meat constitutes 80% of 3,610 calories they consume daily per capita, which is approximately a third more than is consumed by African and Australian hunter-gatherers for which data are available.

The Alyawara of Australia

In an analysis of a different sort, O'Connell and Hawkes (1981) have employed the diet breadth model to account for foraging behavior of the Alyawara of central Australia and to explain postcontact changes in their diet and particularly the recent deletion of ripe grass and tree seeds from the aboriginal subsistence repertoire. With regard to the latter, it is argued that the difficulty of collecting and processing of these native seeds caused them to be among the lowest-ranked traditional foodstuffs. Accordingly, as access improved to higher ranked traditional plant foods and nontraditional foodstuffs in the form of governmentally supplied rations, seeds were the first item to be dropped from the native diet.

The Alyawara study has proven to be a fertile source of hypotheses about the culture history of hunter-gatherers. The evidence used to explain why tree and grass seeds were the first items to be dropped from the aboriginal foraging repertoire can be taken a step further to suggest that seeds were probably the last traditional foods to enter the diet prehistorically (leading to the general rule that the last resource to enter the diet is the first to be deleted from the diet). From this it follows that parts of Australia where seeds constitute a major part of the potential food supply (e.g., in the arid interior) would have been occupied relatively late in time. O'Connell, Jones, and Simms (1982) subsequently extended this logic to develop a model for the colonization of the Great Basin of North American. In a parallel to the Australian case, it is argued that population growth depleted highly preferred resources in what might be termed optimal habitats. Aboriginal groups then found it increasingly expedient to draw upon additional less desirable resources, initially in optimal settings and subsequently in more marginal areas—specifically the Great Basin of North America—where less desirable species were available in abundance.

Arctic and Subarctic Foragers

Ethnographic applications of optimal foraging theory are by no means confined to lower latitudes. Winterhalder (1977, 1980, 1981) and Smith (1980, 1981) have employed optimal models to "retrodict" a variety of foraging behaviors for Arctic and Subarctic hunter-gatherers. As among the Alyawara, a point that clearly emerges here, is the potential power of these models to explain the behavioral changes that accompany culture contact. For instance, Winterhalder shows how access to Western technology differentially affected foraging patterns in two instances among the Cree. In that case, early access to nets, steel traps, and firearms substantially raised the speed and reliability with which fish and game could be taken once they were encountered (i.e., it lowered their handling times and, thus, raised their ranking). In accord with the predictions of the diet breadth model, this caused prey that had been previously considered too small or too difficult to capture to become Cree foraging targets. Subsequently, access to boats and snowmobiles decreased the search time associated with foraging. In accord with predictions, this reversed the earlier trend toward increasing diet breadth: As search time decreased overall, Cree foragers grew more selective in their choice of prey.

Measuring Forager Affluence:
Southern Africa and Western North America

Because it employs a standard measure of caloric efficiency, foraging theory is particularly useful as a basis for comparative studies. Hawkes and O'Connell (1981) have used this feature to challenge the widely accepted view of the !Kung as affluent foragers. In particular, they question the basis of that claim, which lies in the observation that !Kung spend only a few hours each day in the field foraging for food (e.g., Sahlins 1968; Lee 1968). As they indicate, that estimate excludes the amount of time needed to prepare resources for consumption. When overall foraging efficiency (i.e., including processing time) is considered, the !Kung seem to be working about as hard as the Alyawara of Australia—who have never been characterized as affluent. The implications of this are particularly telling with regard to the vaunted mongongo nut, the abundance of which is generally assumed to account for !Kung affluence (cf. Lee 1968). Hawkes and O'Connell argue that when both procurement and processing time are taken into account, the mongongo nut yields only about 700 calories per hour, which is as low or lower than any traditional staple consumed by the !Kung and roughly comparable to the lowest ranked foods consumed by the Alyawara. Given this, it seems likely that the mongongo nut would be among the first resources the !Kung would drop from their diet in the event of improved access to other more highly ranked resources.

A case parallel to that of the !Kung and the mongongo nut exists with regard to the major dietary staple of aboriginal California, the acorn (*Quercus*, *Lithocarpus*). The nearly unlimited natural abundance of this resource has been the source of much comment and traditionally held to account for the apparent affluence and observed sociopolitical complexity of hunter-gatherers in that region (e.g., Heizer 1958). As with the mongongo nut, however, the appearance is deceptive. The extensive pounding, leaching, and cooking required to render acorns edible make it comparable to lowest ranked traditional foods of both the !Kung and Alyawara. Starting with shelled nuts, a skilled processor can prepare the equivalent of 1,660 calories of cooked acorn mush per hour (Goldschmidt 1974). Adding harvesting and shelling time would probably put the overall rate of return for acorns somewhere between the 700 calories per hour estimated for mongongo nuts and 500 calories per hour estimated for Australian grass and tree seeds. Further, as in both those cases, given their low rate of return, it is likely that acorns entered the aboriginal California economy relatively late in time, when other, more attractive, resources were no longer capable of supporting the native population (Basgall 1987). In short, to argue that the abundance of acorns permitted dense aboriginal populations in California is correct but misses the important point: Dense populations *required* the use of the acorn. Using marginal foraging efficiency as a measure, it would appear that native Californians were roughly equivalent in "affluence" to the !Kung and Alyawara, all three being demonstrably less affluent in this respect than the Aché.

Processors and Travelers

In comparison to ethnographic examples, archaeological applications of optimal foraging theory are fewer in number but equally convincing. One example is provided by Bettinger and Baumhoff (1982), who have joined the diet and patch models to deduce a theoretical continuum of hunter-gatherer strategies (Table 4.1) that superficially resembles Binford's forager-collector series; but unlike Binford's, that model has the advantage of specifying precise relationships between population and resources, on the one hand, and settlement and subsistence patterns, on the other.

In the traveler-processor model, as population increases from low densities (the traveler situation) to high densities (the processor situation), diet breadth increases and, along with it, processing, that is, handling, costs (both absolutely and proportionally), and overall dietary cost. At the same time, because overall return rates and return rates for time spent foraging within patches both drop, the benefits of travel between patches decrease. Consequently, time spent within any given patch increases and, for this reason and because patch selectivity itself declines, the overall proportion of time spent traveling between highly productive patches declines concomitantly.

Apart from its more obvious implications regarding basic patterns of subsistence and settlement, which are of archaeological as well as ethnographic interest (e.g., range of plant and animal species represented, diversity of extractive tools, presence of residential and storage facilities, and so on), the traveler-processor model carries a series of more subtle expectations regarding subsistence technology and demography. For instance, because increasing population density necessarily implies a greater utility (and thus demand) for processing time, it follows that overall increase in population ought to be followed by an overall increase in the size and elaboration of assemblages of processing tools. Further, because food processing is a task that almost universally falls to females (e.g., cooking, seed grinding), population increase would seem to produce a greater economic demand for females. Preferential female infanticide might well be expected to decrease under such conditions.

Table 4.1. Ideal Characteristics of Travelers and Processors[a]

	Travelers	Processors
Duration of settlement residency	Brief	Extended
Distance between settlements	Long	Short
Population density	Low	High
Sensitivity to demographic change	High	Low
Resource selectivity	Narrow spectrum	Broad spectrum
Sex ratio	Female-poor	Female-rich
Major costs of subsistence	Travel, search, scouting	Procurement, processing
Competitive fitness	Low	High

[a] After Bettinger and Baumhoff 1983.

The implications of population growth are much less appealing for males. In particular, because extractive costs decrease proportionally as overall diet costs increase, males, who in comparison to females typically expend proportionally more of their time extracting resources than processing them, would seem to become proportionally less economically important as population increases. That the proportional contribution of high-ranking patches and proportion of time spent in travel between patches both decrease as population grows larger further contributes to this decline in the economic importance of males for it typically falls to males to scout new productive patches during the course of dispensing their other wide-ranging extractive activities (e.g., hunting).

One of the more surprising implications of the traveler-processor model is that it predicts that in many cases hunter-gatherers are likely to solve economic problems occasioned by population growth by short term means that in the long term only encourage further population growth, making the problem worse and the appropriate solutions more drastic. The most obvious avenue leading to this is that in which, as suggested, female infanticide is curtailed to make more female labor available for resource processing. This leads to increased population both by definition and probabilistically: by definition because in the near term more individuals will survive past infancy and probabilistically in the long term (and this effect is substantially much more important) because the near-term increase represents a proportional increase of the reproductive individuals of the population (i.e., females).

Because it relies upon explicit theoretical constructions drawn from formal microeconomics as well as on simple and well-documented anthropological observations about population, subsistence, settlement, and sex-differentiated tasks, the traveler-processor model constitutes one of the more coherent and general explanatory and predictive accounts of variability in regional subsistence-settlement systems among hunter-gatherers. By standardizing description and analysis of regional subsistence-settlement systems in explicitly systemic and materialistic terms, it is a particularly powerful tool when used as a basis for comparative studies.

Bettinger and Baumhoff (1982) mention some interesting specific archaeological cases where their model might profitably be applied. In particular, they use it to account for the late prehistoric northward and eastward spread of Numic-speaking peoples from southeastern California into the Great Basin. It is argued that this population movement was precipitated by growing demographic pressure in southeastern California that eventually led groups there to adopt a processor strategy that emphasized low residential mobility in combination with the intensive use of low-quality resources requiring extensive processing, particularly small seeds. For reasons already noted, the increased investment in resource processing led to curtailment of female infanticide, which had the effect of putting further pressure on local resources.

With this processor strategy firmly entrenched by A.D. 1000, aboriginal groups in southeastern California were preadapted for expansion into adjacent parts of the Great Basin. Those areas were occupied at the time by groups embracing traveler strategies that emphasized high residential mobility and the selective use of high-quality resources, large game in particular. Bettinger and Baumhoff show that, in general, groups with processor strategies enjoy fundamental competitive advantages over groups with traveler strategies. Most important, processor strategists compete for all of the resources that are important to traveler strategists whereas traveler strategists compete for only a fraction of the resources important to processor strategists, ignoring the lower ranked ones. Further, because of their intensive use of a broad range of resources, processor strategists can sustain themselves on tracts of land too small or too marginal to sustain traveler strategists.

Given these circumstances, processor strategists can gain footholds in territories occupied by traveler strategists in at least two ways: (1) by occupying small, unused (and thus uncontested) tracts; and (2) by occupying more favored locations where, by virtue of their more generalized subsistence patterns and more stable residential patterns, they generally concentrate in greater numbers than traveler strategists who might contest for access to the same place. Bettinger and Baumhoff (1982) argue that this is exactly what happened in the case of the Numic spread. Driven by continuing population growth arising from the importance of female labor in resource processing, Numic-speaking populations spread from southeastern California across the entire Great Basin in less than 1,000 years. Several lines of archaeological evidence relating to settlement patterns and subsistence technology seem to support that argument.

Foraging Experiments

One of the greatest obstacles preventing broader archaeological application of optimal foraging theory lies in the determination of return rates associated with specific foraging activities. How does one set about calculating the search and pursuit times applicable to mammoths, for example? Controlled harvesting and processing experiments with resources still available for study (e.g., plants) offer one obvious and potentially fruitful approach to the problem (e.g., Simms 1984). Unfortunately, it is often difficult to replicate through modern experiment many of the parameters that undoubtedly contributed to prehistoric foraging efficiency and foraging decisions. It is often unclear, for instance, by what means and under what conditions a given resource was procured. More fundamentally, it is likely that to be even minimally productive, many resources demanded an exceptional level of foraging expertise acquired only through patient instruction by informed elders and long periods of apprenticeship during childhood and adolescence. Further, it is entirely thinkable that resources wholly unproductive to the novice are capable of producing much higher yields than those resources that the novice finds most productive (i.e., the resource rankings of expert and novice foragers may be different). This suggests that resource return rates obtained experimentally by wholly untutored and comparatively inexperienced modern foragers may often be of relatively limited utility in archaeological contests. Foraging experiments are obviously valuable, but such data should be used with caution.

CRITICISM OF OPTIMAL FORAGING THEORY

The models of optimality we have examined here are intentionally idealized to reveal certain properties basic to economic decision making. This makes it easy to appreciate their potential use in understanding foraging behavior among hunters and gatherers. As we have seen, those models treat foraging behavior as resulting from straightforward choices made by optimizing individuals among alternative behaviors confronted as momentary contingencies. In all these cases, decisions (and thus predictions about behavior) are unambiguous because the decision-making algorithm is specified precisely and because the costs and consequences of each available alternative are treated as though they were perfectly known. That is what makes foraging models potentially so powerful: They explain complex behaviors in simple terms. This quality has attracted much interest and gained foraging theory many adherents. It is also the object of much questioning and criticism, some constructive, some not. Given the diversity of theory within anthropology, this is unsurprising. Skepticism regarding novel (and particularly untested) theories is a predictable and potentially healthy component of science both during and between times of paradigm crisis (Kuhn 1962). It should and will continue as optimal foraging theorists seek credibility for their models. Of course, not all of the criticism leveled against optimal foraging theory is equally interesting or telling, and much is rhetorical rather than substantive.

A remarkably large fraction of the nonconstructive criticism of foraging theory derives from humanistic philosophies seemingly opposed in principle to simple explanations. There is no chance for productive dialogue here. By rejecting its utility *a priori*, such criticism fails in any useful way to come to grips with the issues that foraging theory is intended to address. In particular, the objection raised by some that foraging models ought not to be entertained seriously simply because they contain what are said to be unrealistic assumptions about human motives and about conditions in the real world misses the point of such models altogether (to this one might add that because no one can really know what or how the native thinks, that view is arrogantly ethnocentric to boot). Foraging models are meant to produce specific expectations, predictions if you will, about what foraging behavior would look like were it generated according to a particular logic (the decision-making algorithm) in the presence of certain external conditions, prey density, and the like. Simply put, foraging models are about behavior. In this sense, whether the inner mechanics of native logic conform to the model algorithm that is used, or whether external conditions are specified in sufficient detail is not, in the last instance, subject to objection on theoretical grounds. The real test is whether observed behavior conforms to expectations arising from the models.

The Middle-Range Critics of Optimal Foraging Theory

Given its distinctly material and behavioral cast, one would expect optimal foraging theory to find staunch advocates among those individuals who have figured prominently in middle-range theory in archaeology. Surprisingly, this is not the case. Middle-range theorists have been among the harshest critics of optimal foraging models. Binford has been particularly outspoken in the matter. His objections, however, are as curious as they are unconvincing. He protests, first, on the grounds that he, "cannot understand how *constant* properties can guide us to understand and explain cultural diversity" (Binford 1983b:219, emphasis supplied; see also Binford 1978a:455). There is little merit in this claim: Science is full of constant properties useful in understanding diversity and replete with models in which constant, nonreducible elements are employed to produce a variety of outcomes. Indeed, from the transformations of Lévi-Strauss, to the forager-collector continuum, to the double helix, DNA, and Einsteinian physics (e.g., $E = mc^2$), it is difficult to think of a single kind of scientific theory that does not involve constant properties to explain diversity: That is, in fact, what theories are supposed to do.

Binford continues in specific criticism of optimal foraging theories: "If there is one principle that anthropological field studies have affirmed over and over again it is that the intellectual contexts of behavior in different cultures renders rationality a relative phenomenon" (1982:220; but compare Binford 1978a:453). There is no mistaking what is being said here. It is the standard substantivist criticism that, as a version of formal economics (microeconomics), optimal foraging theory is flawed because it ignores specific cultural values and arbitrarily separates economy from other parts of culture. Perhaps this is so—but the alternative has been demonstrated to be far less useful: *Norms* guide human behavior. Substantivisim is the penetration of ordinary functionalist thought into economic studies. The substantivists, in particular Dalton (1961, 1969; Dalton and Kocke 1983) and Polanyi (1957), argued that economic behavior was the result of individuals acting on the basis of enculturated norms; the acquisition and use of language was the analogy (itself being a matter of some dispute). This was in contrast to the formalist view that individuals act in their own self-interest under partial constraints imposed by cultural norms (cf. Davis 1973). It is noteworthy that the substantivists consistently failed to account for the source of their normative variation and so, in essence, their explanations of economic behavior are merely descriptive. Does Binford believe this the proper approach to the study of hunter-gatherer economic systems? If so, that is clearly a sharp reversal from his earlier stands and in particular his vehement criticism of normative models. Certainly it contradicts the very same premises upon which a great deal of his own recent work has been built (see later discussion).

Note also that unless Binford is claiming that rationality is *entirely* cultural—which would put him squarely in the camp of such extreme substantivists as Sahlins (1976) and eliminate any active role for either materialist theory or archaeology in anthropology—his suggestion that deductive models of objective rationality are without analytical value is groundless. Weber (1948:184-185) addressed this issue precisely (cf. Davis 1978), when he stepped into the debate between the Romantic "German Historical School" of Schmoller and the "Austrian Marginal Value Theory School" of Menger (see Chapter 2). Weber posited that human rationality consisted of two parts, which he termed *substantive* and *formal*. The former (behavior consistent with a specific set of ultimate values) corresponds to Binford's (romantic/substantivist) concept of culturally conditioned rationality; the second (behavior limited only by efficiency in attaining goods) corresponds to objective rationality, that is, as a formal economist, microeconomist, marginal value theorist, or optimal foraging theorist would see it. In recognizing this distinction, Weber showed that the fact that rationality was culturally conditioned did not obviate the utility of analyses grounded in concepts of objective rationality; quite the contrary, the former required the latter. He argued that individuals are held in constant tension between the actions dictated by cultural rationality and actions dictated by the objective rationality of self-interest. Recognizing this tension requires that subjective and formal rationality be distinguished analytically so that the tautology could be broken and the relative effect of each could be weighed.

This is precisely what optimal foraging theorists have argued (Smith 1983; O'Connell and Hawkes 1981; see also Bettinger 1980): Such studies provide a yardstick of objective economic rationality as a basis for the comparative study of human behavior. Without this yardstick it would be impossible to know whether human behavior was governed by cultural norms and ideas or by rational, self-interested incentives. This is a common and very power kind of simple theoretical analysis. We often use "ideal types" as analytical instruments in situations where we do not expect predictions to be completely accurate. Actually, this justification is as old as microeconomic theory itself:

Political economy considers mankind as occupied solely in acquiring and consuming wealth. . . . Not because any political economist was ever so absurd as to suppose that mankind are really thus constituted, but because this is the mode in which science must necessarily proceed. (This is followed by an analogy with the assumption of frictionless engines in mechanics; J. S. Mill 1836 [quoted in Burrow 1966:74])[1]

Discussion

It should be clear from the forgoing that, when examined, the criticisms that Binford has to this point leveled against optimal foraging theory fall to the ground. Indeed, in the last analysis Binford's objection to optimal foraging theory seems to stand on grounds no more secure than that from which utilitarianism was rejected originally, namely an "unanswerable refusal . . . to believe that pain and pleasure . . . [are] . . . the only sources of human motive" (cf. Burrow 1966:70). It can be shown with equal clarity that certain other criticisms recently leveled at optimal foraging theory from the camp of middle-range research are similarly wanting. It seems worth considering those in order to clarify issues and set the record straight.

Note first that optimal foraging theory *is* middle-range theory in the senses intended by both Merton and Binford. It employs a few generalities about utility and economizing (those we have reviewed) and sets forth explicit and testable predictions. That prominent middle-range theorists have taken issue with the model is all the more puzzling, given that it is merely a more formal statement of the same phenomena upon which much recent middle-range research, including their own, is based. This is particularly clear in the case of Binford's (1978a:15-38) well-known and widely used (cf. Thomas and Meyer 1983) model of butchering strategies. As noted earlier, in this model different skeletal elements are scaled from highest to lowest utility according to their by-weight complement of meat, marrow, and grease. It is obvious that this scaling is formally identical to the ranking of items of diet/patches by utility in optimal foraging: Both assume that economic utility governs the value assigned to different

---

[1]To follow the parallel a step further, in this light the middle-range critics of optimal foraging theory seem to be taking much the same stand as J. S. Mill took against utilitarianism. In reference to the analogy between utilitarian theory and models of frictionless engines in physics, Mill noted that, although for some purposes such simplifying assumptions might be useful, they alone could never result in a comprehensive accounting of actual cases. That was so because such disturbing causes as friction often caused expectations arising from simple principles to be wrong when put to empirical test and more important because those disturbing causes were not merely random noise but rather forces important in their own right, subject to their own laws, and, therefore, a legitimate and necessary subject of study (cf. Burrow 1966:74). The analogy between J. S. Mill's "disturbing" forces and middle-range "processes of site formation" can hardly be overlooked here.

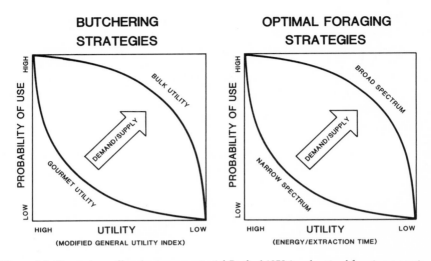

Figure 4.8. Comparison of butchering strategies (cf. Binford 1978a) and optimal foraging strategies. In both cases, resources are ranked from high utility on the left to low utility on the right. The curves indicate probability a resource is used under varying conditions of supply relative to demand. When demand is relatively low (i.e., supply is high), only high-utility resources are used resulting in gourmet-utility butchering and narrow-spectrum diet breadth. When demand is high, low-utility resources are used in addition to high-utility ones resulting in bulk utility butchering and broad-spectrum diet breadth.

commodities by foragers/consumers and that this value, however justified in cultural terms, determines forager/consumer behavior with respect to these commodities (Binford 1978a:38-39). It is equally apparent that optimal foraging theory faithfully predicts the conditions under which one would expect the two basic butchering strategies postulated by Binford (1978a:81): *bulk utility*, in which all but the very lowest utility items are taken, and *gourmet utility* in which all but the very highest utility items are left behind. Indeed, Binford's suggestions that the bulk strategy is to be expected when demand is high, the gourmet strategy when demand is low (Binford 1978a:44), is little more than a restatement of the basic optimal foraging principle that the use of specific items varies according to demand. This similarity is illustrated in Figure 4.8, in which butchering strategies predicted by Binford are compared with exploitative strategies predicted by the optimal foraging model of diet breadth.[2]

---

[2]Metcalfe and Jones (1988:495) argue that the diet breadth model differs from Binford's modified general utility curve in that the contingency model predicts that the use (or disuse) of an item will be complete rather than partial (an item is either in the optimal set or it is not). By this logic, one would expect all skeletal elements representing body parts above a given utility threshold to be equally represented (or unrepresented) in archaeological assemblages; that is, they would not be differentially represented according to their individual utility as Binford's utility curves imply. In

It should now be clear that whatever the inspiration for his recent suggestion that human rationality is relative and that optimal foraging theory is accordingly flawed, nearly the whole of Binford's work with faunal assemblages is predicated on the assumption that human behavior is economically rational (Binford 1978a:38, 44, 453). It is equally clear that optimal foraging theorists had anticipated many of Binford's basic notions regarding economic behavior ten years prior to his work in middle-range research. That Binford cites a standard introductory work in optimal foraging theory and evolutionary ecology (Binford 1978a:38; cf. Emlen 1973) to defend his views regarding the relationship between utility, rationality, and the universals of behavioral economy only underscores the intellectual debt his own model owes to microeconomic/micro-evolutionary theory.

That is not the only time Binford has found it useful to call upon principles formally identical to those in optimal foraging. Elsewhere he has brought them to bear to explain late Pleistocene/early Holocene dietary shifts and the origins of agriculture as a consequence of growing populations:

> The hunter who formerly killed moose and put up the meat for storage now finds he must make do with animals of smaller body size—ducks, or fish, or in coastal areas even shellfish. In short, he is progressively forced to move down the chain of animal body sizes, as he is constrained spatially. Eventually, inevitably, he is drawn away from animals and towards plants, because plants are aggregated in small amounts of space. (Binford 1983a:211; compare Hawkes, Hill, and O'Connell 1982; Bettinger and Baumhoff 1982)

If we grant that optimal foraging theory is grounded in the same basic principles that less formally guide much middle-range research, then it follows that all the objections that have been raised against the application of optimal foraging theory are equally applicable to middle-range research. Thus the claim that optimal foraging models are difficult to operationalize is admittedly correct; but the criticism applies equally well to middle-range theories (e.g., the ones that deal with butchering). It is no more difficult to ascertain whether prehistoric groups were foraging rationally than it is to ascertain whether prehistoric butchers were carving their game rationally. Indeed, as we have just shown, the latter is a special case of the former.

If we are correct in our arguments regarding the logical similarities between middle-range research and optimal foraging theory, then why do the

---

practice, however, the utility indexes obtained for individual skeletal elements are probably best regarded as means representing the central points of a presumably large range of variation. This and other sources of error, including those made in butchering and judging utility, make the probabilistic utility curve at least as realistic as the nonprobabilistic contingency alternative.

most ardent proponents of the middle-range theory find optimal foraging theory so objectionable? Evidently it is because optimal foraging theory has been linked to an overarching general theory, sociobiology, that these individuals find objectionable (cf. Thomas 1986:258-261; Binford 1983a:242; 1983b:221). As it is clear that middle-range theories are ultimately governed by more general theories and as optimal foraging theorists have attempted to articulate their middle and general theory while the middle-range theorists have not, such criticism seems inappropriate. Indeed, as noted earlier, middle-range theorists have been conspicuously silent on the matter. One would gather from various clues that Binford still allies himself with neofunctionalism—witness his reference to homeostatic devices that function to maintain hunter-gatherer groups at optimum sizes (1983a:213), his vaguely phrased appeal to the explanatory power of "ecological relationships" (Binford 1980:19), his preference for models that stress equilibrium (1983a:221), and his emphasis on systems and adaptation (1980). Unfortunately, his specific assumptions have not been made clear, so one cannot be sure. The failure to specify how concepts relate to theory is the core of the problem with current middle-range research and the source of the current confusion over what middle-range research is and why optimal foraging is or is not acceptable.

SUMMARY

The recent shift in archaeological objectives away from the development of general theory toward the more modest endeavor now termed middle-range research was undeniably beneficial in many respects. By the mid-1970s American archaeology was so riddled with such far-fetched and untestable theories it was hardly clear what was real and what was not—or whether that mattered (cf. Flannery 1973, 1982). In their haste to put aside unproductive theorizing, however, middle-range theorists seem to have accepted the myth that their research can proceed in the absence of general theory (cf. Binford 1981:29; but see Binford 1977a:7), which clearly it cannot. Widespread confusion regarding the nature of middle-range research is one result. Misplaced criticism of optimal foraging theory is another. Purportedly it centers on matters of practicability and verifiability; actually it turns on more deeply hidden general theoretical suppositions. In this way, the rhetoric of middle-range research has caused an issue of general theory to be treated as though it were a problem of middle-range theory and operationalization. The lesson, then, is clear: Attempts to do without general theory necessarily result in vague and poorly articulated general theory because middle-range theory must be derived from some one or more basic postulates. In short, as the example of Binford shows, covert general theory is as bad as overblown general theory.

It is time that archaeology once again owned up to its dependence upon generalizing theories and confronted the knotty issues lurking therein. If it has been recently convenient to act as if middle-range research is independent of generalizing theory, that is only because this permits eclectic movement between different theoretical positions without declaring commitment to some coherent theoretical framework. At our convenience, humans are rational here (Binford 1978a:453), irrational there (Binford 1983b:220, cf. Binford 1983a:241). This strategy has, in short, allowed us to avoid all the messy problems one confronts when attempting to apply ideal models to the real world. Inevitably that strategy produces poor science.

Chapter 5

More Complex Models of Optimal Behavior among Hunter-Gatherers

One problem in evaluating the potential utility of foraging theory in anthropology is that the results of critical behavioral tests are seldom clear-cut. Historically, where optimal models have been applied to real cases (see Chapter 4), the fit between expected and observed behavior has been close enough to satisfy advocates and loose enough to encourage critics. Because alternative theories weigh facts differently, such empirical indeterminacies are unavoidable. Constructive critics of foraging theory have made this a productive area of research. They regard the inevitable mismatches between observed and expected foraging behavior neither as devastating (providing an excuse to ignore such models) nor as uninteresting (to be dismissed as noise reflecting faulty or incomplete data). Rather, the constructive critics of optimal foraging theory see such mismatches as opportunities to develop better models. These alternative models all sacrifice some of the simplicity of explanation that characterizes the foraging models previously discussed by introducing additional assumptions and logical complexity. In each case it is assumed that the loss in elegance is justified by gains in predictive accuracy or in model realism.

Two aspects of the simpler optimal foraging models are regarded as particularly susceptible to criticism and alternative interpretation that would require the construction of alternative models. The first centers on the definition of optimality and the model constraints through which it is operationalized; choice of appropriate foraging currencies and the potential effects of resource variability and risk are key issues here. A second, and more fundamental, source of dissatisfaction relates to what might be called "model structure." The social context of foraging and the mutually causal interaction between foragers and prey are particularly problematic in this regard. A third area of dissatisfaction that has also led to the development of alternative models turns on assumptions about the fundamental mechanisms that produce foraging behavior itself (e.g., genes or learned behavior). At issue here ultimately are the forces that might cause humans to forage optimally. That is a problem of higher order than those that have given rise to the models in question here. It falls more properly within the domain of general theory and is, hence, beyond the scope of this chapter. We will, however, return to the issue and some foraging models that have arisen in response to it in Chapter 7. For the moment, we confine our attention to models of optimality in the original and more limited perspective of foraging behavior.

FORAGING CURRENCIES
AND RESOURCE CONSTRAINTS

An obvious question with regard to foraging currency is whether energy is the correct currency with which to measure efficiency (optimality). Optimal foraging theorists seem divided on this point, but most would concede the choice is essentially pragmatic: Energy is a provisional currency. Arguably, there are other currencies that might work as well; it is difficult, however, to think of another one that alone would work better. Clearly, then, if the question of foraging currency boiled down to something as simple as "which one?", there would be little to debate. In point of fact, the principal issue with regard to foraging currencies hinges on a question that, at first glance, seems no more complicated, that being, "how many?" As it turns out, however, if we ask that question and decide that more than one currency is needed to characterize the goals of foraging behavior adequately, it follows that we must model optimality in terms of multiple constraints (one for each currency) and then, for reasons made clear later, we can no longer evaluate foraging decisions in terms of momentary contingencies exclusively.

When we get down to cases, the real issue with regard to defining the number and kind of currencies and constraints is whether foraging can be modeled properly as an infinitely repeating string of momentary contingencies in which behavior is guided (i.e., constrained) only by the goal of maximizing rate of energetic return, which is the picture presented in the assumptions of the simpler models of optimality. The more realistic—and more complicated—alternative would be to envision foraging behavior in terms of an overarching plan or strategy designed to reconcile certain finite environmental constraints regarding the amounts of time, space, and resources available against minimum acceptable dietary requirements. Ultimately, it is the choice between these alternative interpretations of foraging constraints that determines what foraging currencies are chosen and the kinds of algorithms that are needed to produce optimal solutions.

The situation is readily illustrated with reference to the standard diet breadth model that evaluates an array of alternative choices in terms of their performance measured by the ratio of one utility variable (either single or multicomponent) against one cost variable (again, either single or multicomponent). Because the performance standard against which the simpler optimal foraging solutions are measured is a finite benefit/cost ratio, all decisions must necessarily be cast as dichotomous contingencies: A resource either exceeds the critical ratio, or it is excluded from the optimal set. Because that is so and because contingency models cast decisions as momentary events in which past events and long-term goals have no bearing, desired levels of more than one currency cannot be satisfied unambiguously. To illustrate the point, envision a very simple hypothetical problem in which we specify that both fuel and water are needed daily in some prescribed mix—say 10 parts fuel to one part water. A contingency solution would make sense here only if it were required that fuel and water be ingested only in the prescribed ratio (certain primitive organisms lacking the ability store fuel or water and certain kinds of internal combustion engines are two examples where these kinds of restrictions might well apply). Accordingly, a resource containing five units of fuel and one unit of water would be valued the equal of one containing 10 units of fuel and one-half unit of water: Each contains one-half a unit of the required 10 to 1 fuel-water mix (i.e., each one contains five units of fuel and one-half unit of water).

Further, following the terms of a contingency analysis, in the strictest sense, resources containing only fuel or only water would have no value whatsoever because they lack any of the desired mix. In short, because they do not include additional information (e.g., regarding current system state), contingency models make no provision for weighing the relative values of individual components (here, fuel and water) when they are encountered separately. Of course, because more fuel than water is required in this problem, one would suspect that a unit of the former might be more highly valued than a unit of latter, but a policy of always taking a unit of fuel rather than a unit of water when the two are offered at the same cost might easily result in a take consisting of fuel units alone—which would not be optimal. Clearly, to evaluate the relative values of fuel and water here requires additional information about the current balance of fuel and water within the system relative to a specific set of requirements or constraints. This step takes us beyond contingency models of optimal foraging and into the area of noncontingency models of which linear programming is the best known (see also Keene 1979, 1981 and Reidhead 1979, 1980 for detailed discussions and Bettinger 1980 for a simpler review).

Noncontingency Optimality: Linear Programming

Linear programming models initially identify two things: (1) a series of currencies relevant to the problem to be solved (a prospective car buyer might deem style, color, and comfort relevant "currencies," for example); and (2) a series of resources or products that vary in cost and contain at least some of at least one of the relevant currencies. In a "minimization" linear programming problem, minimal acceptable quantities are specified separately for each relevant currency, and the goal is to find the cheapest mix of the available resources that satisfies the minimal thresholds for all currencies simultaneously. In the "maximization" linear programming problem, on the other hand, the goal is to maximize the obtained quantities of all currencies given limitations in the availability of resources and/or the cost that can be incurred obtaining them. Most anthropological applications of linear programming take the minimization form.

A simple hypothetical example showing how a minimization linear programming problem is set up and solved will help to illustrate the differences with respect to choice of currency and limiting constraints that separate this technique from the more familiar contingency optimal foraging model. To make matters easier, we will choose a problem of diet.

As in that of optimal foraging, the linear programming model of diet presents a forager with an array of items that vary with respect to per item (or unit) costs and benefits. In contrast to the optimal foraging model where benefit is measured in strictly caloric terms, in linear programming an item may (and generally does) produce benefits in more than one dimension, that is, of more than one kind. In the case of a diet problem, for example, nutritional benefits of resources might include—in addition to calories—protein, trace minerals including calcium, phosphorus, and iron, and vitamin C. In a further departure from the familiar contingency model that contains no specifics regarding rate of caloric return, the minimization linear programming model of diet defines minimum required amounts for each of these different nutritional components. The problem is to achieve these various amounts in the cheapest way possible given the costs of different resources from which they are obtained. To illustrate the process with a concrete example, consider a case in which there are six foods: beef, ham, salmon, broccoli, potatoes, and lima beans, the prices and nutritional attributes of which are as shown in Table 5.1. Also shown are desired daily intake levels of the six nutrients these foods contain in varying quantity. Which mix affords the cheapest means of satisfying (or exceeding) the minimal desired level for each nutrient?

However unappealing it may seem, the linear programming answer to this problem (the derivation of the solution is too complex to be shown) is a daily diet consisting of 9.42 pounds of potatoes and 1.52 pounds of broccoli at a cost of

Table 5.1. A Linear Programming Model of Optimal Diet

				Resource attributes (per lb)			
	Cost ($)	Calories (kcal)	Protein (gm)	Calcium (mg)	Phosphorus (mg)	Iron (mg)	Vitamin C (mg)
Beef[a]	2.00	984	72	42	720	11	0
Ham[b]	3.00	1,264	58	35	657	9	0
Salmon[c]	6.00	886	76	0	1,201	0	0
Lima beans	.90	223	15	94	258	5	52
Potatoes	.15	279	8	26	195	2	73
Broccoli	.70	113	13	364	276	4	400
Daily requirement:		2,800	60	800	800	10	60
Solution:	9.42 lb potatoes						
	1.52 lb broccoli						
Cost:	$2.48						

[a]Beef is chuck (entire).
[b]Ham is fat-call (entire).
[c]Salmon (Chinook) steak.
Note: This example is intended to be purely hypothetical, but the values given are those of the USDA (1963) and the National Academy of Sciences (1968).

$2.48. That mix offers the cheapest means of attaining the desired nutritional goals when only these six resources are available at the prices shown.

As this example illustrates, the chief difference between contingency and noncontingency optimal foraging models has to do with constraints: Linear programming problems demand a specific solutional configuration within which optimality must be achieved (e.g., a particular mix and level of nutrients in the case just reviewed). The contingency-model solution is free to take any configuration provided only that it is optimal (i.e., maximizes rate of return). Because solution costs are monotonic, nondecreasing as constraints are added (i.e., constraints cannot decrease the cost of a given kind of solution but may increase it), linear programming analyses of diet will almost always predict higher costs than contingency analyses.

The principal objections to linear programming models by those optimal foraging theorists who favor contingency models have to do with the elegant theoretical (and, arguably, computational) simplicity of contingency models and both empirical and theoretical reservations regarding the degree to which the many nutritional elements typically included in linear programming analyses (e.g., calcium) actually affect human foraging (cf. Hawkes, Hill, and O'Connell 1982; Hill et al. 1987; O'Connell and Hawkes 1981, 1984). There is some justification for that view. For instance, when the diet problem used here to illustrate linear programming is reanalyzed following the usual diet breadth procedure of ranking resources according to their calorie:cost ratio, the results are strikingly similar to those obtained by the more lengthy linear programming calculations. In both cases potatoes are clearly the highest ranking resource.

Potatoes	1,860 kcal/$1.00
Beef	492 kcal/$1.00
Ham	421 kcal/$1.00
Lima beans	248 kcal/$1.00
Broccoli	161 kcal/$1.00
Salmon	148 kcal/$1.00

Although they are worth keeping in mind, the objections generally raised against linear programming models do not seem telling. Linear programming models, no less than the more familiar contingency models, have a place in the analysis of human and nonhuman foraging because they address a dimension of important variability wholly ignored by contingency models. Because foraging space and the resources within it are finite, it is conceivable that a forager acting in compliance with optimal foraging models and foraging at his optimal rate may end up with an insufficient quantity of resources to survive. Given this, one might observe that optimal foraging models seem most robust where resources and space are relatively abundant. Where these conditions do not pertain, linear programming models become increasingly more realistic (Bettinger 1983). Perhaps a better way of putting it is this: Investigators should feel free to add constraints to their models—but only when they can provide a good reason for doing so.

RESOURCE VARIABILITY AND RISK

Diet breadth, patch choice, and central place foraging models have often been criticized because they center on choices between alternative behaviors that are characterized in terms of fixed rates of return. Granting that in the real world rates of return associated with individual behaviors are likely to vary, the use of fixed rates remains quite reasonable provided we assume that the best foraging behaviors are those that maximize expected rates of return (provided, of course, that the fixed rates chosen represent the central tendencies associated with each behavior). If one regards maximization of expected long-term rate of return (i.e., mean return) as the goal of foraging behavior, short-term variability does not matter.

Many students have, of course, contended that variability in rates of return seems centrally important to many hunter-gatherers. It is clear in such cases, however, that it is not so much variability in foraging rates *per se* that is at issue (though this might sometimes be important) but rather the degree to which that variability entails some probability of resource shortfall. When put this way, it is clear that variability does not assume importance in foraging models unless we assume that there is a minimum rate of return, a threshold, below which survival is increasingly threatened. Diet breadth, patch choice, and central place models make no such assumption and thus properly ignore variability.

Because there do seem to be ample theoretical and empirical grounds for assuming that minimal foraging return thresholds are important to hunter-gatherers, models that take this into account may sometimes be more satisfactory than those that do not despite the increased complexity and empirical demands that accompany these models. Of the models that have been advanced that contain this feature, the Z-score model of Stephens and Charnov is perhaps the simplest and most general.

The Z-Score Model

The Z-score model takes its name from the statistic, Z, which, as many will recognize, is the standardized normal deviate of a normally distributed population with mean, u, and standard deviation, s. For any such population, Z describes a ratio between the amount an individual measurement, say, n, departs from the mean of the population relative to the standard deviation of that population. Thus, Z varies directly with n relative to u; it is negative when n is smaller than u, and, holding s constant, from there decreases (becomes more negative) as n decreases. Conversely, it is positive when n is larger than u, and from there increases as n does. In formal terms

$$Z = (n - u)/s \qquad (5.1)$$

Every value of Z is associated with a probability corresponding to the amount of a normal curve with mean u and standard deviation s that lies on either side of it (i.e., Z). These probabilities are tabulated in the appendexes of most elementary statistics texts.

In the Z-score model, u and s correspond to the mean and standard deviation of the return rate for a given behavior and n corresponds to a specific return-rate threshold below which survival is increasingly threatened. Accordingly, Z corresponds to the probability that the behavior will result in a return rate below the threshold. Given these definitions, note again with reference to Equation 5.1, that if the threshold, n, is below the mean, Z is negative, that is, it is small, and that if n is above the mean, Z is positive, that is, it is large. This leads to the generalization that to minimize the possibility of falling below the threshold, foraging behavior should minimize Z: Threshold-sensitive optimal foragers should be Z minimizers.

The goal of minimizing Z holds some rather counterintuitive implications for the manner in which variability in rate of return, here represented by standard deviation, s, affects probability of resource shortfall. Specifically, when mean return is greater than the threshold (i.e., when $u > n$), Z is negative; then, increasing variability increases Z (by making it a smaller negative number, i.e., less negative), which increases the probability of falling below the threshold. Conversely, when mean return is below the threshold (i.e., $u < n$), Z is positive; then increasing variability decreases Z and thus the probability of falling below the threshold. In short, variability will either increase or decrease the probability of shortfall depending on whether the expected mean return of a behavior is above or below the threshold. This means that threshold-sensitive foragers (Z minimizers) should follow two rules: (1) when expected returns are above the required threshold variability should be minimized and (2) when they are below the threshold variability should be maximized. In simpler terms: Don't take chances unless you have to.

The utility of the Z-score model can be extended by reworking Equation 5.1 into a form in which mean rate of return, u, is a function of its standard deviation, s. Thus

$$u = n - Zs \qquad (5.2)$$

This expresses the relationship of the mean rate return for a behavior, u, to its standard deviation, s, as a ratio of $-Z$ (i.e., negative Z) relative to a specific threshold return rate, n. Equation 5.2 can be depicted as a line on a graph in which s is represented by the X axis and u by the Y axis, and the slope of the line (the ratio of u to s) is equal to $-Z$ and the intercept of the line on the Y axis is n (see Figure 5.1). The formula is of particular interest because a line plotted for given values of n and $-Z$, defines a series of mean/standard deviation combinations that are equivalent to each other with respect to the probability they will produce rates of return below the threshold rate, n. With respect to Figure 5.1, for instance, all of the mean/standard deviation combinations that fall on line A are equally likely to produce rates of return below n.

Because it features lines the slope of which are negative Z ($-Z$), Equation 5.2 can be used to produce graphic solutions to problems in which the goal is to minimize the probability of falling below a specified threshold. To see this, remember first that the slope of the regression line is $-Z$ (negative Z). Therefore when Z is very small (a large negative number, for instance) $-Z$ is very large, and conversely. This means that Z, the quantity to be minimized, decreases as the the slope of a line anchored at a given n swings counterclockwise from steeply negative to steeply positive, as shown in Figure 5.1; this counterclockwise movement corresponds to a shift in the values of Z from positive (large) to negative (small). Thus, with respect to the goal of minimizing Z, for any two lines originating at the same threshold n, the higher one is superior: It defines mean/standard deviation combinations with a lower probability of falling below the threshold. Note further, with reference to the two rules established earlier for minimizing Z, that for means below n, Z decreases (the line rotates counter-

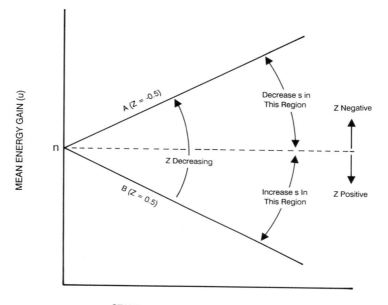

Figure 5.1. Z as a ratio of standard deviation of energy gain (X axis) to mean energy gain (Y axis) relative to a specified threshold (n). Z corresponds to the probability that an activity with a given mean and standard deviation of energy return will produce an outcome below the threshold. For means below the given threshold, Z is positive and decreases as standard deviation increases. For means above the threshold, Z is negative and decreases as standard deviation decreases. Given the specified threshold, all the mean-standard deviation combinations falling on line "A" are equivalent with respect to Z ($= -0.5$). The same is true for all points on line "B" (except $Z = 0.5$).

clockwise) as s increases and that for means above n, Z decreases as s decreases. This is the same as saying that increasing variability decreases the probability of shortfall when $u < n$ and that decreasing variability decreases the possibility of shortfall when $u > n$.

Problems of Z minimization are solved graphically by plotting the mean and standard deviation combinations for the return rates associated with the various behaviors being evaluated (Figure 5.2). Then the line with the highest slope originating at the specified threshold and intersecting one of the combinations identifies that combination as the one that minimizes the possibility of falling below the threshold (see Figure 5.2).

The graphic approach to problems of Z minimization can also be used to assess the extent to which the behavior of threshold-sensitive foragers will differ from the behavior of mean-rate maximizers, that is, foragers insensitive to variability. Stephens and Charnov (1982) have explored this issue with respect

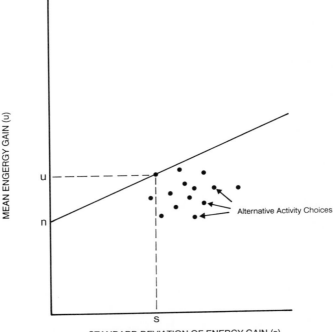

Figure 5.2. Graphic solution to Z-minimization problem. Mean-standard deviation combinations are plotted for various alternative activities. For a given threshold, n, the highest line from the threshold through one of the activities identifies the mean-standard deviation that minimizes Z and thus the activity for which the probability of falling below the threshold is the lowest.

to the problem in which foragers must decide at what point to abandon foraging within a patch and search for another. As detailed in Chapter 4, mean-rate maximizers follow the marginal value theorem of Charnov (1976): They leave a patch when rate of return there falls to the point where it is equal to the expected net rate of return associated with travel to and foraging in a new one (i.e., the mean rate of overall return for the environment counting both travel to patches and foraging within them). In that case, the amount of time required to locate a new patch is treated as fixed. Stephens and Charnov obtained a Z-minimization solution for a series of hypothetical mean/standard deviation return-rate combinations associated with different patch residence times when travel time between patches is variable rather than fixed and compared the result to the optimal patch residence time indicated by the marginal value theorem. They found that, for those hypothetical values at least, threshold-sensitive foragers would behave much the same as mean-rate optimizers so long as the threshold value does not depart radically from the maximum mean rate of return. Because the mean/standard deviation combinations they generated indicate that the standard deviation of return rate increases as patch residence time decreases from the value that produces the maximum mean rate of return, risk-sensitive foragers should adopt shorter residence times than rate maximizers when their threshold is greater than the maximum rate of return and longer residence times when it is less than the expected rate of return (Figure 5.3).

Winterhalder (1986a,b) has performed a similar sort of experiment in relation to the diet breadth model in which costs and returns associated with different prey types are variable rather than fixed as they are when the model is usually applied. His results parallel those of Stephens and Charnov in that the

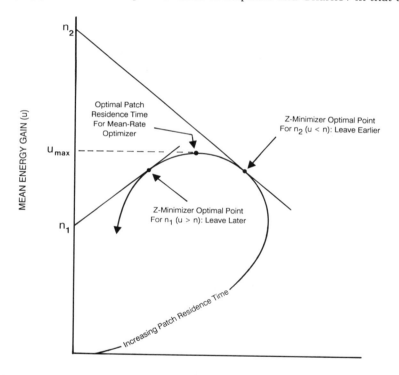

Figure 5.3. Effect of varying thresholds on patch residence times (after Stephens and Charnov 1982). As shown, different patch residence times are characterized by different mean-standard deviation combinations. With respect to mean-rate optimizers, who leave the patch at u_{max}, Z minimizers will leave sooner for thresholds above u_{max} (e.g., n_2) and leave later for thresholds below u_{max} (e.g., n_1).

behavior of risk-sensitive foragers is generally quite similar to rate-maximizing foragers. Because, as might be expected, the standard deviation of return rate decreases as diet breadth increases, risk minimizers ought to restrict diet breadth when confronting a threshold greater than the maximum expected rate of return and expand diet breadth when confronting thresholds below the maximum expected rate of return.

The Social Context of Foraging in Relation to Variability: Sharing

As do nearly all microeconomic formulations, the risk-minimizing and rate-maximizing foraging models we have examined so far are directed toward understanding the behavior of individual actors that employ external means (e.g., resources) in the attainment of self-interested goals (e.g., maximum rate of energetic return). These assumptions are intimately related to, and severely constrain, the range of behaviors predicted by such actor-based models. The Z-score model examined in the previous section, for instance, makes it clear that, in the presence of variable rates of return of nonstorable resources, individuals sensitive to minimal foraging thresholds can only insure themselves against shortfall by sacrificing foraging efficiency: Losses in mean rate of return must be traded for gains in risk minimization.

It is far from clear, however, whether it is reasonable to model human foragers as independent individuals whether we mean by that either true (i.e., single) individuals or unified collectives that act as individuals. The matter of risk is particularly germane here because it would seem that in many cases individual hunter-gatherers ensure themselves against resource shortfall primarily by pooling and sharing resources rather than by expanding or contracting diet breadth, patch choice, patch residence times, and so on. If that is so, the Z-score model is likely to be a poor approximation of human behavior because it predicts behaviors appropriate for independent individuals rather than for multiple interacting ones. Fortunately, the effects of sharing on risk are relatively straightforward, and it is easy to examine the benefits of such behavior in comparison to the benefits that derive from alternatives that assume action only at the level of the individual.

The work of Winterhalder (1986a) on this problem makes it clear why sharing is likely to be so effective as a means of reducing risk among hunter-gatherers. Using hypothetical data generated to study the way in which variability in return rates might affect choices of diet breadth (see previous discussion), Winterhalder observes that varying diet breadth alone can provide only modest incremental increases in risk reduction and that these are accompanied by relatively large reductions in foraging efficiency. In that simulation, where resources were randomly distributed and the coefficient of variation (i.e., s/u, where s is standard deviation and u is mean) of pursuit time for all of them was set at .33, increasing diet breadth to minimize Z reduced standard deviation in return rates by 8% and foraging efficiency by 6%. By contrast, given the same simulated conditions, sharing between just two foragers whose rates of return are independent of each other reduces the standard deviation in the rate of return of each one by 30% and without affecting the mean rate of return of either one. This effect derives from the simple statistical relationship between sample size, equivalent here to the number of sharing foragers, and the standard deviation of the mean of a normally distributed population, equivalent here to the standard deviation of pooled return rates of sharing foragers: Standard deviation of the pooled mean rate of return decreases directly in proportion to the square root of the number of individuals that share.

As Winterhalder points out, the preceding result is perhaps less general than it might seem because it assumes the foraging rates of individuals are independent of each other, which may sometimes not be true. It is intuitively obvious, of course, that correlation between foraging rates would substantially affect the size of the potential gain that results from sharing. Thus, if the foraging rates of two individuals are perfectly correlated directly, so that when the return rate of one is above the mean, the return rate of the other is above the mean by the same amount, sharing confers neither any benefit because neither ever has more or less than the other. On the other hand, if the foraging rates of two individuals are perfectly correlated inversely, so that when the return rate of one is below the mean by a certain amount, the the return rate of the other is above the mean by the same amount, then sharing between just two individuals will always result in a pooled rate of return exactly equal to the mean. The influence correlation has on the potential reduction of variability in pooled rates of return can be generalized in terms of a simple equation

$$G = g \left[\frac{1 + (N - 1)R}{N} \right]^{1/2} \tag{5.3}$$

where

   G is the average coefficient of variation for an individual forager when part of a sharing group of size N

   g is the average coefficient of variation for an individual foraging without sharing

   R is the average correlation in foraging rates between the N individuals in the sharing group

It is clear from Equation 5.3 that sharing increases in utility as N increases (the more the merrier) and R decreases. When R is positive, however, that is, when forager return rates tend to vary together directly, the gain from sharing that results from increasing group size, N, steadily decreases as N grows large and reaches an asymptotic limit at $G = gR^{1/2}$. Put another way, when R is positive, the standard deviation of the pooled rate of return can never be less than $R^{1/2}$ percent of the individual standard deviation of return rate. On the other hand, when R is negative, relatively small increases in N can reduce the standard deviation of the pooled rate to 0, yielding a constant return rate. At $R = -0.5$, it only takes three foragers to produce a pooled rate of return that never varies; at $R = -0.1$, it takes 11.

Whether R is positive or negative, the greatest reduction in the standard deviation of pooled return rates, that is, the greatest incentive to add more members to the sharing group, occurs when groups are relatively small. Consider the case cited before, for instance, where $R = -0.1$ and a sharing group of 11 individuals assures a constant pooled rate of return. Assuming the group started with one individual to which members were added one at a time, the first addition to the group (i.e., its second member) reduced the standard deviation of the pooled group rate by 33%, the last addition, the eleventh group member, reduced it by only 10%. The diminishing effect of increasing size is even more pronounced when R is positive. In relation to this, Winterhalder reasons that as group size increases, the costs associated with the addition of new members (in resource depletion, for example) would eventually outweigh further gains that would result from reduced variation in pooled rates of return. Working from this premise, he calculates that relatively small groups capture most of the benefits of risk reduction associated with sharing. Indeed, whatever the correlation between their rates of return, six foragers will obtain 60% of the total possible reduction in mean rate variability that can be achieved by sharing.

Discussion

The preceding analysis makes it clear that the potential benefits in risk reduction associated with resource sharing are substantially greater than those associated with foraging strategies that minimize Z. It follows that where minimum thresholds and risk are important, hunter-gatherers are more likely to resort to cooperative alliances with a small number of other individuals than they are to modify foraging patterns. In this sense, the Z-score model is more appropriate to situations in which individuals—single individuals or individual groups—are forced to act independently, either because they are isolated or because they are in competition.

Before turning to other matters, the point should be made that our statistical analysis of sharing is easily extended to the problem of storage in an environment in which the expected rate of daily return is held constant. In that case, the question centers on the amount of food that should be stored to assure minimal fluctuations in daily food intake. As with group size, the costs associated with protecting and maintaining stored food increase with the amount that is stored. Similarly, as with sharing, the potential utility of food storage also depends on the correlation between return rates on successive days (i.e., the autocorrelation of return rates): Perfect positive correlation makes storage irrelevant because every day is the same and perfect negative correlation means that one-day stores assure a constant rate of food availability. By analogy with our observations regarding group size and sharing, it would seem that relatively small stores—roughly the equivalent of the mean amount foraged in a 6-day period—will achieve 60% of the total possible reduction in daily food intake that can be obtained by storing.

FORAGER/FORAGED-FOR INTERACTION: CARRYING CAPACITY

The analysis of sharing just discussed explores the implications that arise when it is assumed that foragers do not live in isolation but rather in a social environment that contains other similar, self-interested individuals. That one assumption leads us to expect very different sorts of behaviors than we would anticipate for isolated individuals. This makes it reasonable to ask whether the simple, individual actor-based optimal foraging models overlook other potentially salient interactions that might profoundly affect forager behavior. Perhaps the most obvious interaction of this sort is that which exists between the forager and the foraged for, that is, prey, which is the crux of the diet breadth model.

Because it is couched in terms of momentary contingencies, the simple diet breadth model assumes that prey availability is unaffected by foraging behavior. Although in the short run—that is, for any one contingency—this is true, in the long run it is not: When time and resources are finite, predator/prey interactions are likely to be important. Of course, the problem can be easily avoided merely by stipulating that the diet breadth model applies to those long-run situations in which forager-forage densities are at equilibrium in which case foraging would have little or no affect on prey densities. To take this tact, however, severely limits one advantage claimed for the diet breadth model—that it predicts behavior under variable conditions. The assumption is further constraining in the sense that it prevents understanding of behavior when forager demand and prey availability vary as a function of each other before equilibrium is reached. It prevents us from asking, for instance, what effect might result from variations in population density, resource density, or amount of time spent foraging. Obviously, to resolve such questions requires a much more complicated formulation than the simple diet breadth model. The effort seems worthwhile, however, in the sense that these issues are fundamentally related to a topic of perennial controversy among anthropologists—carrying capacity. Resolution of the matter in the context of foraging theory would contribute substantially to a unified understanding of the ecology of humans, hunter-gatherers and otherwise. Once again, Winterhalder (Winterhalder *et al.* 1989) has taken the first step in tackling the matter.

The analysis of Winterhalder is far too complicated to review in detail here. In simple terms, however, he models a forager-prey situation in which the levels of both prey and forager conform to logistic growth curves that mimic actual values for humans and mammals. Following the standard equation for population growth, the forager and prey populations grow at rates determined by their intrinsic growth rates, r, and their carrying capacity, K, in the following way:

$$dP/dT = rP[(K-P)/K] \qquad (5.4)$$

where

> dP is change in population size
> dT is change in time
> r is the intrinsic rate of population increase
> K is the carrying capacity of the environment
> P is population size

Equation 5.4 will produce the familiar s-shaped logistic growth curve in which, beginning with small populations, population growth is initially slow because P is small, gains momentum as numbers (P) increase, and finally slows again as carrying capacity is approached (i.e., as P approaches K). It is clear from this that population growth is greatest when population just equals one-half of the carrying capacity, that is, when $P = K/2$. Ideally, this is the size at which the foraging population would like to maintain its prey.

To perform the analysis, Winterhalder further defines several other variables pertaining to the forager population including its size, the caloric requirements for each individual, number of hours spent foraging, caloric costs of foraging, and rate and radius of foraging. Prey populations are also specified with respect to density.

The preceding values are incorporated in a simulation in which capture of an individual prey reduces the size of the prey population, affecting its density and potential for growth, and at the same time provides a caloric return for consumption by the human group. The simulation is designed so that when foraging returns more calories than are needed to sustain the existing forager population, population growth occurs. Conversely, when returns fall below those needed to sustain the population, it will shrink. Because the size of forager and prey are interactively related, growth in one necessarily results in decline in the other. Presuming extinction does not occur (one outcome of these simulations), the two populations eventually reach an equilibrium at which both populations are either stable and do not vary or oscillate regularly within fixed limits.

One of the more interesting questions addressed by this simulation is the intuition of many that hunter-gatherer groups stabilize at population levels well below carrying capacity (cf. Hassan 1981). It is surmised that this provides insurance against short-term environmental fluctuations. Alternatively, it has also been suggested that foragers might stabilize at levels that maximize environmental productivity. Flannery (1968), for instance, seems to assume this was the case in preagricultural Mesoamerica. As Equation 5.4 shows, this would be true if human foragers harvested resources in such a way that the standing population of those resources were exactly at one-half their long-term carrying capacity. At this point the maximum sustainable yield of such a resource would be equal to $.25rK$ (this is obtained by substituting $K/2$ for P in Equation 5.4: $dP/dT = rK/2[(K - K/2)/K] = .25rK$).

A second interesting problem addressed by the simulation is the effect that varying work effort has on population size and economic viability. Bettinger and Baumhoff (1983), for instance, have suggested that intensification of work may confer competitive advantages for expanding hunter-gatherer groups.

The results of the simulations performed by Winterhalder are as interesting as they are counterintuitive. They show first that increases in the amount of time spent foraging result in long-term decreases in human populations. A bit of reflection shows why this is so. Assume that at a given population level and individual caloric requirement, prey availability is less than required to sustain the forager population. Then increasing work hours acts to depress further the size of the prey population, which results in further energetic shortfalls. In short, hard-working hunter-gatherer populations are sparse ones.

An equally interesting result of the simulations was that increases of the density of a prey or the rate at which its population grows do not result in equivalent changes in human population size. For example, doubling the density of a prey does not result in a doubling of the forager population, nor does doubling the rate of prey population growth result in a concomitant increase in forager density. In both cases this has to do with the effect that foraging has on prey population growth: Forager population growth adversely affects prey population growth. It is further the case, that the effect of increasing prey carrying capacity and rates of increase diminish as the amount of time spent foraging increases. As before, this is because extending the work period reduces the rate at which prey must be captured, which results in greater relative depletion of prey populations, inhibiting their potential for growth. However counterintuitive it might seem, it follows from this that foragers can maintain relatively high population densities and still work long hours if they increase their minimal caloric requirements. This makes sense because, holding the number of hours worked constant, an increase in minimal caloric levels will cause populations to cease growing before they reach levels that threaten prey populations. Without this corrective limit, foragers that work long hours risk extinction.

Perhaps the most important lesson to be learned from this exercise is the same one now being learned by those engaged in modeling evolutionary processes: Even the simplest systems that contain interactive elements often behave in unexpected ways. We cannot begin to understand how such systems work without going through the difficult process of building and testing quantitative models. With regard to the specific problem at hand here, simple contingency models of diet breadth are without question useful in understanding some sorts of behaviors. It would be a mistake, however, to assume that the properties we observe in contingency models are of general application in the real world, where behaviors are conditioned by and highly dependent on the consequences arising from similar previous behaviors.

Chapter 6

Marxist and Structural Marxist Perspectives of Hunter-Gatherers

THE NECESSITY OF GENERAL THEORY

The entirely unnecessary confusion regarding the differences between middle-range and optimal foraging theory reviewed in Chapter 4 indicates the kinds of problems that arise when research is conducted in the absence of a firm understanding of how it relates to general theory. Middle-range theorists to the contrary, like any other scientific enterprise, hunter-gatherer research requires a decent body of general theory. In the sense I intend here, to be viable that general theory must present, minimally, a coherent explanatory matrix in which materialist explanation and a concern for evolutionary processes figure prominently. I assume, further, that just as these features will characterize any modern theory of hunter-gatherers, so must they characterize any modern general theory of anthropology. These stipulations reflect my own theoretical perspective and assumptions regarding the quintessential role of hunter-gatherers in anthropology. Note further still that by invoking these stipulations and the body of theory underlying them, I am denying deliberately any possible role here for what has been called "post-processual archaeology" (Hodder 1982a,b, 1983). As Yengoyan (1985) notes, that approach effectively precludes any chance of doing comparative or generalizing research, which is assumed to be the principal purpose of all the theories, limited and general, in question here (see later discussion).

The history of hunter-gatherer research hints that among all the possible remaining alternatives we might conceivably consider as candidates for a general theory, only three seem potentially viable: neofunctionalism, neo-Marxism, neo-Darwinism. Chapter 2 reviewed the central tenets of neofunctionalism and found it flawed, probably fatally, in two respects. One is its emphasis on homeostasis as a natural condition or guiding goal of cultural systems; the other is its reliance on philosophical/methodological collectivism and explanation by means of group-level processes (e.g., selection). That neofunctional theory fails to justify either of these basic (and highly problematic) assumptions would seem to make it a poor candidate for a general theory useful in understanding hunter-gatherers. That leaves Marxism/structural Marxism and neo-Darwinism. It is the former that occupies us in this chapter.

HISTORICAL MATERIALISM, MARXISM, AND STRUCTURAL MARXISM

That it is arguably the most politically conservative subdiscipline of American anthropology may explain why archaeology—which otherwise prefers materialist arguments (cf. Bettinger 1980)—has remained so obstinately ignorant of Marx, whose writings constitute the earliest—and in certain respects the most sophisticated—contributions to modern cultural materialism (Harris 1968a, 1979). For whatever reason, that Marx is so little read by archaeologists makes it useful to preface our discussion of recent Marxist studies of past and present hunter-gatherers with a few introductory observations regarding his more important contributions to theory in the social sciences.

Historical Materialism and Capitalism

It is most important to understand that Marx was interested primarily in capitalism and that his interest was in part politically inspired. Marx's purpose was to show that capitalism had resulted from a series of idiosyncratic, that is, historical, circumstances peculiar to Europe following the "voyages of discovery" (Marx and Engels 1967:79-86); this was decidedly in opposition to the Social Darwinist thinking of his contemporaries, particularly those who followed Adam Smith in presenting capitalism as a natural, indeed desirable, economic form resulting from progressive cultural evolution and particularly as a system in which selection was free to winnow inferior forms from superior forms. Marxism is, thus, historical in the sense that it attempts to portray much of world history, and particularly capitalism, as consisting of changing and transitory phenomena, as opposed to lasting and natural ones (Marx 1967:598-599, 667-668). To the Social Darwinists, process was progress, whereas to Marx process was often anything but progress—particularly in the case of capitalism a principal characteristic of which was its increasing emiseration of the masses.

Marx, of course, was a materialist in the sense that in the last analysis he saw material conditions as explaining social systems and social change (Marx 1977:389). It was a materialist analysis that led him to argue that capitalism was a transitory state, inherently self-contradictory and carrying the seeds of its own destruction; this same analysis, in turn, led him to reject many tenets basic to social science then and now—including that of empirical objectivity. He rested his analysis of capitalism on Ricardo's labor theory of value (Marx 1967:46, 84-85), which holds that under ideal, that is, free market, conditions, the value of any product derives primarily from the labor expended in producing it (supply and demand and the cost of materials were also elements of price but substantially less important than labor). From Ricardo's theory, Marx deduced first that the concept of "profit," which is basic to formal economic theory, was inherently flawed—a mystification of reality: Profit was merely the peculiar form in which the capitalist exploited the worker. This followed in the sense that in any self-sustaining system of production, the worker must be paid the cost of sustaining himself (to feed, shelter, and reproduce himself), which is equal to the cost that can be asked for his product in the marketplace. But because in capitalism, the capitalist owns the means of production, he dictates the conditions of production and thus is free to extract surplus labor from the worker (beyond that needed to reproduce the worker); that, less the cost of capital depreciation and contributions to the state (e.g., taxes), is his profit. In short, in contradistinction to formal economics where profit is dictated primarily by supply and demand, for Marx profit was dictated by exploitation (Marx 1967:500).

Marx argued that according to the labor theory of value, capitalism contained a fatal contradiction, which he articulated through what has been termed the laws of motion of capitalism. In simplest terms, competition among capitalists could only be waged by economizing—by producing the same item for less; other things being equal, this had to be done by increasing the efficiency of production to gain savings in labor; that is, by increasing the contribution of "constant" capital (machinery, for example) and at the same time decreasing the amount of labor invested in a given product (the law of capital accumulation; Marx 1967:582-589). And herein lay the contradiction: As the amount of labor invested per unit of output decreased so did the profit in the system. Capitalist competition resulted in a declining spiral of value (the law of declining rate of profit; Marx 1977:488-492).

This had a number of further implications. One of these was that through competition and the elimination of the smaller by the larger, capital organizations would grow fewer and larger in compensation for the lesser value in the market (Marx 1967:587-589). A second implied consequence was that capitalists would seek out production situations less pressed by capitalist competition, that is, those containing greater value, as in the Third World, for example (Marx and Engels 1967:83-84). In this way, capitalism necessarily preyed upon precapitalist systems. This response, however, worked only as a stopgap measure and after a long period of escalating class struggle capitalism would fall away, replaced by a utopian socialist state.

To make this scenario at all credible, Marx had to explain two things further: (1) why the worker allowed the capitalist to exploit his labor and (2) why classical economists were unable to see profit as exploitation. To do so, he set forth a structure in which technology, social relations, and ideology were all important (Marx and Engels 1970:57-82). In the first instance, of course, he had little trouble establishing that the organization of the state reproduced the exploitative hierarchy and other necessary conditions of capitalism and that capitalists controlled the juropolitical machinery of the state (e.g., laws, courts, police, and prisons). Marx did not confine his analysis of capitalism to material conditions alone, however. Unlike many other materialists, he found explanatory utility in the concept of ideology (witness his fascination with Hegelian idealism) in the sense that ideology manifest as "false consciousness" permitted both worker and economist to rationalize exploitation of the former (worker) as the legitimate profit of the capitalist. Yet as a materialist, and thus one unalterably opposed to theories grounded in idealism such as Hegel's, Marx was forced to explain ideology in material terms without "reducing" the former to the later (i.e., without arguing that ideology faithfully recreates objective material conditions). This naturally implied the existence of rather complex relationships between humans and nature and between humans and humans.

For Marx, humans were not merely animals but social animals and as such organized themselves into groups within which perceptions were shared (Marx and Engels 1970:49-52). This sharing meant that individual perception was never objective, being instead always measured with reference to a common "group perception" that in some degree distorted reality. Ideology was thus a group phenomenon—a class phenomenon, more precisely, because for Marx the principal groups into which humans organized themselves were classes. It was understandable thus that the capitalist would willingly perpetuate the myth of his "legitimate profit" to justify his behavior both to himself and to the worker; in turn, the worker, having no independent access to the means of production and forced to "reproduce" this system by his own participation, saw his condition as in some sense "natural" and accepted the confusing and distorting myth that explained it.

Of equal importance to its ideological implications, the sociability of humans also governed the process of production and so the relationship between humans and between humans and their environment. For Marx, production articulated specific social groupings (classes) with specific resources and technologies. All labor could in this sense be construed as a social process. All this was expressed more elegantly (and, unfortunately, more vaguely) with reference to the concept of *mode of production* (Marx and Engels 1970:50; Marx 1977:202)—the basic structure through which humans organize production. Each mode of production consists of the *forces of production*, which includes resources, the instruments of labor, and the labor process, and the *social relations of production*, which dictate the manner in which what is produced is distributed and the reproduction of the system.

As described, the mode of production constitutes the economic base or infrastructure of society, in addition to which there is the superstructure—jural, political, and ideological systems—that arise primarily in response to dictates of the economic base, though not in any simple way so that, for instance, we might reduce them to motives inspired by the base. For the most part, Marx traced relations of production back to the forces of production yet in some instances he implies that other segments of the social formation may impinge on these relations as well.

Thus in response to the two questions posed, Marx held that (1) the worker allowed the capitalist to exploit him because (a) of political oppression through the institutions of the state and the consequent domination of capitalist production and (b) his perceptions mystified reality; and (2) that the formal economists perpetuated the myths of supply, demand, and profit because they, too, were a part of the system and therefore mystified and because it fell to them to perpetuate their own myth. The latter has a number of serious ramifications not the least of which is that no less than any other group, scientists are blinded by their own social existence and thus practice science by means of myths that legitimize their existence and that of the social relations that underwrite that existence (e.g., Marx and Engels 1970:109-114). Elster (1985) suggests that it is this special concern with ethics alone that distinguishes contemporary Marxism from other social theories, many of which incorporate other important elements of Marx's theories.

For Marxists, objectivity is always a myth, and (non-Marxist) science has the implicit political purpose of reproducing the system in which it exists. That is why Marxists find empiricism and positivism so objectionable: Both are dependent on a "surface reality" that distorts deeper truths. Unfortunately, it also follows that Marxist criticism of alternative theoretical schemes is by definition *ad hominem* (the theoretical basis for this notwithstanding). That is one reason why the Marxist literature is so easy to ignore—polemics, epithets, and all (cf. Harris 1979:216-217).

For those engaged in hunter-gatherer research, however, there has been a far better reason to ignore Marxist thought: There is little in the literature on the subject that deals with hunter-gatherers (cf. O'Laughlin 1975:354); in reference to social formations of this kind, both Marx and Engels relied entirely upon Morgan's evolutionary formulations or other similarly conceived schemes (Engels 1972; Marx and Engels 1967:79). Predictably, therefore, their accounts are of limited value and provide no clues whatsoever regarding the "laws of motion of hunter-gatherers." Engels to the contrary, that Marx portrayed the history of culture as a history of class struggle has made all the more problematic the application of such theories to hunter-gatherers that, although not without their own forms of inequality, seem to lack anything that approximates classes in the usual sense of the term as set forth by Marx and others. French or structural Marxism developed directly in response to the neglect of prefeudal societies in classical Marxist theory.

STRUCTURAL MARXISM

Structural Marxism is, as the name implies, an approach that combines certain elements of Lévi-Straussian structuralism with Marxism (Berger 1976; Bloch 1983). As we shall see, it differs from mainstream Marxism in putting more emphasis on the social relations of production (i.e., social claims on production and distribution), which it casts in a dominant role, than on the forces of production, which is almost certainly what Marx believed to be the forge of most cultural causation (Pasquinelli 1983:198-200). The French Marxists who struck this odd marriage between structuralism and Marxism did so on the basis of what they perceived to be underlying similarities in the two programs of research. The most important of these was the premise that like structuralism, Marxism investigated phenomena that could not be explained with reference to surface appearances but only in terms of underlying "structures" (Godelier 1972:xix). As Harris (1979:219) and Bloch (1983:151) both note, this similarity is singularly unconvincing, as all science seeks causation at some deeper level than surface appearances; that is, after all, what distinguishes science from common sense. But the French theoreticians claimed further similarities between Marxism and structuralism because both emphasized the concept of transformations, outward change that preserves intact an inner, basic structure consisting of irreducible components. Again, it is difficult to see in what way this might be peculiar only to Marxism and structuralism, for as we have already remarked with reference to Binford's curious position regarding constants, in some sense all scientific endeavor seeks to explain variable phenomena as "transformations" of basic structures.

Setting false pretensions aside, the French Marxists, Althusser (1970; Althusser and Balibar 1970), for example, contended that Marx's analysis of capitalism contained a model of "structural causation" that could be applied directly to primitive societies. Critical to this scheme was the notion that social relations could not be explained in terms of (i.e., reduced to) the forces of production, as in "vulgar materialism," but had a reality of their own, being in this sense separate from those forces (e.g., Godelier 1984:53-54). In what would seem a major departure from the materialism in which the work of Marx was grounded, the structural Marxists codified the special relationship between the forces and relations of production by arguing that the former were determinant, the latter dominant. By this is meant that, operating within the basic "ground rules" set down by the forces of production, it is the relations of production that give each mode of production its distinctive character. The separation between the forces and relations of production provides in part the "tension"—that is, structural contradictions—that are the source of culture motion, that is, change (cf. Pasquinelli 1983:200). Ironically, this view clearly aligns the structural Marxists with the "possibilism" of Kroeber (1939), Forde (1934), and Wissler (1926). As for them, for Friedman (e.g., 1975:163), and other structural Marxists (e.g., Bender 1981:150), the forces determine only what cannot be, not what will be, which is governed by social relations.

Althusserian structural Marxists (e.g., Rey, Terray, and Meillassoux) postulate that a second source of contradiction in precapitalist social formations derives from the universal presence of multiple modes of production that are imperfectly connected (i.e., articulated rather than integrated) and of unequal importance. Within a given social formation, this causes the dominant mode to distort (i.e., impinge upon) the other modes without completely changing their character. The articulation between traditional (e.g., primitive) and capitalist modes of production, in which the capitalist mode dominates the traditional mode, is most frequently the subject of such analyses. It is argued, however, that the same general approach can be adapted for use in the absence of capitalist penetration, that is, in completely traditional societies. Among Great Basin hunter-gatherers, for instance, at least three modes of production might thus be identified: *individual hunting*, *individual gathering*, and *communal hunting*; each one defined by a distinctive combination of forces and relations of production. Of necessity all three modes are articulated within a larger subsistence-settlement system but only imperfectly because each one constitutes a fundamentally different realm of activity, with its own logic and internal constraints. Further, among these three, individual gathering would be identified as dominant and thus a source of distortion in the other two modes of production. In this way, the interests of women, who are responsible for individual gathering, might be seen as being in conflict with the interests of both men, who are responsible for individual hunting, and the larger groups constituted of both sexes that conduct communal hunts.

For some structural Marxists, it follows from such an analysis of conflicting modes of production that primitive societies lacking conventionally defined social classes actually contain internal divisions that in some sense substitute for the class structure that is necessary to traditional Marxist theory (Bloch 1983:160). For example, age (i.e., old vs. young; e.g., Rey 1979) and gender (men vs. women; cf. Begler 1978) might represent quasi-class structures among hunter-gatherers (cf. Rey 1979; Meillassoux 1972; see also Siskind 1978). That argument, however, is singularly unconvincing: Age and gender differ from classes in fundamental ways. Age sets have no fixed membership, and age and gender groups are both wholly incapable of reproducing themselves independently and always have some vested interest in the well-being of the opposing group or groups, which is an inevitable, indeed, necessary, transformation of their own. It is in the interest of both capitalist and laborer to be concerned with the well-being of each other, of course, but few laborers will be capitalists, and even fewer capitalists have aspirations to be laborers (see also Bloch 1983:161). In short, age and sex cannot easily be substituted for classes of the kind Marx had in mind (but see Bloch 1983:163-164).

Recognizing some of the problems noted, Godelier has taken a different course and denied that multiple modes of production, and the quasi-class structures they imply, are necessary to successful structural Marxist analysis (Godelier 1982; cf. Bloch 1983:163; see also Terray 1972:172). In particular, he rejects the idea that each social formation necessarily contains more than one mode of production. That assumption, he suggests, often leads to economic reductionist arguments in which modes of production are essentially what an archaeologist would call "procurement systems," the fundamental characteristics of which are determined by environment and technology. For Godelier, the separation of the forces and relations of production that constitute any individual primitive mode of production inherently contains by itself sufficient contradictions (i.e., between relations of production and forces of production) to produce conflict and change in the absence of quasi-classes or additional modes of production (Godelier 1982:277-286; cf. O'Laughlin 1975:357-358). That is because, in the last instance, Godelier sees underlying psychological structures as the principal determinants of the social relations of production. This causes the structural-psychological logic of the relations of production to be in conflict with the technoeconomic logic that governs the forces of production.

Applications: Ethnography

Even after a cursory reading of the literature, it is difficult to avoid the conclusion that most structural Marxists grasp very little of hunter-gatherer behavior and even less of the traditional anthropological theories that have been advanced to explain that behavior. No careful reading of Steward (1938), for instance, would ever permit Pasquinelli the claim that traditional anthropology has argued that primitive societies are determined by kinship and social organization rather than by technology and environment (1983:197). On the contrary, as we have seen in Chapters 1 and 2, the opposite assumption (i.e., that technology and environment dominate hunter-gatherer behavior) is basic to anthropology. If, as she avers, this was a major insight of Godelier, he got the right answer—a hundred years late. Again, if Godelier believes, as Bloch avers (1983:165), that he was saying something new in arguing that technoenviron-mentally caused social change is mediated by preexisting sociocultural struc-tures, he could have saved a lot of time and learned a great deal by reading Murdock (1949; in this case he was only 30 years late). The suggestion of Terray (cf. 1969) and Meillassoux (cf. 1972; Moseley and Wallerstein 1978:270) that the force of environment and technology lessen—and the force of culture grows—as technology improves, would merit much the same kind of comment from Powell, Spencer, Steward, and Hippocrates: "We already knew that." What would be news to them, and indeed to all contemporary students of hunter-gatherers, is that incest prohibitions are not universal among hunter-gatherers; such, at least, is the observation of Godelier (1977; cf. Pasquinelli 1983:201; as one might expect, this carries some rather unfortunate consequences for the emphasis he places on the "structural" qualities of Australian section systems [see later discussion]). Finally, had Hindess and Hirst (1975) paid heed to Birdsell (1953) or any of the numerous discussions regarding hunter-gatherer band exogamy or the importance of the fission-fusion cycle that typifies many hunter-gatherer groups (cf. Lee and Devore 1968; Service 1962; Wobst 1974), they could have easily avoided the mistake of supposing that individual micro-bands are self-contained units (cf. Keenan 1977:67).

Given these many fundamental misunderstandings, it is not surprising that structural Marxists have consistently failed to produce penetrating analyses of precapitalist cultures and particularly hunter-gatherers (cf. Pasquinelli 1983:200, 202; Keenan 1977:59-62). Substantively, in large part these studies do little more than duplicate the logic and findings of traditional technoenviron-mental studies. Godelier's treatments of Australian aborigines and Mbuti Pygmies, though couched in structural Marxist vocabulary, are in the last analysis standard functional and cultural materialist explanations. When exam-ining the Australian case, Godelier (1975) rediscovers what Yengoyan (1968; see also Harris 1979:83-84) already knew about section systems: They are a response to the need to be able to draw on kin ties over large areas in regions of resource shortage. In his analysis of the Mbuti case, he again rediscovers what virtually every student of hunter-gatherers knows: that the Mbuti are bound by their environment and technology and develop social relations responding to these conditions (Godelier 1973:51-62). In neither case does he make good on his claim to show the priority of structural elements in determining these organiza-tions; neither does he succeed in demonstrating in what way these structural elements interfere with the way in which the Australians or Mbuti go about making a living.

Though it does not deal with hunter-gatherers specifically, Friedman's discussion of Kachin society in a similar way fails to establish the explanatory importance of what he argues is a basic structural contradiction that causes oscillation between *gumsa* and *gumlao* forms of organization. In explaining how this seemingly endless loop is exited to newer more complex social formations (i.e., genuine transformations), such as characterize the neighboring Shan, Friedman falls back on technoenvironmental explanations (1974:456; 1975:187, 194). In short, Friedman seems to concede that his structural Marxist model of the Kachin case accounts for small-scale, short-term phenomena and that simple (vulgar) materialism is necessary to explain large scale, long-term phenomena. Few vulgar materialists would disagree (see Moseley and Wallerstein 1978:270-271).

Comparable explanatory shortcomings are evident in the works of other kinds of structural Marxists. Meillassoux, for example, argues that the origins of stratification cannot be found among hunting bands and suggests that it might instead have begun among some ill-defined "fishing stage" of culture (1973:201). As with Friedman, this seems a clear admission that large-scale phenomena result from technoenvironmental conditions and not from relations of production. Thoroughly knowledgeable about hunter-gatherers, Michael Asch (1979:90-96) has no difficulty in finding one of these groups to illustrate social formations in which the relations and forces of production are not in contradiction; but he also is forced to illustrate such contradictions not with reference to the hunter-gatherer groups with which he is familiar but with reference to Friedman's analysis of the Kachin.

Such failures are quite telling. If it cannot derive its basic structure—the social class or something like it—from the early, primitive stages of cultural development, it is doubtful that structural Marxism can lay any valid claim to sufficiency as a general theory of cultural evolution. Repeated failures of this sort probably explain why it is that some of the most influential structural Marxists have turned their attention to the articulation of modes of production and particularly the contemporary penetration of capitalism into primitive societies, where there is no question as to the presence of contradiction and conflict (e.g., Meillassoux 1972:101-103; Terray 1972:162; Bradby 1980; Wolpe 1980).

Applications: Archaeology

The attempt to introduce structural Marxist theory into archaeology is equally troubled. British archaeology, in particular, has taken structural Marxism to its logical extreme, putting so much emphasis on social relations that the result no longer bears much resemblance to either vulgar materialism or Marxism but has become substantivism instead. In these analyses, "no part of the system is determinant, but the social relations of production are dominant" (Bender

1981:154; Gamble 1981:215; see also Kus 1984; Faris 1979), that is, culture comes from culture. It is hardly surprising therefore that structural Marxism has been of no greater help to archaeology than to ethnography, and perhaps less.

It is symptomatic that such analyses are typically grandly abstract, didactic in tone, and phrased principally in vague generality and assertion. When Bender attempts to link the agricultural revolution to social demand for surplus production among hunter-gatherers, for example, she is willing simply to assume the presence of various social and ceremonial obligations she believes demanded that surplus (1979). Of course, if we assume universal cultural demand for social surplus, it is no trick at all to explain agriculture in this way, because for a structural Marxist, agricultural production is to be construed not in economic but social terms. Unfortunately, commitment to the explanatory power of socially demanded surplus occasionally leads Bender to less forgivable excesses — as for instance when she (Bender 1985:58) suggests that in the eastern United States Late Archaic, labor intensification occurred in absence of population growth. One wonders on what basis such stable population densities are inferred. Insofar as I am aware, authorities on this question generally deny there are any reliable data that speak to this, but if pressed to speculate, would suggest that the data that exist indicate population growth during Archaic times (e.g., Caldwell 1958; Willey and Phillips 1958:201-202; Griffin 1983:249; Funk 1976:312; 1978:27; 1983:320; Asch, Ford, and Asch 1972; Salwen 1975:52-54; Dragoo 1976:22; Winters 1968:Figures 1-3; 1974:x-xi). I am aware of no authority who has argued that overall population either remained stable or declined during Archaic times.

Finally, it is perhaps most revealing of Bender's theoretical bind that, despite her denial of the utility of technoenvironmental explanations of hunter-gatherer organization (1981:149), she is compelled to argue that harsh environments precluded the development of social differentiation in the Great Lakes region of North America (Bender 1981:155) and that productive environments led to social complexity in the American Midwest (Bender 1981:155) and coastal Peru (Bender 1979:217). This same tendency, identical to the one already observed in ethnology, holds for many other Marxist and structural Marxist archaeological analyses: They advocate the dominance of social relations but employ standard technoeconomic causation when speaking to real situations (e.g., Gamble 1981:226; Gilman 1984).

MARXISM, STRUCTURAL MARXISM, AND NEOFUNCTIONALISM

If, as suggested, Marxism and structural Marxism have produced little in the way of remarkable insights about hunter-gatherers, then why do they enjoy any following at all in hunter-gatherer studies? The answer, at least in part, would seem to be that Marxist/structural Marxist theory shares much in principle with the brand of neofunctionalist interpretation that gained popularity with the rise of the new archaeology in the United States and analytical archaeology in Great Britain (cf. Clarke 1968). Harris (1968a) by word and Sahlins by deed (compare Sahlins 1963 and Sahlins 1972; see also Sahlins 1976) have shown just how narrow the gap is between neofunctionalist/cultural materialist explanation, on the one hand, and Marxist/structural Marxist explanation on the other.

In this regard, two conceptual resemblances between neofunctionalist and Marxist theory are particularly notable. First, like those of neofunctionalism, Marxist interpretations assume that culture process occurs by means of system transformations. In both theories, change takes place through alterations effected from within cultural systems that retain their unique identities despite these changes. In short, as revealed in its emphasis on the concept of "structural causation," reduced to basics, Marxist theory is essentially a special kind of general systems theory and thus inherently transformational. In this sense, both Marxist and neofunctionalist interpretations are quite compatible with the new archaeology's stated preference for theories capable of generating explanations in which culture change responds to structural conditions existing within a system rather than conditions wholly external to it (e.g., migrations or climatic change; cf. Clarke 1968; Binford 1968b; Flannery 1968; Faris 1979; Dunnell 1980). Second, and equally salient, Marxism/structural Marxism and neofunctionalism resemble each other in their use of philosophical collectivism as a framework for explanation and methodological collectivism as a strategy for research. In this respect, a special appeal of structural Marxism would seem to lie at least in part in the stress it places on the social relations of production, a view consistent with the important role given to social organization in the theories that grew popular with the new archaeology (Binford 1962; Hill 1968; Longacre 1968; Rathje 1972; see also Rappaport 1970; Flannery 1972).

Unfortunately, neither of these conceptual features contributes significantly to the utility of either Marxism/structural Marxism or neofunctionalism as general theories suitable for understanding hunter-gatherers. Rather, both are serious liabilities: The failure of general systems theory is by now quite apparent (cf. Salmon 1978), and it is equally evident that philosophical/methodological collectivism and explanation by group selection are plausible only in the presence of specified conditions the grounds for which remain unestablished in both Marxist and neofunctionalist theory.

Disregarding these mutual deficiencies, it can be observed that the Marxist emphasis on culture change would seem to make it more attractive as a candidate for a general theory than neofunctionalism, which lacks a theory of culture change and, thus, appears poorly qualified to address the problem of cultural evolution. Marxist theory, at least, offers a means for hunter-gatherer specialists to avoid the neofunctionalist pitfall of assuming that hunter-gatherers are adapted, which makes them an unlikely source of new, more highly evolved, cultural formations. It is in the unrelenting search for conflict, contradiction, and the unintended and destabilizing consequences of behavior—all potential sources of change—that Marxist theory most deliberately departs from neofunctionalist research, where the search for order and homeostasis is paramount. This is particularly apparent from the way in which neofunctionalism and Marxism approach the problem of maladaptation.

What constitutes maladaptive behavior, of course, remains unsettled in both the social and natural sciences. In biology, for instance, certain predator/prey interactions seem to reduce the fitness of both species (i.e., seem to be mutually maladaptive), which appears inconsistent with the general Darwinian assumption (see Chapter 7) that behaviors ought to be understood in terms of the ways in which they enhance fitness. In any case, in the sense used here, a maladaptive behavior is one in which the rational attainment of some culturally valued goal compromises energetic efficiency or genetic fitness. In Weber's terms, cultural maladaptations are "subjectively rational" on the one hand and "objectively irrational" on the other: rational in the mind of the actor but irrational in the mind of an objective and impartial observer (see Chapter 4). The emphasis on adaptation and homeostasis in neofunctionalism essentially precludes the possibility of studying such phenomena and, arguably, denies their existence altogether. Alternatively, Marxism, in its emphasis on contradiction, conflict, and mystified exploitation, suggests that all systems (excepting, of course communism) are maladaptive owing to the manner in which one class exploits another. In Marxism, it is maladaptations that drive evolutionary change and make it inevitable.

There is now little doubt that the Marxist approach is the more correct of the two. The shortcomings of the alternative neofunctionalist approach have been made particularly apparent in the recent reconsideration of the Tsembaga cycle among the Maring of New Guinea by Foin and Davis (1984). This compelling reconsideration of the now-classic original study of the Maring by Rappaport (1968) reveals fundamental flaws in the basic neofunctionalist concept of equilibrium (see also Winterhalder 1984). The work of Foin and Davis establishes that, despite Rappaport's every effort to demonstrate to the contrary, it is unlikely that the Maring system is or ever was in equilibrium. Indeed, as shown by another restudy of the Maring, it is impossible to imagine how the Tsembaga cycle itself could have ever evolved into the form described by Rappaport in the first place (cf. Peoples 1982). Moreover, as Rutz (1977) demonstrates, even in cases where systems are in equilibrium this need not be the result of group-level, goal-seeking behavior; it is just as likely to be an unintended consequence of individual self-interest expressed in the aggregate. For these reasons, it cannot be assumed that systems in equilibrium have any tendency to remain so or to return to equilibrium after being disrupted.

Hunter-Gatherers and the Penetration of Capitalism

The Marxist search for conflict and contradiction offers at least one additional advantage to those interested in hunter-gatherers. This premise has led Marxists and structural Marxists to address an important topic largely ignored in the contemporary ethnographic literature on hunter-gatherers, namely the attempt to understand the penetration of capitalism into precapitalist modes of production (cf. Comaroff 1984; but see Schrire 1984). To advocate the significance of such studies does not require that we assume that contemporary hunter-gatherers are qualitatively different from prehistoric ones; superficial criticisms of the kind that suggest that because the Nunamiut use snowmobiles they have little to tell us about prehistoric hunter-gatherers are easily rejected (Binford 1978a:452; see also O'Connell and Hawkes 1981:113). Be this as it may, modernization is an accomplished fact for many contemporary hunter-gatherers. It is fruitless to attempt to compensate for this by trying somehow to subtract its effects and then pretending that one has eliminated and thus need not consider further the obvious influence capitalist or socialist industrial states have had on these groups (or, indeed, the effect complex preindustrial social formations had on prehistoric hunter-gatherers; e.g., Parkington 1984). It seems more profitable to face the problem squarely and actively investigate the ways in which this articulation has distorted these precapitalist systems and to consider in detail the implications of this for their economic and social behaviors (e.g., Denbow 1984; Bradby 1980). It is quite thinkable, for instance, that, prevented by public opinion and law from directly exploiting certain economically valuable but endangered species (e.g., fur and ivory bearers), capitalists find it in their interest to keep Arctic hunter-gatherers in a suspended state of development in which their appearance of primitiveness creates the appropriate justification for such exploitation. The use of primitive hunter-gatherers as guides for sportsmen and the military, as portagers, and as laborers in lumber camps are all well-established alternative motives for wishing hunter-gatherers to remain "primitive" (e.g., Wilmsen 1983; Gordon 1984). There is every reason to suspect that the "rationality" of such hunter-gatherers is highly colored by this contact with capitalism. Indeed, it is scarcely conceivable that, in everything from choice of prey and settlement location to choice of mate, the economic decisions of contemporary hunter-gatherers are not ridden with "hidden" motives ultimately grounded in the demand of First-World economies for Third-World labor and products (e.g., Hoffman 1984; but see Brosius 1988; Sellato 1988; and Kaskija 1988). Such distortions should not be ignored.

Marxists and the Environment

To be entirely fair in our weighing of the relative merits of neofunctionalism and Marxism/structural Marxism as general theories, it must be noted that although vastly superior to neofunctionalism in many respects, Marxist theory is clearly inferior in one critical (and perhaps more important) respect: Marxist theory and Marxist theoreticians from Marx himself to Godelier are uniformly naive in the manner in which they treat the environment and human/environmental interaction. For all their flaws, neofunctionalism and neofunctionalist-like theories produced as part of the new archaeology are rich with environmental fact and interpretation and are clearly the better for it. In the final analysis, this flaw above all others might well prove fatal to conventional Marxism — at least insofar as hunter-gatherers are concerned. Whether or not one accepts the theory of multilinear evolution, no scholar reasonably well versed in the literature that deals with hunter-gatherers would deny that Steward (1938) produced a technoenvironmental interpretation of ethnographic adaptations in the Great Basin that is almost certainly correct in broad outline, if not in particular detail; neither can it be denied that this interpretation would have been impossible had not Steward had an intimate understanding of the Great Basin environment and its aboriginal human ecology. Likewise none who are familiar with the recent literature on hunter-gatherers would deny that proper interpretation of these groups must proceed hand in hand with similarly intimate understanding of environment and technology. This is not to say that the environment is sufficient to explain behavior — only that behavior cannot be understood apart from a specified technoenvironmental setting, which Marxist interpretations have consistently failed either to appreciate or to act upon. To the contrary, Marxists have denigrated such efforts.

CONCLUSIONS AND IMPLICATIONS

Two concluding observations seem in order. The first is that from an evolutionary perspective, neofunctionalist and Marxist/structural Marxist accounts of hunter-gatherers both suffer from a problem outlined in Chapter 1: the entrenched assumption that hunter-gatherers are adapted to their environments and that the analysis of hunter-gatherers should center on an examination of the ways in which that is true. As noted in that discussion and the preceding one in this chapter, it is the working assumption of neofunctionalism that this holds true for all societies and groups, regardless of complexity or technological sophistication. As noted in Chapter 2, this makes it difficult to produce neofunctional accounts of evolutionary change for hunter-gatherers or any other kind of group without resorting to external conditions.

Equilibrium and stability are not assumed by Marxists or structural

Marxists, however. They take it as given that every social formation contains inherent structural contradictions that are constantly working to produce change. This assumption has caused Marxists theorists no end of trouble in the hunter-gatherer case. In many instances, it has led to the stretching of empirical facts (e.g., regarding the presence of classes) in order to make hunter-gatherers fit a mold suitable for investigation through Marxist theory. These efforts are perhaps helpful in articulating that theory but are wholly devoid of utility in understanding hunter-gatherers, who emerge from the analysis looking nothing like hunter-gatherers at all. Fortunately, most structural Marxists have rejected that alternative and thrown their lot in with traditional anthropology by accepting hunter-gatherers as a distinct socioeconomic category that require distinctive kinds of explanations. The explanations advanced, however, are not distinctively Marxist.

Despite their revolutionary predilections, most structural Marxists (e.g., Asch, Rey, Terray, and Meillassoux) simply accept hunter-gatherers as a counterinstance to the general assumptions of Marxist theory in the sense that they are unable to find clear instances of exploitation, classlike groups, or inherent structural contradictions. As noted, this has led them either to produce accounts of hunter-gatherers matching those of traditional anthropology or to turn to cases in which the necessary structures of class and contradiction result from the penetration of capitalism. In this sense, the problem with Marxist/structural Marxist interpretations of hunter-gatherers is not that their analyses are incorrect but rather that they are not grounded in the precepts that distinguish Marxist/structural Marxism from traditional anthropological theories grounded in materialism. Because this is so, they lack most of the explanatory advantages Marxist theory enjoys over these traditional theories, particularly neofunctionalism. This parallels the case of progressive social evolutionary theory, which like structural Marxism, produces no evolutionary account of hunter-gatherers but rather interprets them in terms of natural environment and ecology.

The second concluding point of interest concerns the larger influence of Marxist and structural Marxist theory on contemporary theory in archaeology. Here it can be argued that the central themes of what has been called "postprocessual" archaeology (e.g., Hodder 1982a,b, 1983; Shanks and Tilley 1987) are directly traceable to Marxist/structural Marxist thought (Shanks and Tilley 1987:194). Principal among these concepts are the notions of the power of ideology, the idea of behavior as meaningfully constituted, the idea that exploitation and control are universal, and the conception of traditional anthropology as a tool of Western capitalism. This is no place to review postprocessual archaeological theory, in large part because, like Marxist/structural Marxist theory, postprocessualism speaks very little to the case of hunter-gatherers. Much of this work attends more to the criticism of anthropologists than their specific anthropological interpretations, and most of it deals either with more complex prehistoric societies or (with increasing regularity) the interpretation of modern material culture. What is worthy of remark is the way in which from Marxism to structural Marxism to postprocessual theory, ideology and meaning have been assigned ever-increasing explanatory importance whereas technology and material conditions have at the same time been accorded increasingly less importance.

Ultimately this has meant, for Hodder at least, that ideology, symbol, and meaning have become the fundamental elements through which existence is mediated and thus constitute the real arena in which conflicting interest groups oppose each other. Thus among the Ilchamus of Kenya (Hodder 1986), for example, men exert power over women by excluding them from public discourse; the women reexert their independence and authority by decorating calabashes. Without denying the importance of symbols, this is dangerous nonsense. Mao's famous dictum reestablishes a sense of the real situation: "Political power grows out of the barrel of a gun." Events in Tian'anmen Square seem to support Mao against Hodder: Tanks, not talk, constituted the "meaningful context" in Beijing, and no detailed consideration of deep structure or hidden meaning was needed to understand what happened.

Shanks and Tilley seem to grasp more clearly the immediate realities of political context and accordingly reject Hodder's views as inherently subjective, relativistic and, thus, out of touch with reality. Their postprocessual alternative places more emphasis on the understanding of real power and power politics. Unfortunately, this leads them to view the conduct of traditional archaeology as an essentially political act, being inevitably embedded in Western capitalist imperialism. In compensation, they advocate that archaeologists use archaeology as an instrument of social change.

> A critical archaeology is value-committed, a willed personal act with the aim transforming the present in terms of its conceived connection with the past. (Shanks and Tilley 1987:213)

This is equally dangerous nonsense. It allows Shanks and Tilley to indulge in the delusion that in doing archaeology they can contribute to social reform. An informed cynic might well observe that this is exactly what the entrenched capitalist-imperialist power structure would like them to believe. The capitalist undoubtedly sees the situation thus: Archaeology is harmless enough, and it serves to keep those with potentially dangerous ideas (e.g., Shanks and Tilley) off the streets. In real terms, archaeology contributes little to what is right or wrong with the world. If Shanks and Tilley really want to do something about social reform they are in the wrong field. Better they should get off the sidelines and follow the lead of those Marxist anthropologists who have left comfortable positions to work in places where they have a chance of actually making a difference.

In a larger sense, Hodder and Shanks and Tilley both seem to be engaged in a scarcely concealed attempt to control archaeology by dictating the nature of debate on unequal terms that give them all the advantages. Cloaking themselves in righteous criticism of the capitalist-imperialist hegemonic science of anthropology, Shanks and Tilley can easily dismiss views counter to their own as self-interested distortions designed to legitimize existing power structures: There is no need go to the trouble of consulting archaeological evidence at all (Just for record, however, it would appear that insofar as distortion of empirical cases is concerned, it is not traditional, i.e., Western, capitalist anthropologists but more often their critics who seem to be guilty; cf. Beidelman 1989; Brosius 1988; Sellato 1988; Kaskija 1988; cf. Hoffman 1984).

Hodder's gambit is more subtle. As a younger archaeologist, Hodder found it quite acceptable to engage in positivistic debate: That allowed his interpretations to be weighed on equal terms against those advanced by older and more well-established archaeologists. Himself finally in a position of power, Hodder finds it convenient to deny the merits of positivism, which would offer his junior colleagues the same advantages he once enjoyed. Rather, now it is a case in which there are no "correct" interpretations and no objective basis for weighing the merits of two opposing arguments. Here, a cynic would observe that such a program has the insidious effect of "freezing" existing relations of power. In such cases, the nod for the argument considered most persuasive always goes to individuals with the most prestige and influence. This is precisely the situation that led to the introduction of positivism into archaeology in the first place (Binford 1968a:16). Hodder and Shanks and Tilley indict processual archaeologists as being more concerned with the form of an argument than its content; in point of fact, however, in their schemes, it is form alone (or personal prestige) that provides the basis for evaluating interpretations (see Meltzer 1990 for a slightly different perspective).

Both Shanks and Tilley and Hodder seem to believe that they have discovered some fundamental new truth in the observation that science is subjective and that it has very little to do with the "truth." That suggests that they grasp very little of the nature of scientific research, the basic rules for which are actually quite simple: At any moment, the best theory is the one that explains (accounts for) or predicts the greatest number of facts with the fewest assumptions. To suggest, as Shanks and Tilley do, that additional points ought to be scored for theories in conformance with "correct" political views, turns the debate immediately into a matter of weighing the relative merits of different kinds of politics. Worse yet, it opens the door for either good or bad political views—Fascist or antifascist, feminist or antifeminist—depending on the social circumstances prevailing at the moment. Here, the lesson of history is quite clear: The consequences of mixing politics and science are potentially far more devastating (e.g., Nazi Germany) than beneficial. Ultimately, the best protection against the devastating effects is to keep politics out of the scoring system altogether.

Chapter 7

Neo-Darwinian Theory and Hunter-Gatherers

In previous chapters, the general theories we have attempted to apply to hunter-gatherers derive, directly or indirectly, from the social sciences. In this chapter, we turn for the first time to a theory drawn directly from the natural sciences, specifically from biology. The body of general theory in question is neo-Darwinism.

DARWINIAN AND NON-DARWINIAN SOCIAL THEORIES

As it is used here, the term *Darwinian* applies to theories that explain macrolevel phenomena as the cumulative consequence of explicitly defined processes (e.g., selection and others) acting on a microlevel, specifically on reproductive individuals. Social Darwinism, Marxism/structural Marxism, "early" cultural materialism (cf. Harris 1968a), and neofunctionalism proceed in the opposite direction: They assume that macrolevel phenomena (e.g., cultures) are of paramount importance. This makes the study of process a matter of generalizing about macrolevel phenomena. In a manner of speaking, Darwinian theories move from process up to consequence, non-Darwinian social theories from consequence down to process (see Chapter 9). The theory of "early" cultural materialism, for instance, often seems to be more a statistical generalization than an explanation.

> The probability that India's sacred cattle complex is a positive-functioned part of a naturally selected ecosystem is at least as good as that it is a negative-functioned expression of an irrational ideology. (Harris 1966:59)

151

Like the European swan (which is white simply because all European swans are white), a behavioral trait is probably adaptive because behavioral traits are more likely to be adaptive than not. In neither case, swans or cattle, do we have any satisfactory account of why this should be so as a matter of process.

These philosophical differences carry significant implications for the relevant operational units that are the subject of Darwinian and non-Darwinian social theories. In Darwinian theories, individuals are always important, in non-Darwinian social theories, they almost never are. In most non-Darwinian social theories, processes are essentially generalizations about the behavioral characteristics of groups. That is, their explanations are derived out of philosophical collectivism—conceptual frameworks in which various collectives of individuals (interest groups, populations, cultures, social formations, etc.) are the most important unit of process. In such a framework, the group is an organic whole the behavior of which cannot be reduced to the aggregate behaviors of its individual constituents and must be understood in terms of behaviors appropriate to, and understandable in terms of, the larger unit (see also Elster 1985; Vayda 1986). As we have seen in Marxism (Chapter 6), for example, it is classes, class interest, and class conflict that provide the context for discussing social theory. In Darwinian theories, on the other hand, individuals are essential to explanation: Their interests cannot be ignored. It is the self-interested individual that must make real and metaphorical choices about reproduction and the selective risks associated with different courses of action.

In combination, the previously mentioned differences cause Darwinian and non-Darwinian social theories to differ regarding the mechanisms through which change occurs. Social Darwinism, the various forms of Marxism, cultural materialism, and neofunctionalism explain culture change as a consequence of transformational processes. They envision process in terms of the metamorphosis of collectives that maintain their essential identity despite change, external (morphological) and internal (structural; see Dunnell 1980). Thus, tribes become chiefdoms, feudal formations become capitalist formations, and England progresses and becomes industrialized. By contrast, neo-Darwinian theories of culture are selectional rather than transformational. They assume that it is the presence of variability that affects selective fitness of reproductive units and determines the presence of reproductive mechanisms by which this variability—somewhat reduced by selection—is carried from unit to unit (i.e., the differential persistence of variability).

For the most part, these differences in philosophical approach carry over to methodology. Neofunctionalism, "early" cultural materialism, and the various forms of Marxism specify groups (rather than individuals) as basic units for observation and study and are thus methodological, as well as philosophical, collectivist theories. Social Darwinism (Spencerism), on the other hand, implied the need for a methodological individualist approach. It held that selection and acquired variation acted on individuals and that this produced group transformations and progress. As we saw in Chapter 1, however, the Spencerists— Spencer in particular—did little to put this model of process into action and seldom engaged in first-hand research with individuals (Kennedy 1978:15-16). Neo-Darwinian theories are invariably methodological individualist in approach. That is because in these theories individuals are always the locus of important selective and reproductive activity. Neo-Darwinian commitment to methodological individualism carries no necessary implications regarding the scale at which evolutionary processes will operate, however. These may be manifest at either the group or individual level. Accordingly, neo-Darwinian theories cannot be unambiguously characterized as committed philosophically either to individualism or collectivism (see Dawkins 1976).[1]

Having distinguished it from non-Darwinian social theory, it is useful further to distinguish within Darwinian social theory two schools: evolutionary ecology, in which all human behavior is interpreted—or can be thought of as being interpreted—in terms of genetic fitness, and dual inheritance, in which human behavior is judged partly in terms of genetic fitness and partly in terms of cultural fitness. It is evolutionary ecology that concerns us in this chapter.

EVOLUTIONARY HUMAN ECOLOGY

Evolutionary human ecology is the first attempt to develop a coherent theory of sociocultural behavior in terms of exactly the same principles that guide biological theories of evolution. Despite the novelty of its approach and its relatively recent appearance, evolutionary ecology had no trouble finding a home in hunter-gatherer studies where it is seen as participating in a tradition of technoenvironmental materialist explanation that extends through Steward

---

[1]Unfortunately, the possibility of group-level phenomena is denied by many evolutionary ecologists in anthropology who take the position that the individual is the only relevant unit of reference. This, of course, has never been maintained by Darwinian theorists in the natural sciences: Many potent biological models involve population-level phenomena and variables, for example, logistic growth rates, predator/prey interactions. Philosophical individualists suggest that even the rare cases of group selection are best explained by the presence of individuals who underwrite the cost of public goods (i.e., act in ways that benefit larger groups of unrelated individuals) because in helping the group, those individuals help themselves. This argument is easily disposed of (see "prisoner's dilemma"). When it comes down to cases, the suggestion that the explanatory point of reference ought to be the individual even when selection acts on a group is just too simplistic a reductionism: Where groups are involved, one cannot predict what is rational for the individual without reference to what is good for the group as it competes with other groups. It may seem to make things tidier and more parsimonious to argue that all phenomena can be explained at the individual level but that idea rests on semantics not substance or logic. In sum, in some cases behavior cannot be explained in terms of individuals only but in terms of individuals and groups.

back to Mason, Powell, and McGee. Within this tradition, evolutionary ecology represents an effort to escape the traditional contradiction between the idea that hunter-gatherers are important to the understanding of evolutionary processes, which implies that they are to be understood in terms of how culture changes, and the idea that hunter-gatherers are adapted to their technoenvironmental situation, which implies that they are to be understood in terms of equilibrium and stability, that is, how culture stays the same. Evolutionary ecology makes it possible to produce accounts of change and stability in hunter-gatherer groups under the same theoretical umbrella without shifting explanatory framework. As we shall see, however, evolutionary ecologists have not taken full advantage of this opportunity. Most frequently they have chosen to produce explanations that are in keeping with traditional anthropological interpretations in the sense that the hunter-gatherer groups under study are assumed to be in equilibrium (i.e., adapted). Thus, as in the case of Marxism/structural Marxism, the advantages of evolutionary ecological theory remain to be exploited fully.

Despite their many differences, evolutionary ecologists agree that human behavior can ultimately be understood in terms of genetic fitness: Any specific behavior should have the effect of increasing the likelihood that some or all of the genes of an individual will be passed to another individual. The logic of this is quite simple: If behavioral variability (whatever its source, i.e., genetic or otherwise) results in differential genetic fitness and if such behaviors (again, regardless of source) are transferable from one individual to another, then this transfer necessarily carries with it the implication of genetic fitness.

Note in particular that it is not essential to this argument that behavior be tied to genes in any but the loosest sense, that is, that certain behaviors and certain genes must necessarily reside within the same individual even though the behaviors are not dictated directly by the genes (some of the more prominent sociobiologists, of course, think that they are, e.g., Lumsden and Wilson 1981). For example, one might imagine that in the past selection for the properties of individual decision makers resulted in individuals that chose fitness optimizing behaviors, even though no variability now exists for such genes. By this view, the same processes that underlie natural selection in the animal world apply in general terms to the human case. Thus if the behavior of an individual causes him/her to produce more offspring and if these offspring are encultured with his/her behaviors, then whether or not these behaviors are genetic or cultural in origin they will flourish just as the genes of that individual will flourish. Put another way, evolutionary ecology does not require that behavior be genetically linked, although it uses the same measure of behavioral viability as Darwinian models grounded wholly in genetics: genetic fitness.

The Problem of Altruism

From the perspective of genetic fitness, it is easy to understand how the traditional conundrum for evolutionary ecologists came to be that of explaining the recurrence of apparently altruistic behavior in humans (cf. Rosenberg 1980:185). By definition, altruistic refers to behaviors in which an individual sacrifices individual self-interest (compromises personal genetic fitness) to further the interest (genetic fitness) of other individuals.

In a book widely read by anthropologists and pointedly attacked by the evolutionary biologist George Williams (1966), Wynne-Edwards (1962) argued that this problem could be resolved by postulating that selection was in these cases acting at the group level. This solution was intuitively attractive: Groups consisting of individuals genetically programmed for altruism might well outdo groups constituted of members preoccupied with their own selfish interests. Upon reflection, however, it was clear that this could occur only where the selective gradient between groups was steeper than the selective gradient between individuals within groups—which is presumably rare in the real world. Ordinarily, groups consisting of altruistic individuals are too susceptible to invasion by individuals lacking altruistic motives to permit this to happen. In such a situation, the self-interested invaders benefit from the altruistic behaviors of others and soon replace them. Put another way, where there is any degree of migration between different groups, self-interested individuals gravitate to groups constituted largely of altruists, where they (i.e., self-interested individuals) can enjoy the benefits of the cooperative efforts of others without paying any of its costs. This acts to reduce the selective differences between groups relative to the selective differences between individuals within groups (i.e., between altruists and self-interested individuals), which eventually leads to the extinction of the altruists.

The Prisoner's Dilemma

As the case of group selection illustrates, altruism is problematic from an evolutionary standpoint because the interests of interacting individuals often conflict in ways that prevent them from cooperating together, even when cooperation would benefit all concerned. This paradox is captured in the classic case of the prisoner's dilemma (Hardin 1982). We can model the dilemma for a hypothetical hunter-gatherer society that consists of two individuals. Let us say they are hunters—campmates—Bogg and Thogg, who have the choice of consistently hunting close to their camp, which will eventually bring about the extinction of local game, or regularly forcing themselves to hunt further away at greater personal cost. Both Bogg and Thogg have two options: (1) to sacrifice and satisfy group interest, i.e., to hunt far away from camp; or (2) to be greedy

and satisfy self-interest, i.e., to hunt close to camp. The benefit to local game
herds resulting from either one of the hunter's sacrifice—that hunter's contribution to public goods for the group—is PG, and his cost in contributing to the
public good (i.e., hunting far away) is S.

The payoff matrix of this situation shown in Table 7.1 follows standard
game theory format. It keeps score with reference to payoffs received by Thogg
depending on the joint behaviors of Thogg and Bogg. Note that this is merely a
formal device for scorekeeping and does not assume any intrinsic disadvantage
to Bogg, who faces an identical payoff matrix in which the roles are reversed.

We cannot deduce the proper (self-interested) course for Thogg without
knowing the values of PG and S. If $PG/2 < S$, he acts greedily and hunts close
to camp because this produces better payoffs regardless of what Bogg chooses to
do. That is, when $PG/2 < S$, then $PG/2 > PG - S$, and $0 > PG/2 - S$.
Thogg's refusal to sacrifice given these conditions constitutes evidence he is truly
greedy only if he is acting on the knowledge (or belief) that Bogg will sacrifice. In
that case, he receives a full share of the group benefit generated by Bogg without
paying any of its cost. On the other hand, Thogg might refuse to sacrifice not
because he is greedy but merely to protect himself because he thinks Bogg is
likely to be greedy; for if Thogg sacrifices and Bogg does not, Thogg receives the
so-called "sucker's payoff" $(PG/2 - S)$, which results in a net loss to him when
$PG/2 < S$.

Suppose, however, that $PG/2 > S$. Then Thogg will sacrifice and hunt far
from camp no matter what Bogg does, because when $PG/2 > S$, then $PG - S >
PG/2$, and $PG/2 - S > 0$. Put in plain words, unless the collective group benefit
(PG) generated by Thogg's sacrifice is more than twice as large as the cost of that
sacrifice (S), Thogg will not sacrifice. Whether Thogg cooperates or not is purely
a matter of self-interest.

Note further that the payoff of greedy behavior relative to sacrificing
behavior will increase as we add more individuals; that is, as more individuals
cooperate to produce a public good, each individual's portion of the total public
goods produced decreases and the wages of greed increases (Boyd and Richerson
1985:228-229). Thus, in many cases, even though there are clear benefits for
cooperation, self-interest may prevent such behavior; given the choice, some
self-interested individuals are going to be greedy no matter what the situation.

Table 7.1. The Hunter's Dilemma

		Bogg	
		Sacrifice	Greed
Thogg	Sacrifice	$PG - S$	$PG/2 - S$
	Greed	$PG/2$	0

Of course, we might offer a counterscenario in which Bogg and Thogg agree to a pact in which each will limit his kill of local game and will be subject to punishment by the other should he be caught; this would certainly make it more costly to be greedy and in this way encourage cooperation and sacrifice. The argument, however, is just as easily countered by noting that although punishment produces benefits via the conservation of game, it levees costs on those who must punish. Punishment, it turns out, is simply another kind of sacrificing (cooperative) behavior and as such can be analyzed by exactly the same kind of analysis used here with respect to cooperation in game management. This time we would again find that unless half the benefit in being a punisher is greater than its individual cost, neither hunter would find it in his self-interest to engage in coercion. Further, as in the previous example, analyses that cast one player as an individual and the other as a group make it clear that as the size of the group increases the benefits of greed (i.e., refusing to engage in punishment) increase. Given the presence of many others willing to punish, an individual might find it in his interest to cooperate (i.e., on pain of punishment), but it would never be in his interest to engage in punishment personally. The implication is that however beneficial cooperative behavior might be for collective bodies and their constituents, it should not occur except when it is in the self-interest of individuals as individuals.

Group Size

Circumstances such as those surrounding the prisoner's dilemma are likely to interfere in a variety of ways with our attempts to observe rational economic behavior among human groups. Let us suppose, for instance, that there is an optimal group size for hunting a certain kind of game—say, 15 individuals—and that the return per individual when hunting in such groups is substantially larger than when hunting alone. Suppose further that beginning with a group of size one, individual returns increase monotonically as groups increase in size until they reach 15 and thereafter monotonically decrease in quantity until that for a group of 40 the rate of return per individual is equal to that which could be obtained by hunting individually. Now it is clear that although we might be able to predict an optimal group size, it is unlikely that in reality we would find individuals sorting themselves into groups of that size. That is so because self-interested individuals have no commitment to the group, only to their own rate of return. Thus an individual deciding whether to hunt alone or join a group of size 15 will clearly take the latter option even though it will depress overall return rates for the group. Further, unless prevented from doing so by members of the group, which might prove quite costly, individuals would continue to attach themselves to this group until it reached size 40, at which point all its individuals would do better alone. Clark and Mangel (1984) who have analyzed this situation suggest that after its dissolution, individuals would quickly re-form into larger groups and eventually stabilize as two groups of equal but suboptimal size.

Hunter-Gatherer Group Size: Inuit Hunting Parties

Smith (1981) has reviewed the problem of hunter-gatherer group size from the perspective of evolutionary ecology. He discusses some of the advantages potentially accruing to groups of individuals that cooperate in foraging, information sharing, resource sharing. As he notes, as compared with individuals, groups may often be more efficient in finding and taking prey, particularly large prey. Further, group foraging coordinates the activities of individuals, who might otherwise unduly interfere with each other. Finally, as in the case of resource storage, foraging groups that pool and share resources have the effect of "smoothing" the variation in daily capture rates between individuals (see Chapter 5). That is, because "lucky" individuals split their take with "unlucky" individuals, as the group grows larger, the daily individual share approaches the expected long-term mean rate of return. It is clear, then, that in theory hunter-gatherers working in groups enjoy many advantages over individual foragers. The question is whether individual self-interest is important enough to offset these advantages and prevent groups of optimal size from forming.

As part of his discussion of hunter-gatherer group size, Smith (1981) examined variability in foraging group size for ten kinds of hunts commonly conducted by the Inuit Eskimo of Canada. Drawing on the principles of evolutionary ecology, he hypothesized that if the Inuit were acting optimally that (1) for any hunt type the modal group size observed ought to be the one associated with the highest mean rate of return per individual; (2) for any hunt type the frequency of occurrence of different- sized groups ought to be correlated with their mean rate of return per individual; and (3) between hunt types, modal group size and optimal group size ought to be positively correlated.

The first and second hypothesis were confirmed for prey of smaller individual size (i.e., birds and fish), for which single individuals constituted both observed modal "group" size and optimal "group" size in terms of energetic efficiency. Interestingly, for larger prey—seal and caribou—the observed modal group size differed from the optimal group size. In the three hunt types that targeted seals, hunting groups were consistently larger than the optimal one (i.e., the one that produced the highest rate of return per individual). For instance, in the case of breathing-hole seal hunting, in which individuals may cooperate by taking stands at different ice openings used by one seal, the optimal group size was three whereas the observed modal group size was four. In the one hunt type targeting caribou, on the other hand, the observed modal group size was smaller than the optimal one. As a consequence of the latter discrepancies between expected and observed group behavior, Smith (1981:64) was able to report only a moderate correlation between optimal and observed modal group size across all Inuit hunt types.

These results are relevant to earlier observations regarding the potential conflict that exists between groups and self-interested individuals. In the case of smaller, more numerous prey, such as fish and birds, it may be that required level of skill is low enough and the encounter rate high enough to offer little incentive for individuals to attempt to "horn-in" on the activities of other individuals. In such instances, individuals can do as well or better working alone as they can if they join others.

On the other hand, as the optimal group size increases, individuals suffer substantially lower returns than groups and are thus increasingly tempted to join them. That this diminishes the rate of return per individual within such groups is of little interest to the outsider, for whom the diminished rate is still higher than the rate of return the outsider obtains when working alone. Such incentives of self-interest would seem to account for the tendency of Inuit seal hunters to work in groups larger than are optimal.

Surprisingly, the same principles that may keep Inuit seal hunting groups larger than optimal may also explain why Inuit caribou hunting groups are consistently smaller than optimal. This could happen in two ways. With regard to the first, note that the optimal caribou hunting group consists of between six and seven individuals, whereas the observed modal group size is about half that, between three and five individuals (Smith 1981:63). It is reasonable to assume that individual hunters would be tempted to join caribou hunting groups consisting of seven members because groups of that size enjoy the optimal rate of return for that activity. Suppose, however, that the rates of return for caribou hunting diminish sharply when groups grow much larger than seven so that the return rate for groups of between eight and ten is about the same as that obtained by lone hunters. Following the analysis of Clark and Mangel (1984; see preceding discussion), if this were so, the addition of an outsider to an existing caribou hunting group of seven would eliminate the benefits of group participation for all eight individuals and cause the group to dissolve and re-form into groups of about half that size (between four and five individuals), which is roughly the observed modal size of Inuit caribou hunting groups. In this way, Inuit caribou hunting groups might constantly display a cycle of incremental growth followed by fission into smaller groups. The alternate (and less likely) possibility is that some caribou hunting groups of suboptimal size might be stable (i.e., capable of resisting invasion by additional members) given the presence of other, larger, hunting groups whose return rate is higher. Then unattached individuals would choose to join the larger group, leaving the members of the smaller group to enjoy the steady (but suboptimal) benefits of their cooperation. It might also be that only groups of close kinsmen can exclude newjoiners and groups are therefore suboptimally restricted to close kin.

Much of the preceding analysis is speculative. The lesson, nevertheless, is that one ought to be extremely skeptical of attempts to explain hunter-gatherer group size in terms of the benefits enjoyed by the group without considering the disruptive effects unattached individuals might have on such groups. Further, given this, it would be extremely unwise to assume that groups that form for cooperative benefit, particularly those of "optimal" size, represent stable evolutionary equilibria (Smith does not make this assumption). On the contrary, such groups are seldom likely to be stable for any length of time.

Inclusive Fitness

To this point, the problem of altruism and cooperation has been couched only in terms of pairs or groups of unrelated individuals. In this sense, the conclusions that can be drawn from the preceding analyses, which suggest that cooperation is unlikely, are less general than they might seem because they treat payoffs as though they were important only to individuals. In evolutionary terms, that assumption is correct when the interacting individuals are unrelated because then the genetic fitness of one individual is either independent of (or in opposition to) the genetic fitness of all other individuals. However, that assumption does not hold when there is some degree of relatedness between interacting individuals because they share certain genes in common. It follows that in such cases the genetic "interests" of different individuals are not independent and, thus, need not be opposed. This should make it easier for cooperation to evolve.

Using this as a starting point, Hamilton (1963, 1964) ultimately offered what would appear to be the soundest explanation for altruism from an evolutionary ecological perspective: the principle of inclusive fitness. According to this principle, the sacrifice of individual somatic interests might actually increase individual genetic fitness, if the individual somatic sacrifice increases the fitness of close genetic relatives. Put another way, inclusive fitness theory argues that in some cases the best way to pass along one's genes is indirectly through aid given to close relatives who are genetic near copies. This means that one should measure genetic fitness not in terms of the individual but in terms of the individual's genes ("identical by common descent"). It follows that it is the inclusive fitness of a group of closely related individuals that offers the best reference for genetic fitness. Hamilton (1963, 1964) formalized this argument via a simple inequality

$$PG/S > 1/r \qquad (7.1)$$

where

PG is the benefit of the sacrifice to the individual receiving it
S is its cost to the individual making it
r is the genetic relatedness of giver and receiver

In conversational terms, Inequality 7.1 amounts to the statement that an individual should act altruistically toward another (or others) if the ratio of recipient benefit to donor cost exceeds the reciprocal of the genetic relatedness between them. For example, brothers, whose degree of genetic relatedness is one-half, should act altruistically to each other when the benefit the recipient brother will derive is greater than twice the cost the donor brother must incur. This means that in groups of related individuals, altruistic behavior and cooperation might be more common than one would anticipate from the prisoner's dilemma, where the interests of the players are independent and altruism is "rational" only when the private benefits exceed costs.

Tit-for-Tat Strategists

A somewhat different approach to the prisoner's dilemma than the one presented earlier suggests that under some circumstances cooperation may be evolutionarily favored. In these cases, the game is repeatedly played between the same pair of individuals, who may follow different courses of action (i.e., cooperation or greed) at each turn. Under these conditions, one possible strategy is what as been called "tit-for-tat": The player cooperates (acts altruistically) in the first interaction and subsequently mimics the behavior of his opponent in the previous interaction; if the opponent cooperated, he cooperates; if the opponent acted noncooperatively, he follows suit. In this way, tit-for-tat strategists can take advantage of the potential for cooperation with other tit-for-tat strategists while protecting themselves against exploitation by individuals who refuse to cooperate (often termed *defectors*).

Studies of this situation suggest that when pairs are formed from unrelated individuals, cooperation is likely to persist only if the frequency of altruists and tit-for-tat strategists is large initially or if the interactions between pairs continue for a reasonable length of time. When most individuals are noncooperators and the interactions between pairs are brief, the altruists are eliminated and the tit-for-tat strategists quickly revert to a pattern of noncooperation. The same analyses show, however, that when there is a small degree of assortative (i.e., nonrandom) pairing between individuals (as might characterize groups formed on the basis of genetic relationship) and the number of interactions between such pairs is large (thus increasing the potential benefits to be gained), cooperation and reciprocity are evolutionarily stable and that tit-for-tat strategists can invade populations dominated by defectors (i.e., noncooperating individuals; cf. Axelrod and Hamilton 1981; Axelrod 1984; cf. Boyd and Richerson 1988).

Because hunter-gatherer groups are often small and composed of close relatives that frequently interact on a regular basis, it is possible to argue that the cooperative behavior these groups commonly display (e.g., in sharing) can be explained as resulting from the same kind of evolutionary process that favors the persistence of cooperation between pairs of tit-for-tat strategists. However, as Boyd and Richerson (1988) have shown, the potential for cooperation between groups (as opposed to pairs) of individuals is highly sensitive to the size of the group and the number of times it interacts. By analogy with the two-player case, when working in groups, the intolerant tit-for-tat strategists always cooperate in the first interaction but subsequently cooperate if and only if all the other members of their group cooperated in the previous interaction. Under these conditions, if groups are randomly formed of unrelated individuals, cooperation cannot persist unless it is relatively common to begin with *and* the expected number of interactions between the group is relatively large *and* the size of the group is quite small. In general, Boyd and Richerson's results suggest that the conditions needed to favor cooperation among tit-for-tat strategists are unlikely to be realized in groups consisting of more than about eight individuals. They further show that genetic relatedness between the individuals that form groups produces only a moderate increase in the size of groups within which cooperation is favored.

In sum, although cooperative behavior is likely to evolve between pairs and small groups of tit-for-tat strategists, as group size increases, the prisoner's dilemma reemerges: The conflict between group- and self-interest discourages altruism and rewards defection. It is possible, thus, to produce an evolutionary explanation for the cooperation between small groups of closely related hunter-gatherers that regularly interact but not for the cooperation that is often observed between larger, less-regularly interacting aggregations composed of unrelated or distantly related individuals (e.g., war parties, communal fishing groups).

By now, the point should be clear: The aggregate consequences of individual self-interest make it exceedingly difficult to study human behavior from the perspective of economic optimizing in cases where the behaviors of the actors interact because so much of this activity is cast in groups in which group benefits are generally at odds with individual interest. For groups, at least this generally means that behaviors may appear to be suboptimal. As suggested for Inuit hunting parties, one suspects that rather than any inherent adaptive circumstance that rewards flexibility (cf. Lee and DeVore 1968:9; Binford 1983b:220; Turnbull 1968), it is the tension between group and individual interest that accounts for the endless fissioning and fusing that characterizes the sociopolitical organization of many hunter-gatherer groups (cf. Woodburn 1968:155).

TESTING THE MODELS
OF EVOLUTIONARY ECOLOGY

Despite its parsimony and intuitive appeal, evolutionary ecology—sometimes termed *sociobiology*—has proved difficult to test directly in the human case. In large part the problem lies in establishing a linkage between particular kinds of behavior and genetic fitness. We have already commented on the difficulty of evaluating human behavior, which is so often cast by groups, in terms of optimal self-interest. The whole basis for optimal foraging analysis in contemporary hunter-gatherer research, further, rests on the assumption that to forage optimally promotes genetic fitness. It is not at all clear that this is so, however—at least it is not clear in what way it is so. If optimal foraging theorists really mean to claim only that if everything else were equal, that an economically rational forager will be more genetically fit than one who is not, that is more tautology than revelation—how could it be otherwise? The question, in any event, is whether things are ever equal or, more to the point, how we would know they were.

Put another way, the optimal foraging theorists claim that, all other things being equal, more efficient strategies will be favored over those less efficient and imply that this claim is relevant to the analysis of individual cases (O'Connell, Jones, and Simms 1982:233). However, they are really claiming more than that. The hypothesis is that, in the overall scheme of things, foraging efficiency is *the* strong force: It is so important that, by comparison, all other things can be thought of as though they *are*, in fact, equal in any given case one might want to examine. They assert that all things other than efficiency are essentially random and hence mutually offsetting (i.e., on average neutral) in effect; these other things are, in short, simply noise. This hypothesis may be true, but as Orans (1975) notes, to make good on it in any individual case requires that "all other things" (i.e., all other relevant factors) be specified and weighed in terms of their effects to see whether, in fact, they sum to zero. It is because such individual enumeration, weighing, and summing is patently impossible that Orans recommends a cross-cultural approach, in which (presuming no other biases) as the number of cases increases the assumption of *ceteris paribus* become more reasonable.

Presumably the position taken by optimal foraging theorists is only a provisional one—an extreme view taken to sharpen the lines of discussion and establish benchmarks against which field data can be compared. All the same, it is subject to precisely the same criticism optimal foraging theorists have sometimes leveled against normative culture historians who explain assemblage variability in terms of ethnicity or culture groups:

> Attributing variation in material culture to "preference" or "cultural identi-
> ty" tells us nothing; it simply eliminates the question by definition. (O'Con-
> nell, Jones, and Simms 1982:228)

The same point scores just as easily against optimal foraging theory. Thus:

> Attributing variation in material culture to "optimality," "efficiency," or
> "rationality" tells us nothing, it simply eliminates the question by definition.

To paraphrase early critics of microeconomic versions of political economy, optimal foraging theory is either universally true, and therefore trivial, or
it is not universally true—and then merely false (cf. Burrow 1966:69). That is, if
one agreed that all behaviors were indeed economically rational, the interesting
questions would immediately cease to involve economic optimality at all and
would then shift to consider explanations of the conditions that cause optimality to take different forms: environmental variability, technology, population, and the like (cf. Rosenberg 1980:66). Without supporting arguments,
attributions of variation to either cultural preference or economic optimality
both suffer the same flaw: They are either trivial or false.

The only case in which this indictment of explanations made on the basis
of cultural preference would be more persuasive than the structurally identical
indictment of optimal foraging theory would be that in which the principles of
cultural preferences were left unspecified or specified in less detail than those of
optimality; but that is not—at least need not be—the case. Those who discount
categorically models of cultural preference and identity proposed by archaeologists (e.g., Ford 1954; Clarke 1968) and anthropologists (Douglas 1962), which
are admittedly simple, should note that microeconomists have steadfastly held
that the the principles of rational choice and optimality are as legitimately
applied to cultural preferences, that is, in taste and esthetics, as to problems that
have to do with the material provisioning of society (e.g., subsistence). In short,
the nature of their construction *per se* offers no basis for preferring models of
economic optimality to models of cultural preference. Put another way, if
humans act rationally in the pursuit of symbolic goods dictated by cultural
preference, in what way can it be argued that the rational pursuit of subsistence
goods is necessarily more interesting or important?

For optimal foraging theorists, then, the criticism of explanations that deal
with cultural preference is more than a mere criticism of models and explanatory
elegance—it amounts to an evaluation of the relative importance of different
kinds of behavioral data. It is a claim, in effect, that behavioral variability with
regard to cultural preferences, ethnicity, and style is unimportant, that behavioral variability with regard to economic efficiency is all that is important. This
is not an issue of verifiability or testability at all. For many archaeological and

ethnographic situations, it is as easy to predict assemblage composition on the basis of style as on the basis of economy or function.

I have often heard models of cultural preference dismissed in the spirit of early cultural materialism (cf. Harris 1968a:574-575, 580-582, 601-604; 1968b:360-361) with the claim that, "It doesn't matter what they think, it only matters what they do." Such notions are foolish. Presumably the claim here is more than simply that individuals are often confused about and unable to understand clearly their own motivations and the consequences of their behavior. As every undergraduate in anthropology knows, Durkheim, Freud, and Lévi-Strauss made this observation long ago without concluding that because they did not mirror perfectly behavior and consequences at every (or any particular) level externally observable, individual motive and perception were of no consequence. But the evolutionary ecological contention often seems to be just that: Conscious motives—the construction of choices—are unimportant. This is a little like arguing that one should not be interested in the physical composition and construction of the human hand but only in what it does. The problem, plainly, is that if we take this approach we shall never be sure whether it is the construction of the hand or the situation in which it is used, or a combination of the two, that dictates what we see when the hand is in use.

Evolutionary ecologists may find it useful momentarily to ignore cultural preference in order to disentangle the complexities of human behavior. But what is a useful heuristic device should not be allowed to harden into dogma that dismisses the importance of much interesting cultural behavior as essentially "phenotypical," which implies that it is not subject to evolutionary analysis. Likewise, optimal foraging theorists may find it useful to assume as a working hypothesis that the groups they study are doing things rationally and that subsistence behavior determines their existence. Yet this, too, can harden into dogma that causes counterinstances to be explained away or simply ignored. In this sense, many evolutionary ecologists can be seen as falling into the traditional trap of assuming that hunter-gatherers are "adapted"—which makes it all the harder to incorporate hunter-gatherers into a larger theory in which evolutionary change is as important as stability and equilibrium.

In the last analysis, it seems highly unlikely that human perception and motivation, and by extension, cultural preferences, are not somehow intimately linked to behavior, though not necessarily in any simple or direct way. The conviction that this is so is, in fact, what separates other disciplines from anthropology, which arose in the nineteenth century when European observers of more primitive Asian and African societies concluded that it would no longer due simply to dismiss native customs practices as merely irrational or disgusting. As Burrow (1966:76) puts it: "Irrational and disgusting they might be but men were prepared to murder and die for them and seemed to become quite literally demoralized when deprived of them."

Those who are convinced that these distinctly cultural phenomena are wholly unimportant are by any objective measure in the wrong business: It would be easier and far more profitable to work with another species on which any number of experiments can be performed and where there is no need to consider and circumvent by deference and respect alternative systems of thought and custom. In short, where the data are not, as Harris (1968b:361) puts it, "emically contaminated." Surely the study of economic optimality would be simpler without the "epiphenomenon" of culture—without having to work around quaint native misunderstandings of the world as it actually is. An alternative view of cultural preference is presented in Chapter 8, which explores models that explain symbolic variation and cultural preference in Darwinian terms without assuming that such behaviors contribute to genetic fitness directly.

Solution of the Problem through Analysis of Opportunity Costs

Winterhalder (1983) offers one possible escape from the impasse we have reached between models of economic rationality, on the one hand, and models of cultural preference, on the other. He does so by means of a model in which it is possible to weight the value of subsistence efficiency relative to other, potentially competing, objectives through a microeconomic analysis of the opportunity costs couched in terms of fitness-enhancing behaviors. The concept of *opportunity cost* applies to situations in which resources are scarce relative to demands for alternative commodities so that spending resources to obtain one necessarily reduces the resources that can be spent to obtain others. In these terms, the *opportunity cost* of a commodity is the value of the amount of some alternative commodity that could have been obtained given the same expenditure of resources. Models of opportunity cost follow a format unfamiliar to many, but the concepts are useful, and it seems worthwhile to explain how the model works to make Winterhalder's argument clear.

Winterhalder divides fitness into foraging and nonforaging components, (that is, into the fitness contribution of foraging and the fitness contribution of nonforaging behaviors, for example, childrearing) and asks how time and energy might best be allocated between these two components to maximize overall fitness. Following conventional microeconomic modeling of opportunity cost, the relative values of the two limiting commodities (time and energy) are established by means of indifference curves (Figure 7.1). These plot the various possible combinations of these two commodities for which the utility is the same. Because in this kind of analysis, utility is the only basis for a rational decision, any of the points along such a curve are equally rational choices, which is to say the consumer is indifferent to (i.e., he has no rational basis for preferring) any one over any other; hence the term *indifference curve*.

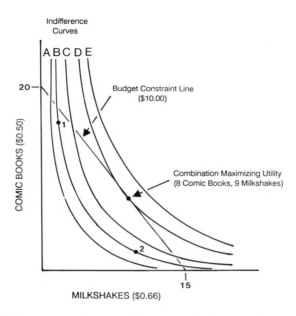

Figure 7.1. Indifference curves relating the relative utility of two different resources: milkshakes (X axis) and comic books (Y axis). Each indifference curve (A-E) plots combinations of the two resources that are equal with respect to utility. Note that the relative value of the two resources depends on their abundance. On utility curve "B," when the consumer has 16 comic books and 2 milkshakes (1), he would give 6 comic books to get 1 milkshake. When the same consumer has 9 milkshakes and 2 comic books (2), he would give only one-half a comic book to get 1 milkshake. Given the fixed prices for milkshakes ($0.66) and comic books ($0.50), and a budget of $10.00, the consumer with these indifference curves attains highest utility by purchasing 8 comic books and 9 milkshakes (curve D).

The distinctive concave or J-shaped contour of indifference curves establishes that the ratio of the utility of a unit of one of the items to the utility of a unit of the other (its opportunity cost) varies according to the proportion of each in the specific combination being considered. Where one item is rare relative to the other, its value per unit is great relative to the other, and vice versa. In other words, when an item is scarce its opportunity cost (how much of the other commodity one would give up to get another unit of it) is high. Irrespective of the height of the curve, its overall slope reflects the relative value of the two commodities to the consumer — steep curves indicate the commodity on the Y axis is relatively less valued, shallow curves that it is relatively more valued.

An example may help to clarify what is meant here. Take the hypothetical indifference curve plotted in Figure 7.1. For the utility curve B, the consumer assigns one milkshake a marginal value of six comic books (i.e., would give six comic books to get one milkshake) when he has 16 comic books and 2 milkshakes; yet the very same consumer assigns the same milkshake a marginal value of only one-half comic book (i.e., would give only one-half comic book to get one milkshake) when he has 9 milkshakes and two comic books. A series of nested indifference curves (A–E in Figure 7.1) plot these shifting ratios of value for an individual consumer, the higher the curve (the farther from the origin), the more of both kinds of items there are, and the greater the overall utility.[2] Now suppose we assume the consumer has $10.00 to spend and wishes to secure the combination of items that will yield the highest utility that can be obtained for this amount. This is a budgetary constraint and can be represented by a straight line connecting various combinations of the two items that total $10.00 assuming a fixed price for each, say $0.66 for a milkshake and $0.50 for a comic book. We now have enough information for the consumer to make a constrained rational choice. The utility curve to which the budget line is tangent, (D in Figure 7.1) indicates the maximum level of utility available to the consumer given his budgetary constraint of $10.00 and the intersection shows the mix of comic books (8) and milk shakes (9) that will assure this level of utility.

In the model of Winterhalder (Figure 7.2), utility is taken to mean fitness resulting from various combinations of time (X axis) and energy (Y axis) expended in nonforaging activities, which is assumed to equal the net amount of energy acquired in foraging activities (i.e., the amount beyond the minimal needs to keep the forager alive). The "budget line" in this case is the net rate of energy acquisition in foraging activities. It is assumed that total time available is expended either in foraging or nonforaging activities is finite. From this it follows that if the rate of energy acquisition is known, for any amount of time expended in nonforaging activities, the corresponding amount of time expended in foraging is also known, as is the total amount of energy available for expenditure in nonforaging activities (this being assumed to be equal to the net amount of energy acquired in foraging). Winterhalder adds two further constraints, these being minimal and maximal rates of energy expenditure in nonforaging activities, within which the solution must fall.

Where the shape of nonforaging fitness curves is known, the solution to the problem is indicated by the highest fitness curve tangent to the foraging budget line. Their intersection indicates the amount of time and energy that should be expended in nonforaging activity and the maximal fitness obtainable from that expenditure. Not surprisingly, depending of the shape of the fitness curves, as the net rate of energy acquisition increases, time and energy expenditure in nonforaging activities increases at various rates, as does fitness resulting from these activities.

Winterhalder's model advances the case for optimal foraging research by embedding it in the broader context of genetic fitness where activities other than

---

[2]The shape of indifference curves is determined by the relative valuation of the items they relate. Specifically, indifference curves tend to be oriented perpendicular to the axis that represents the more highly valued resource.

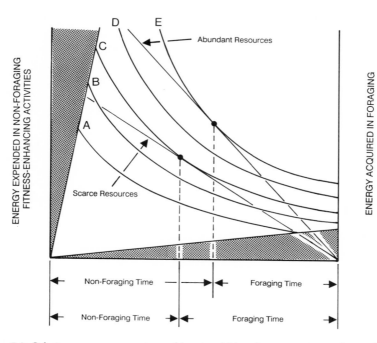

Figure 7.2. Solution to an opportunity problem in which a forager maximizes fitness through optimal allocation of time to foraging and nonforaging activities. Increasing foraging time results in acquisition of energy that may be expended in nonforaging fitness-related activities but decreases time for the same non-foraging activities. Indifference curves (A-E) graph combinations of nonforaging time and nonforaging energy expenditure that are equal with respect to fitness enhancement. The fact that their orientation is more nearly parallel to the X axis than the Y axis indicates this forager is energy limited (time is more abundant than energy). The near-vertical shaded area marks unacceptably high rates of nonfitness energy expenditure, the near-horizontal area unacceptably low rates of nonfitness energy expenditure. The two lines originating in the lower right are budget lines indicating rates of energy acquisition under different environmental conditions (scarcity and abundance). The utility curve tangent to these acquisition-rate lines determines the division between foraging and nonforaging time that maximizes fitness. Increasing resource abundance results in less time spent foraging and more energy spent in nonforaging. For time-limited foragers, the change will be relatively more pronounced for time (greater investment of time in nonforaging activities) than energy. For an energy-limited forager, the reverse will be true.

foraging make important contributions to fitness. Unfortunately, the model itself is a long way from operationalization. That is so because in the human case it is exceedingly difficult to ascertain the shape of the nonforaging fitness curves. Even where this is possible the meaning of the solution may be highly ambiguous because the solution identifies nonforaging activities only by their aggregate rate of energy expenditure, which is not very specific.

This solution is further complicated because it is often uncertain where foraging activity ends and nonforaging activity begins. That a forager might expend nonforaging time and energy by foraging for highly valued prey or by following tactics that bring high-prestige hints at some of the complexities involved here (see later discussion). Perhaps the most important lesson here is that even in the context of models of fitness there is no reason to expect *a priori* that subsistence behavior will conform to expectations derived from simple economic rationality. Any comprehensive model of fitness demands that optimal foraging theorists be as willing to entertain the possibility, indeed, should be ready to expect, that the behaviors they observe are economically irrational as they now seem predisposed to believe that these behaviors must somehow be rational. The next study illustrates the point nicely.

Aché Food Sharing and Inclusive Fitness

The operationalization of sociobiological theory has proven so difficult that a reasonably thorough review of the literature reveals only one example in which its central neo-Darwinian hypothesis of kin selection has been carefully put to empirical test against other kinds of explanation in the hunter-gatherer case (but see Borgerhoff-Mulder 1988). That study, by Kaplan and Hill (1985), deals with the explanations of food sharing, specifically, patterns of food sharing among the Aché, hunter-gatherers of eastern Paraguay. The problem to be explained was why Aché hunters, particularly good hunters, are so willing to share the game they take. The work is particularly commendable for the care and detail with which the investigators develop and consider explicit hypotheses derived out of various rival theories that have been advanced to account for the general phenomenon of food sharing: inclusive (genetic) fitness, conservation, cooperative acquisition, tolerated theft, and tit-for-tat reciprocity.

Hypotheses arising from the theory of inclusive fitness in general suggested sharing ought to be preferentially directed toward close kin. The conservation hypotheses, derived from the cultural materialist theories of Harris, are groupselection explanations in which food sharing discourages efficient hunters from overexploiting scarce resources. The cooperation hypotheses predicted the preferential sharing of food among members of groups that jointly participated in the acquisition of certain resources and the preferential sharing of these jointly acquired resources. The tolerated theft hypotheses all assume that Aché food sharing is actually a form of seizure that is likely to occur when the worth of the food being contested is less (counting defense costs) to the "donor" than to the "recipient" (counting seizure costs; a similar model of territoriality has been developed by Dyson-Hudson and Smith 1978). The tit-for-tat hypotheses derive from models of reciprocality developed by Trivers (1971) and Axelrod and Hamilton (1981), among others, and follow the logic to the model of the prisoner's dilemma developed earlier: The benefit to individual participants must be greater than their costs, either directly through the exchange or indirectly through some sort of punishment system.

Despite the care with which Kaplan and Hill develop these hypotheses, the results were highly equivocal and problematic in meaning (Kaplan and Hill 1985:229-230). Because the question here is one of empirical accessibility (testability), it is particularly noteworthy that the investigators were able to derive but one testable hypothesis for the inclusive fitness theory, fewer than for any of the other rival hypotheses (Table 7.2; cf. Kaplan and Hill 1985:235, Table 10). More important for our purposes, that one testable inclusive fitness hypothesis (which held that hunters should share more with relatives than nonrelatives) was rejected.

As a consequence, Kaplan and Hill were ultimately forced to conjecture alternative links between food sharing and their preferred hypothesis of kin selection *ex post facto* (Kaplan and Hill 1985:235, 237). They suggest that successful hunters willing to share their daily catch might reproduce more frequently because women and unsuccessful hunters (who are willing to share their wives) want to keep them satisfied in order to assure a steady supply of meat. Support for this idea is found in the tendency of the best Aché hunters to hunt longer and more frequently than poor hunters. By this point, however, what started out as a simple argument connecting economic rationality with somatic fitness in groups of close relatives has switched into a much more complicated and precarious explanation via sexual selection. Kaplan and Hill display this same tendency to switch between explanatory frameworks in other places, for example, with regard to the extent to which Aché behavior is learned (cf. sharing [p. 236]) or inherited (cf. hunting skill [p. 237]). However strong, the temptation to develop explanatory hypotheses *ex post facto* and to switch between alternative explanatory frameworks to obtain better fits between theory and fact should be resisted. Evolutionary arguments are complex enough when only a single explanatory framework is used; switching between two or more kinds of explanation makes the situation hopelessly convoluted and defeats the purpose (i.e., prediction/explanation) for which evolutionary ecology was introduced to anthropology in the first place (see Ollason 1980 and Gould and Lewontin 1979 for criticisms of such postexperimental explanations).

The Winterhalder indifference model can be used to formalize the logic contained in Kaplan and Hill's sexual selection hypothesis of Aché hunting. It

Table 7.2. Results of Test Predictions Derived from Various Models to Explain Aché Food Sharing[a]

	Untested	Supported	Unsupported	Total
Kin selection	1		1	2
Conservation			2	2
Cooperative acquisition			2	2
Tolerated theft		1	2	3
Tit-for-tat reciprocity	1	2	1	4

[a]After Kaplan and Hill 1985.

would suggest good Aché hunters invest more time and expend more energy in foraging because it is actually a nonforaging activity, that is, it's goal is prestige. If this is so, however, it renders much more complicated any attempt to demonstrate that Aché hunters are foraging optimally from a strictly microeconomic (i.e. subsistence) point of view (cf. Hawkes, Hill, and O'Connell 1982). There are many possibilities to be considered in the sexual selection case. For instance, Aché men might be signaling the quality of their genes, attracting females by displaying forms of hunting prowess unrelated to ordinary fitness. If sexually selected fitness is involved at all, it would be surprising indeed if the best Aché hunters were *not* sometimes — perhaps frequently — hunting under nonoptimal conditions and for nonoptimal (high-status) prey.

The case of Aché hunting, sharing, and reproductive success has recent grown even more complicated as a consequence of new data and further analysis of the original material (Hill *et al.* 1987). What is particularly noteworthy is that it would now appear that, as suspected before, given the foraging opportunities potentially available to them, Aché men seem to be acting suboptimally. When hunting, they obtain a return of about 1,340 calories per hour on average. However, by choosing to gather palm fiber they could obtain nearly twice that quantity — 2,630 calories to be exact (Hill *et al.* 1987:11). Two explanations are advanced to account for this.

First, it is argued that meat might be nutritionally more important than its caloric content would suggest (Hill *et al.* 1987:11). Thus, if meat calories were more than twice as important as vegetal calories it would explain why Aché men choose to hunt rather than gather palm fiber. If that is true, however, it would leave unexplained the basis for Aché subsistence practices as first documented (Hawkes, Hill, and O'Connell 1982). In that study, the handling time for the lowest ranked resource consistently exploited (palm fruit) was approximately the same as the overall rate of energetic intake of the Aché diet (i.e., considering both handling and search time; see Chapter 4). Specifically, the overall rate of caloric intake was 870 calories per hour, the handling rate for palm fruit 946 calories per hour. Now, if meat calories are given added value by doubling the amount of calories they contain, it would raise the overall rate of Aché energetic intake more than enough to cause the lower ranked plant resources, certainly palm fruit at least, to be deleted from the diet.

The alternative explanation of this phenomenon (Hill *et al.* 1987:12) reintroduces the notion that sexual selection might explain the anomalous behavior of Aché males. In simple terms, here it is argued that if, through sexual access, Aché females each day rewarded the male bringing home the most food, it might encourage them to undertake the risky strategy of hunting on the chance they might, through hunting luck or skill, succeed in producing the most food. The logic here is that although palm fiber produces higher mean returns, it never produces returns much greater than that, that is, it produces steady returns close to mean. Hunting produces lower means but is highly variable from day to day, thus creating the possibility of a very large return on a given day. Following this reasoning, men engaged in palm fiber procurement would consistently bring home more than the average hunter but less than the best hunter and thus never receive any of the reproductive benefits Aché women confer on the most productive male. However intuitively attractive, this hypothesis can easily be shown to be wrong through a series of simple models.

Modeling Reproductive Payoffs for Aché-Like Situations

We can capture the essence of an Aché-like situation with a model in which there are eight males: seven hunters and one gatherer (as will be seen, the exact size of the group is incidental to the point being made). These eight individuals compete daily for the reproductive favors of all females, a fixed quantity equal to 1.00, which is divided among the males according to the amount of food they bring home. To keep things simple and still mimic the Aché situation, it is assumed that hunting and gathering produce payoffs of fixed size, which for gathering is half that of hunting, that is, a successful hunter has twice as much to spread around in exchange for reproductive favors as a gatherer, whose probability of success we will assume to be equal to 1.00. Now if, in accordance with the Aché data, we set the mean return for hunters at half that of gatherers and, for simplicity's sake, the mean return for gatherers at 1.0, it follows that the package size is 1.00 for gatherers and, thus, 2.00 for hunters. It follows, further, that for a hunter the probability of success must be $p = .25$ (i.e., mean daily intake divided by unit of intake, or $.50/2.00 = .25$).

Given these conditions, the question is whether the short-run successes of the seven hunters in combination prevent the one male gatherer sexual access to females in sufficient degree to cause him to stop gathering and start hunting. Presented in Tables 7.3 and 7.4 are the reproductive payoffs associated with hunting and gathering under the assumption that reproductive opportunities are directly related to quantities of calories obtained. Table 7.3 indicates the reproductive payoffs each hunter receives on the days he is successful in bringing home game. Note that on those days he must split the payoff in sexual access with the one male gatherer (who is always successful) and any other hunters who are also successful, whose contingent probabilities of success are determined by binomial expansion (i.e., where $n = 6$, probability of success $[p] = .25$, and probability of failure $[q] = 1 - p = .75$). On days when there is only successful hunter, he receives two-thirds of the potential reproductive payoff, whereas the gatherer receives only one-third. Table 7.4 indicates the payoffs for the gatherer, who brings home food steadily in small packages and must split his reproductive payoff for this with any successful hunters (whose packages are twice as large), whose contingent probabilities of success are again determined by binomial

Table 7.3. Hypothetical Payoff Schedule for Hunters in Aché-Like Situations

	Probability n other hunters are successful	Group intake for day		Hunter's payoffs	
n	Probability	Hunted	Gathered	For day	Long term[a]
0	$q^6 = .178$	2	1	.666	.118
1	$6q^5p = .356$	4	1	.400	.142
2	$15q^4p^2 = .297$	6	1	.268	.085
3	$20q^3p^3 = .132$	8	1	.222	.029
4	$15q^2p^4 = .033$	10	1	.182	.006
5	$6qp^5 = .004$	12	1	.154	.001
6	$p^6 = .0002$	14	1	.133	—

Total expected payoff on successful days = .381
× Frequency of successful days .25
Total expected payoff = .095

[a]Probability of event × payoff for day.

Table 7.4. Hypothetical Payoff Schedule for Gatherers in Aché-Like Situations

	Probability n hunters are successful	Group intake for day		Gatherer's payoffs	
n	Probability	Hunted	Gathered	For day	Long term[a]
0	$q^7 = .134$	0	1	1.000	.134
1	$7q^6p = .312$	2	1	.333	.104
2	$21q^5p^2 = .312$	4	1	.200	.062
3	$35q^4p^3 = .173$	6	1	.143	.025
4	$35q^3p^4 = .058$	8	1	.111	.006
5	$21q^2p^5 = .012$	10	1	.091	.001
6	$7qp^6 = .001$	12	1	.080	—
7	$p^7 = .0001$	14	1	.070	—

Total expected payoff = .332

[a]Probability of event × payoff for day.

expansion (i.e., where $n = 7$, $p = .25$, and $q = 1 - p = .75$). For example, on days when two hunters are successful, the gatherer receives a payoff equal to only .20 $(= 1/[2 + 2 + 1])$.

It is clear from Tables 7.3 and 7.4 that Hill *et al.*'s intuition that Aché hunters might be enticed by reproductive favors to undertake risky strategies is unlikely to be correct—at least if we assume that reproductive favors of females are exchanged straight across for calories and there are many more hunters than gatherers. In this model, the lone Aché gatherer reaps more than three times the reproductive benefits the Aché hunter can expect to receive. Analysis of the situation in which there are many more gatherers than hunters produces much the same result. For example, if there are seven gatherers and one hunter, the probability that game is taken on a given day is .25 and on that day the hunter receives a payoff equivalent to two-ninths and each gatherer a payoff equivalent to one-ninth. The other 75% of the time, the hunter receives no payoff, while each gatherer receives a payoff of one-seventh. The lone hunter then has an expected payoff of .056 per day (= .25 × 2/9) and each gather an expected payoff of .135 per day (= [.75 × 1/7] + [.25 × 1/9]).

In the terms of evolutionary game theory (Maynard Smith 1982; Maynard Smith and Price 1973), in this model gathering is an evolutionary stable strategy (ESS) but hunting is not. Gatherers obtain more calories and hence receive higher sexual payoffs than hunters whether gathering is common or rare; the hunters can't win.

The payoff schedule would change, of course, if we assumed different rules. Suppose, for instance, Aché women do not allocate reproductive rewards directly in proportion to the amount of food contributed by individual males but rather only to the single male who contributes the largest quantity on a given day, daily ties between males being settled by the Aché equivalent of a coin toss. Now because gathered products come in size 1 and hunted products in size 2, any day any hunter is successful, no gatherer receives any reward. In a group of one hunter and seven gatherers it is now better to be the hunter than one of the gatherers: The hunter receives a payoff of .25 and each gatherer a payoff of .11 (= .75/7). This advantage varies depending on the number of hunters. For instance, if there are seven hunters and one gatherer, the gatherer's expected payoff is equal to .134, which is simply the probability that all seven hunters will be unsuccessful (i.e., $.75^7 = .134$), and each hunter's payoff is simply one-seventh of what is left over (i.e., [1 - .134]/7 = .124). This logic can be generalized to determine the payoffs to hunters and gatherers in any one winner game

$$\text{Hunter's payoff} = (1 - q^h)/h$$
$$\text{Gatherer's payoff} = (q^h)/n-h \tag{7.2}$$

where

n is the number of mates in the group
h is the number of hunters
$n - h$ is the number of gatherers
q is the probability that a hunter fails to bring home game on a given day

By like reasoning, the inequality expressing the attractions of being a hunter relative to a gatherer in the one winner game is

$$(n - h) / n > q^h \tag{7.3}$$

Inequality 7.3 says that if the fraction of gatherers is greater than the probability no hunter will be successful, hunting is favored; conversely, if the fraction of hunters is greater than the probability at least one hunter will be successful, gathering is favored. In small groups of occupational specialists, gathering is never favored and cannot occur whenever $1/n > q^{n-1}$; that is, specialized hunting is a small-group ESS when the probability all hunters will be unsuccessful is less than the smallest possible fraction of gatherers. Likewise, hunting is never favored and cannot occur whenever $1/n > 1 - q$; specialized gathering is a small-group ESS when the probability a hunter will be successful is less than the smallest possible fraction of hunters. Between these extremes both hunting and gathering should be present in small groups of specialists.

Clearly, however, the one winner rule penalizes gathering as groups grow large. Assuming very large groups, in this model hunting is usually an ESS because when hunting is common a gatherer receives no payoff at all (or next to none) unless the individual probability of hunter success is quite low. Gathering, however, is never an ESS provided the probability of hunter success is non-negligible (which is to say, not infinitely small) because in very large groups of gatherers the hunter's payoff is larger than the gatherer's payoff, which becomes infinitely small.

This analysis seems to imply that "only one winner" reward rules might be workable in small, finite-sized groups because the uncertainty of obtaining large prey would cause those bringing in smaller, more reliable prey to be rewarded and thus keep the mean productivity of the group relatively high. If the relative value of different kinds of resources were difficult to calculate (if resources could only be ranked ordinally, for example), such a rule might be favored over one allocating rewards strictly according to productivity even though such a rule (i.e., strictly by productivity) would result in higher group yields. On the other hand, the one winner rule should be quite rare in large groups because it encourages individuals to undertake risky strategies with increasing frequency and would thus substantially depress the overall mean return. The expected combinations of hunters and gatherers associated with various group sizes and degrees of hunter risk under the "one winner" rule are displayed graphically in Figure 7.3. With respect to the Aché case, this model suggests that even if Aché women choose daily to reward only the male bringing home the most food, at least some Aché males ought to opt to gather, which they do not seem to do.

In summary, it is clear that unless meat is much more nutritionally valuable than its caloric content would indicate (which creates problems of another sort), it is going to be very difficult to explain Aché male behavior in terms consistent with evolutionary ecological theory. In light of this, at least two alternative explanations ought to be considered. First, it may be that the Aché are not at a stable evolutionary equilibrium. This, of course, does not preclude the possibility of developing an evolutionary ecological account of their behav-

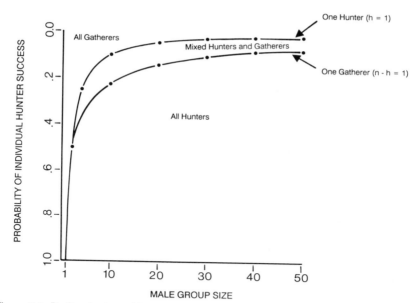

Figure 7.3. Predicted mixes of hunters and gatherers when successful hunters cause successful gatherers to go unrewarded. Group size is plotted on the X axis, probability of individual hunter success on the Y axis. The lower curve traces the conditions under which the group will have just one gatherer and the upper curve conditions in which there will be just one hunter. The proportion of hunters is more sensitive to probability of hunter success when group size is low than when it is high.

ior. To do so, however, would require much more powerful models (and perhaps more data) than those used previously where the problems to be solved were greatly simplified through the assumption of equilibrium.

Second, it may actually be that cultural preferences and prestige are guiding Aché male hunting behavior and Aché female sexual behavior. That, too, would not preclude the possibility of developing an evolutionary account of the Aché. Clearly, however, such an account would differ fundamentally from the kind offered by evolutionary ecologists, who assume that all sorts of human behaviors are susceptible to explanation with reference to inclusive genetic fitness (a prediction seemingly at odds with the Aché). A family of such alternative models is examined in Chapter 8. They differ from evolutionary ecology by assuming that such distinctively cultural phenomena as esthetics and symbolic behavior are subject to evolutionary processes and explanation and thus not to be dismissed simply as situational (i.e., phenotypical) variability. These models incorporate cultural preference and prestige within a larger evolutionary framework in which both genetic fitness and cultural fitness are important.

Discussion

Keeping in mind that sociobiological theories are more easily advanced than tested, empirical failures such as in the case of Aché food sharing loom particularly large, especially if it is recognized that almost all humans act Aché-like and almost all nonhumans act non-Aché-like. It is of some interest, therefore, that Hamilton (1986) himself has most recently found it useful to distinguish between animal altruism—for which he finds a clear explanation in kin selection—and human altruism—for which he sees no obvious explanation of similar kind. Ernst Mayr (1987) has expressed similar views. Coming as they do from two of the more perceptive, prestigious, and articulate theorists of evolutionary biology, these observations poses a serious challenge to the future of evolutionary ecology in anthropology.

THE GENETIC BASIS FOR EVOLUTIONARY ECOLOGICAL EXPLANATION

Entirely apart from the matter of verification, it is the implied linking of genes and behavior that has undoubtedly prevented broader acceptance of evolutionary ecological theory in anthropology. This reflects a very healthy traditional skepticism toward genetic explanations of behavior, which are inherently susceptible to distortion by racists. Even though, as noted, evolutionary ecological theory does not require one to assume a genetic basis for behavior, the matter remains a sticking point to many. This is unfortunate. Evolutionary ecologists differ among themselves on this point, of course. Yet even if, following Harris (1979), we discount the hard-core position of sociobiologists that much of human behavior is genetically based in specific terms or "hard-wired"—a view for which there is little empirical support—genes would still be important in at least two senses.

First, even assuming that all human populations are essentially similar where genes are concerned—that is, they have essentially the same ability to learn, the same drive to reproduce, and so forth—these innate drives and abilities must be genetically influenced and evolutionary in origin; accordingly, one would need to assume that their presence (which is clearly not adaptively neutral) must be maintained by selection, that is, the continued presence of these motives is owed to elimination by natural selection of individuals who lack them or fail to act upon them properly.

Harris (1979:136-137) objects to this more moderate view of sociobiology on logical grounds: If all human populations are genetically identical, then genes are superfluous to explanation. Leslie White (1949:144-145) earlier took much the same position, arguing that, for humans, biology is constant and thus not helpful in understanding cultural variability. It is White's view that seems to give rise to Binford's analogous rejection of optimality theory as simply another constant unhelpful in understanding how humans behave. Obviously, there is some sense to these notions. As an alternative to the genetic explanation, Harris (1979:62-64) postulates the existence of a finite set of biopsychological constants (exactly four) he sees as driving human behavior. It is clear, however, that these constants—his innate motives—must be genetic; they are surely not cultural, at least to Harris. And if genes underlie the motives Harris imparts to human behavior it would be unwise to dismiss them as superfluous. Even were selection no longer acting directly or indirectly on these innate motives, one would have to concede that the motives themselves were originally established by selective forces and, being absolutely central to human behavior, must have once acted and must therefore still be acting to promote genetic fitness. In the final analysis, if we leave genetics out of the equation, the cultural materialism of Harris becomes mere description: If people act the way they do as a consequence of innate drives, then explanations (as opposed to descriptions) of behavior would necessarily require consideration of the origins, bases, and effects of these drives.

Whatever Harris would like to believe, his position is essentially an incomplete version of soft-core sociobiology: The bulk of human behavior is (probably) not genetically determined but on balance human biopsychological predispositions result in genetic fitness and can be understood in much the same terms. In the final analysis, it is in this second sense that there is clear advantage in recognizing the genetic basis for all evolutionary ecological arguments. It produces some rather precise predictions regarding the kinds of behaviors in which we would expect humans to engage. Evolutionary ecologists can give a theoretical account of innate drives that Harris must take as givens. It is precisely with reference to such expectations that evolutionary ecology has been challenged by another neo-Darwinian theory of culture: dual inheritance theory.

Chapter 8

Hunter-Gatherers and Neo-Darwinian Cultural Transmission

Evolutionary human ecologists frequently observe that somatic (i.e., genetic) transmission need not be assumed for Darwinian processes to operate and then drive the point home with reference to the example of Darwin, who knew nothing about genes. The more interesting implications of such an evolutionary philosophy appear to have gotten lost somewhere in the shuffle, however; the same individuals seem equally prone to insist that neo-Darwinian theory must be applied via models in which cultural transmission and evolutionary fitness are treated as simple biological analogs, that is, as though they were genetic. This chapter goes back to evolutionary fundamentals and pursues the original and less-restrictive, agenetic approach to Darwinian processes by means of models of culture in which transmission and reproduction are, to use Leslie White's term, *extrasomatic*. As will become clear, this produces results at odds with traditional evolutionary ecological interpretation. This simple modification in the assumptions about the nature of the transmission/reproduction process leads to predictions about behavior that differ fundamentally from those that follow from the genetic model upon which classic evolutionary ecological analyses rest. In comparison to evolutionary ecology, however, this nonsomatic approach to transmission and reproduction in many ways better accounts for behaviors that distinguish humans from other organisms—behaviors that have from the start interested anthropologists and been the central subject matter of their theories. Among the more important of these are altruism and the tendency of humans to act cooperatively as groups rather than individuals and the value that humans assign to symbols and prestige.

A NEO-DARWINIAN MODEL
OF CULTURAL TRANSMISSION

Though not well known to most anthropologists, the theoretical contributions of Boyd and Richerson (1982, 1983, 1985) toward the formal analysis of the processes and consequences of cultural transmission are a revolutionary advance in the understanding of the principles of human behavior. The central premise of this research is that to understand culture one must understand it as a system of inheritance to which the fundamental prerequisites of evolution by selective processes apply (i.e., populations of variable individuals, a system of transmission of information) but in which the principles by which information is transmitted differ markedly from those that govern genes. In essence, the argument is no more complex than that if there are such things as ideas and if ideas affect behavior, then, owing to the differences in the manner in which genes and ideas are transmitted, it is unlikely that all cultural behaviors can be explained directly in terms of genetic fitness. The processes of cultural transmission are also an essential component of explanations of human behavior. That is, of course, what many anthropologists have said for years—culture has a logic of its own. The problem with most previous explanations of this sort is that they seldom explain why culture should have any logic at all. The standard structuralist response to this query, that the logic of culture is logic that has been hard wired into the human mind, begs the more basic question: Why should the human mind be hard wired one way and not another? The point is not at all trivial given that structuralism contains no account of how this hard wiring came to be, and structuralists as a group are evidently prepared to accept the idea that it lacks any evident selective advantage. The theory of cultural transmission, on the other hand, has formalized the process of transmission via a series of quantitative models that deserve our attention. To understand these, however, requires that some other principles of cultural transmission be understood. Except as noted, both the principles and models presented next follow Boyd and Richerson (1985).

PRINCIPLES OF CULTURAL TRANSMISSION

There are obvious similarities between cultural and genetic inheritance in the sense that nearly all the basic properties of genetic systems have at least rough analogs in culture: Human choice is selective and in some ways resembles natural selection, human invention roughly resembles mutation, change in style looks something like evolutionary drift, and when large bands fission, the resulting smaller bands may differ as the result of founder effects. These similarities are so broadly drawn, however, that any superficial attempt to analyze cultural transmission as a special case of genetic transmission is doomed from the start. At a minimum, to make any sense of cultural transmission requires that we recognize at least one fundamental property in which cultural and genetic transmissions differ: In humans, genetic information is imparted directly by two and only two individuals (mother and father); cultural information, on the other hand, may be transmitted by anywhere from one to some very large number of individuals. In this sense, cultural transmission may be said to be asymmetric to genetic transmission—the two are quite clearly not the same. Put another way, the routes through which genes pass are different from the routes though which ideas pass. In some cases (e.g., Hewlett and Cavalli-Sforza 1986) the routes may be very close (i.e., only slightly asymmetric) or even exactly the same (fully symmetric) but more commonly they diverge widely. For example, a young hunter-gatherer male receives, on average, half of his genes from his father and the rest from his mother. On the other hand, the ideas, values, and behavioral knowledge he gathers and uses in the course of daily life are nearly always drawn from a much larger pool of individuals that includes many unrelated individuals. In this sense, much of the "cultural" information upon which he acts is nonparental.

This is very important: It suggests that if culture is important in behavior, then some behaviors will not result in genetic fitness. This does not mean that cultural transmission will cause humans to be unfit. Quite the contrary, as will be shown later, cultural transmission frequently favors behaviors that are adaptively quite sound and is often more effective in establishing and reinforcing such behaviors than simple genetic transmission. This necessarily implies, however, that cultural transmission and genetic transmission differ with respect to consequences. Because this is so, behaviors subject to cultural transmission will not conform to expectations arising from the genetic model. Whether or not these culturally transmitted behaviors individually result in greater or lesser fitness is a separate question.

The implications of this seemingly obvious difference between genetic and cultural transmission is generally unappreciated by evolutionary ecologists. In this regard, consider Dunnell's (1980:63) syllogistic paraphrasing of the socio-biological reasoning for a biological/genetic basis for human behavior:

> If a given trait is heritable to a measurable degree (the mechanism of inheritance need not be known) and

> if it also affects the fitness of organisms possessing the trait to some measurable degree . . . , then

> the trait must be subject to natural selection and

> (the trait) will be fixed in populations in accord with the biological model.

If we include only its first three parts, the syllogism is correct. If we include the fourth, it is not. That part introduces an assertion regarding the "biological model" for which no basis is established in the initial assumptions. To be correct, the first part of the syllogism would have to be:

> If a given trait is heritable to a measurable degree (the mechanism of inheritance need not be known *save that it must be of a sort identical in effect, i.e., symmetrical, to genetic inheritance*).

And, of course, cultural inheritance is in general neither symmetrical, nor identical in effect, to genetic inheritance. Again for clarity, genetic and cultural transmission are symmetrical only where both follow the same pattern exactly, or nearly so. Parental instruction is a form of cultural transmission that is roughly symmetrical to genetic transmission because children receive all of their genes via their parents. Peer-group learning among children (or adults), however, is a form of cultural transmission that is clearly asymmetrical to genetic transmission. It should be noted that Dunnell (e.g., 1980:86) recognizes this distinction and, thus, the need for separate models of cultural transmission.

Recognizing the asymmetry between cultural and genetic transmission immediately requires that we further recognize an obstacle to the application of Darwinian models to cultural transmission: If individuals can acquire a culture trait (e.g., the length that they make their spears) from more than one cultural parent, and if in so doing they tend to approximate the mean of that trait among the set of individuals (cultural parents) from whom they acquire it, then it follows that cultural transmission would very quickly suppress cultural variability. This is the analog of the classical problem with blending inheritance in biology. Because there is no evidence that cultural transmission is particulate, it potentially arises again in cultural evolution. Variability, of course, is required for natural selection to act; without it the application of Darwinian processes and some loosely analogous cultural processes would be problematic. Expressed quantitatively, when cultural blending of this sort occurs, with each generation the mean of traits within the population remains unaffected, but cultural variance within a population is reduced by a factor proportional to the inverse of the effective number of cultural parents; the greater the number of effective cultural parents, the greater and more rapid the blending (Boyd and Richerson 1985:74). Formally, where randomly drawn parental individuals are equally weighted the effect on population variance is

$$V' = (1//n_e)V \tag{8.1}$$

where

V is the population variance for the trait in question in the population
   before transmission
V' is its population variance after transmission
n_e is the effective number of parents

As noted, the population mean is unaffected by this blending. Thus

$$\overline{X'} = \overline{X} \tag{8.2}$$

where

$\overline{X'}$ is the population mean of the trait after transmission
$\overline{X}$ is the trait mean before transmission

It is my impression that many anthropologists who reject the notion that
culture can differentially affect selective fitness, particularly those whose theory
is firmly grounded in models of economic rationality (e.g., Binford 1978a), do so
out of an intuitive understanding of this effect of cultural blending. Such a
process would quite quickly destroy culture differences between individuals
locally and, depending on rates of migration, from place to place, that is,
regionally. Culture would at this point cease to be selectively relevant, and
learning and rational responses to environmental variability would become the
most potent forces guiding human behavior. This is, I believe, what Harris
(1974b) and Binford (1978a:457) imply when they stress the importance of rules
for breaking cultural rules. In essence, their argument is that selection is more
likely to act on learned behaviors and rational choices than on culture. The
question is, then, whether cultural transmission always results in blending that
reduces cultural variance in given traits to negligible values.

At least four very plausible circumstances might offset the blending effect
and result in the preservation of cultural variation:

1. There might in some cases be only one cultural parent; in this case, the
variance after transmission would be exactly the same as before transmission
(assuming no other factors are involved).

2. If the population of potential parents were not randomly assorted, then
the parent models being selected and blended by one individual might be quite
similar to each other but quite different from the sets of parents selected and
blended by other individuals. Thus, while individuals might have a great many
cultural parents (which ought to increase the blending effect), the variability
within any such set might be quite low relative to the variance between different
groups of parents.

3. The individual being enculturated might err in his approximation of the mean of the trait being copied among his cultural parents. In this case, two individuals blending from the same set of cultural parents might end up with different values of a given trait. In short, random errors in the transmission process might preserve variability.

4. Because many behaviors are complex and consist of a series of component attributes, it is thinkable that an individual might mimic one cultural "parent" for one component of a complex behavior and another for a second component of the same behavior. It can be shown that an enculturative process of this sort would preserve cultural variability within a population (Boyd and Richerson 1985:79).

It is clear, then, that cultural transmission might preserve individual variability in selectively significant cultural behaviors. Unfortunately, it is equally clear that there are potent forces other than transmission that might act to reduce this individual variability. Depending on their strength these other forces might reduce the selective importance of culture. Two of these seem particularly important: (1) individual invention and learning, and (2) the ability to evaluate alternative cultural behaviors rationally. Either of these might cause individuals initially differing in behavior to converge toward a common optimal behavior. Boyd and Richerson (1985) formalize these twin processes, which they term, respectively, *guided variation* and *generalized direct bias*, by means of two quantitative models.

Guided Variation

Guided variation is a model of individual learning cast as a population-level phenomenon by coupling it with a model of inheritance. It assumes that individuals initially mimic the behavior of those around them and through subsequent learning and experiment adjust their behavior to conform to a behavior favored by the inherited rules that guide the learning process (e.g., pleasure, pain). If we assume the behavior is a quantitative trait (e.g., spear length or chimney height), this process can be modeled in terms of its effects on the mean and variance of the trait within the population with each succeeding generation (Boyd and Richerson 1985:97). Here, effect on the population mean is

$$\overline{X}' = a\overline{X} + (1 - a)H \tag{8.3}$$

where

$\overline{X}$ and $\overline{X}'$ are the population means for a particular behavior in a previous and subsequent generation, respectively

H is the behavior favored by the learning rule (which may or may not be
   optimal for the environment)
a is the relative weight of enculturation
1 − a is the relative weight (importance) of learning

The effect of individual learning on population variance of the trait is

$$V' = (1/n_e)(a^2V + (1 - a)^2V_e + \overline{E}) \qquad (8.4)$$

where

a is defined as before
V and V' are the population variances before and after learning, respectively
n_e is the effective number of parents
V_e is the variance in the rate of errors made attributable to individual
   mistakes in learning
$\overline{E}$ is the mean rate of errors attributable to transmission

In simple terms, Equations 8.3 and 8.4 say that with each generation the
cumulative result of individual learning is to move the mean of a population an
increment, 1 − a, from its initial mean, $\overline{X}$, toward a mean favored by the
learning rule, H. If this mean is optimal for the local environment, individuals
with that rule ought to be advantaged over those lacking it, which would allow
individuals with the proper learning rule to become established. Boyd and
Richerson (1985:95) suggest that in this case the size of this increment, which
measures the relative importance of culture (a) and learning (1 − a), is determined by the ratio of learning errors to the weight placed on learning itself, or

$$a = V_e/(V_e + L) \qquad (8.5)$$

where

L is the propensity of an individual to learn
V_e is again the population variance in the rate of errors made by
   individuals in learning

Note that when a = 1, behavior is entirely determined by culture, and
when a = 0, entirely by learning. Between these extremes both have some
influence. In other words, learning moves population behavior toward forms
favored by local environments in direct proportion to the inclination of

individuals to learn and in inverse proportion to the variance in the rate of the errors they make in learning.

To illustrate though a hypothetical example, one might imagine a case in which young hunter-gatherer females initially learn the art of basket making from their mothers. Since this is a complicated task requiring a lifetime to master, after a period of apprenticeship, the daughters might well be expected to develop on their own the finer points of working technique and the steps needed to adopt techniques to different situations, say when working with substandard materials. This would make sense in terms of our model of individual learning because the potential for learning error is greatest and most variable in the case of basic techniques where novices are involved: Basic techniques should be transmitted culturally to novices. Once these techniques are grasped, there is less potential for, and less variability in, subsequent learning error and positive benefits for individuals that learn to adapt their techniques to accommodate changing conditions.

Note that individual learning requires neither initial variability nor selection: Individuals move toward favored behaviors by learning, and the effectiveness of learning is independent of initial variability. This latter feature captures an intuitive assumption of many social scientists, including all of those advancing transformational interpretations of culture: Culture process and change is not selective – at least where individuals are concerned.

Direct Bias[1]

Though it bears superficial resemblance to guided variation, directly biased transmission differs fundamentally in being a selective process; in this context, selection refers to an inherent bias that predisposes individuals with the bias to adopt some and reject other behaviors to which they are exposed. In direct bias, such individuals make their evaluations on the basis of the behavior and its consequences directly. For instance, novice hunters might observe several methods of calling game, experiment with each, and on this basis select that which seems best. In contrast to guided variation, then, the utility of direct bias depends on exposure to a reasonable range of behavioral variability. To avoid unnecessary confusion here, we confine ourselves to a model for the distribution within a population of a behavioral trait that may take two states, c and d, and in which c is locally optimal and favored by a bias. In this very simple case, it can

---

[1]Biased cultural transmission (direct or indirect) is "biased" in two senses. First, the individual receiving cultural information is *biased* in favor of some information (e.g., traits) and against others. Second, biased transmission results in a cultural population that, following cultural transmission, is a *biased* sample of the cultural population before transmission.

be shown that direct bias has the following effect on trait frequency (Boyd and Richerson 1985:138)

$$p' = p + Bp(1 - p) \qquad (8.6)$$

where

> p and p' are the frequencies of variant c, which is favored by the bias, before and after transmission, respectively
> B is the strength of the bias

In other words, direct bias moves the mean behavior of a population by an increment, $B\,p(1 - p)$, from its initial value, p, toward the value favored by the bias until it reaches that value at unity or zero (1.0 or 0.0). If this favored value of p is optimal for the environment, individuals possessing the bias will be advantaged over those who do not, allowing the bias to become established. For example, a hunter-gatherer female might be exposed to two different methods of seed preparation: one used by her mother and another by her mother-in-law. Given the correct bias, she would try both of them out and and settle on the one most effective for her situation with some probability, measured by B. In this respect, she would enjoy an adaptive advantage over females lacking such a bias.

Those who have had an introductory course in statistics may have already recognized that the increment subject to (moved by) direct bias, that is, $p(1 - p)$, is the (binomial) variance for populations consisting of dichotomous characters with frequencies of p and $1 - p$. This underscores that other things being equal the utility of direct bias depends on the variability in the population: The greater the differences in the models to which an individual is exposed, the more effective direct biases become. It also means that as a population moves toward its optimal state the effectiveness of bias decreases: At $p = 1.00$ or $p = 0.00$, bias has no effect, there being no variability upon which it can work (i.e., individuals are not exposed to alternative models). In turn, this implies that if they entail any cost at all, the continued presence of generalized biases in populations must be due to external circumstances that maintain behavioral variability within a population. Immigration is one common activity that would create these conditions: Migration between different local environments would increase the probability that individuals would be exposed to locally incorrect models of behavior and in this sense a generalized bias allowing critical evaluation of behavior would be useful.

In the case where there is migration between two populations that occupy habitats in which two different behavioral variants, say c and d, are selectively favored respectively, individuals genetically biased to evaluate directly the behavioral variants they obtain by observing those around them will increase in number when the following is true (Boyd and Richerson 1985:154)

$$[(1 - p_e)p_e s]b > z \qquad (8.7)$$

where

p_e is the equilibrium value of the behavior favored in the habitat
s is the selective advantage of each trait in its favored habitat, formally defined as

$$s = W_c/W_d - 1$$

where

W_c and W_d are the survival rates associated with individuals characterized by traits c and d, respectively, in the habitats where each is favored
z is the cost an individual incurs in evaluating the relative merits of the two traits

Inequality 8.7 says that direct bias is genetically favored when its costs (z) are low relative to (1) the amount of behavioral variance in a population, $(1 - p_e)p_e$; (2) the strength of the bias, b; and (3) the selective advantage, s, of the favored trait relative to its alternative. In other words, direct bias is an advantage when something like migration maintains lots of locally maladaptive behavioral variation and when the bias is relatively low cost.

Boyd and Richerson demonstrate that biases of this sort are almost certain to be of a general sort—that is, of the kind that maximizes rates of energetic return, for example—rather than habitat specific—that is, of the kind that would specify exact programs of behavior.

Discussion

Superficially at least, guided variation and direct bias are opposite with respect to conditions and consequences: Learning does not require variability but, through errors, produces it. Direct bias requires variability, but works to eliminate it. Despite these differences, both forces are potentially capable of causing populations to move toward optimal behaviors and can in this sense be regarded as sociobiological processes: Whether genetically inspired or not, learning and direct bias should in the long run lead to behavior that results in genetic fitness.

Given the potential power of these two processes to increase ordinary Darwinian fitness, it is reasonable to ask, as some evolutionary ecologists have asked, whether cultural transmission itself is of any particular importance to understanding human behavior, that is, whether quantitative models of culture are needed at all. It is of course true that in environments either endlessly stable or infinitely variable culture is useless: Without environmental variation, genes are easily capable of producing all needed behaviors. In a like sense, unceasing environmental variation renders moot the value of anything learned in one generation and transmitted to the next when environmental circumstances will almost certainly dictate different optimal behaviors. In this case, genes, learning, and direct bias would provide the only tools needed to promote adaptation. There is good reason to believe, however, that between these extremes (which seem inapplicable to any environments inhabited by humans) cultural transmission might be adaptively quite important.

That culture is so rare in the animal world suggests that it is costly. If that is so, the evolution and maintenance of culture would make sense only if culture were capable of solving certain problems more effectively than genes. Moreover, whatever its costs, circumstances are easily envisioned in which cultural transmission would be less costly than either learning or direct bias. With direct bias, for example, as behaviors become more complex, the relationship between behavioral cause and material effect—the basis for directly biased judgments between alternative behaviors—grows tenuous. This is particularly true when there is appreciable time lag between cause and effect. It is even more true when there are interactive effects between seemingly unconnected behaviors such that to change just one of the constituent behaviors results in a completely different outcome. The contemporary world is full of such examples: What makes this businessman a success, that one a failure? Surely that there are so many "how-to-succeed-in-business" books suggests that the key ingredients of the process remain mysterious to most. The hunter-gatherer world is equally mysterious in these terms. That archaeologists continue to debate whether nuances in morphological variability in projectile points represent differences in style or function or whether atlatl weights are decorative or served some useful purpose suggests that function and utility must have been equally difficult for prehistoric peoples to assess. Likewise, that anthropologists still cannot decide whether the Kwakiutl potlatch (see Chapter 2) was functional or dysfunctional makes it highly unlikely that the Kwakiutl were able objectively to weigh the adaptive merits of that system.

Similar considerations limit the potential utility of individual learning: It is inconceivable that any individual acting alone would have the capacity to invent either the modern high-speed computer or the sinew-backed bow. The bottom line here is simply that relatively blind imitation allows individuals to obtain complex adaptive behaviors much more cheaply than they could obtain them by either direct bias or learning. Culturally transmitted techniques can be improved incrementally and cumulatively over many "cultural" generations.

Even if the force of decision-making is relatively weak in any one individual in any one generation, the population-level consequences can be quite spectacular given a lifetime.

The preceding discussion converges toward this: Under some circumstances certain more sophisticated forms of cultural transmission (e.g., frequency-dependent and indirect biased transmission; see later discussion) are likely to be more effective than genetic transmission, individual learning, or directly biased cultural transmission. If that is so, then these processes of cultural transmission must differ fundamentally from that of genetic transmission; as a necessary consequence, they must be capable of producing behavioral consequences for populations that differ from those we would expect were only genes, learning, and direct bias involved.

All of this acknowledges the basic similarities of cultural and genetic transmission. As in the genetic case, cultural transmission is an evolutionarily active system potentially subject to blind selective processes as well as guided variation and direct bias. At the same time, the asymmetry of cultural and genetic transmission means that the results of the selective process can (and should) differ depending on the system.

In sum, if culture exists, it must sometimes act at odds with genetics – not most of the time, perhaps, but at least some of the time. It is in this sense that the study of "maladaptive" behavior takes on importance (*maladaptive* here referring to behaviors that compromise genetic fitness). This is not meant to recommend that we rush to engage in the mindless sort of relativistic endeavor that seeks only to portray culture as a sort of anthropological "freak show," a "That's Incredible" (or "Mondo Cane") approach to culture, so to speak. Quite the contrary, as in high-energy physics, to illustrate the basic properties of culture sometimes requires that we examine them not under ordinary but extreme conditions. This is why we should be interested in maladaptations: Maladaptations from a genetic perspective may not be maladaptive from a cultural perspective. Further, if cultural transmission is important in behavior, then we will not be able to provide an account of behavior in terms of genetic transmission, learning, and direct bias. To do that requires an evolutionary (Darwinian) model of cultural transmission.

We have already noted that the asymmetry of cultural transmission and genetic transmission virtually guarantees the existence of behaviors that compromise genetic fitness. It is perhaps easier, however, to appreciate that point with reference to concrete, albeit contrived, example. Consider a population in which there are two cultural behaviors, say c and d, and individuals are enculturated by just one genetic *parent* and one other individual whom we will term *teacher*. Let us assume further that individuals with behavior c are more likely to become teachers and individuals with behavior d more likely to become parents. In such a case, it can be shown that even if individuals with behavior c are at a selective disadvantage relative to those with behavior d, individuals with behavior c will nevertheless become more common than we would expect were only genetic fitness involved if (1) cultural selection favoring of c is relatively strong and (2) teachers are relatively important in cultural transmission (Boyd and Richerson 1985:182-186). This can be expressed quantitatively in terms of the following inequality, in which variant c increases if

$$(1 - A)/A > - s/t \qquad (8.8)$$

where

A is the weight of parents in enculturation
$1 - A$ is the weight of teachers in enculturation
s is the selective value of c relative to d via parental transmission (the process that favors a trait increasing genetic fitness), formally defined as

$$s = W_c/W_d - 1$$

where

W_c is the probability an individual with variant c becomes a parent
W_d is the probability an individual with variant d becomes a parent
t is the selective value of c relative to d in teacher transmission (the process which favors a trait increasing cultural fitness), formally defined as

$$t = V_c/V_d - 1$$

where

V_c is the probability an individual with variant c becomes a teacher
V_d is the probability an individual with variant d becomes a teacher

In short, the tendency of variant c to increase depends on both $(1 - A)/A$ (the relative enculturative weight of parents and teachers) and s/t (the relative selective advantages of c and d in parental and teacher transmission). If teachers are enculturatively more important relative to parents than c is selectively disadvantaged relative to its enculturative advantage, then c will increase despite its genetic selective handicap, that is, even if $s < 0$ (note that when the latter is true, i.e., when c is selectively disadvantaged relative to d in parental transmission, the term to the right of the inequality is positive).

Of course, one would expect that in the long run genetic selection would work to counter this; specifically, it should favor more fertile parents and in this way decrease the relative genetic fitness of teachers. Yet, by similar logic, we would also expect an analogous effect to cause increased cultural selection against parents because as the teaching variant grows rarer, individuals carrying it in increasingly more exaggerated (i.e., more effective) form tend to be disproportionately represented in successive cultural generations. Selection for increasingly effective teachers might make them more attractive as mates despite their low fertility. In short, just as genetic selection works against genetically maladaptive cultural behaviors, cultural selection works against culturally maladaptive genetic behaviors; in the long run, the two might well neutralize each other. Even more interesting, paying attention to teachers may on average increase genetic fitness even though some traits arise that increase cultural fitness at the expense of genetic fitness. Selection on genes might not favor learning rules that remove such traits if the cost of doing so were excessive. At the very best, then cultural transmission sets up a complex co-evolutionary dynamic between genes and culture that cannot be reduced to the terms of a simple fitness optimizing analysis.

All of the preceding suggests that cultural transmission differs from genetic transmission not only in terms of how it operates but also in terms of its distinctive effects. This establishes the need for a special theory that addresses these special effects of cultural transmission.

MORE SOPHISTICATED FORMS
OF CULTURAL TRANSMISSION

Boyd and Richerson (1985) postulate two ways of acquiring behavioral information via more sophisticated forms of cultural transmission that would appear to be less costly than, and thus preferable to, individual learning and direct bias. Under the proper circumstances, either can result in behaviors that would be difficult to explain solely with reference to genetic fitness. These processes are termed *frequency-dependent bias* and *indirect bias*.

Frequency-Dependent Bias

Frequency-dependent bias refers to an enculturative process in which unenculturated individuals choose among a range of behavioral alternatives on the basis of their frequency. Individuals might survey their local group and adopt the modal behavior (i.e., the one followed by the majority/plurality of individuals). This results in what is called conformist transmission. Reversing this logic produces nonconformist transmission in which the least common behavior is chosen.

As with direct bias, the advantages of conformist transmission are most apparent with reference to the case in which individuals are, as a consequence of migration, exposed to a variety of behaviors, the rarer or most extreme of which are locally suboptimal. Given a frequency-dependent bias, migrants and younger unenculturated locals would find it relatively easy to adopt optimal behaviors. Thus, young hunter-gatherer males might survey the older males in their bands and adopt the behaviors used by the majority of them. In this way, the set of individuals constituting the majority for one behavior might not be identical to the set constituting the majority for another behavior, though that would often be the case. By keeping the locally adaptive trait common, conformist transmission might have much the same effect as direct bias. However, it generally ought to be easier to follow the majority than to figure out the best technique for oneself, so conformity has a decision-cost advantage.

For frequency-dependent bias to work, the unenculturated individual must have access to a minimum of three models: Smaller numbers—one or two—lack information about population frequency. In the three-model case in which there are two cultural variants, frequency-dependent bias has the following effect on the frequency of the two variants (Boyd and Richerson 1985:209)

$$p' = p + D(2p - 1)[p(1 - p)] \tag{8.9}$$

where

> p and p' are the frequencies of one of the two traits in the population before
>   and after transmission, respectively
> D is the strength of the frequency-dependent bias

It is clear from (8.9) that if D is greater than 0 and p is greater than 0.5, then p' will be greater than p: Here frequency-dependent bias increases the frequency of the more common trait, resulting in conformist transmission. Alternatively, if D is less than 0 (i.e., negative) and p is greater than 0.5, then p' is less than p: Here frequency-dependent bias increases the frequency of the less common trait, resulting in non-conformist transmission. Note also that when $p = 0.5$, that is, when two traits are equally common, frequency-dependent bias has no effect, which makes sense because then trait-frequency provides no consistent basis for choice for the population as a whole. Note further that, as in the case of direct bias, the force of frequency-dependent bias also depends on variability in the population (measured by $p[1 - p]$), which is highest when p reaches 0.5. These two properties mean that the force of frequency-dependent bias increases as p moves away from 0, 0.5, and 1, which is to say that it is highest when p is either .25 or .75 for a dichotomous trait.

In light of the aforementioned biological and anthropological interest in human altruism (see Chapter 7), it is of more than passing significance that it can be shown that sufficiently strong conformist frequency-dependent bias can lead to situations in which cultural differences between groups are greater than those within groups—precisely the conditions that are required for group selection to occur (Boyd and Richerson 1985:216-221, 232-236). Thus individuals copying local norms might *unknowingly* adopt some norms that compromise their own fitness but optimize group fitness. As we have said, this is most likely to occur when behavior is complex and individuals are exposed to many possible behavioral models, at least some of which are suboptimal.

Indirect Bias

The second more sophisticated form of biased cultural transmission is termed *indirect bias*. In it an individual uses one trait (termed *indicator*) to select a role model and then adopts other traits (behaviors) displayed by that same model. Indirect bias here refers to the fact that the individual uses a preference for one kind of trait (the indicator) as a basis for choosing other traits, the choices regarding which are thus "indirectly biased" (i.e., biased by another trait). Three kinds of traits are thus involved: (1) the *indicator traits* displayed by potential role models; (2) additional *behavioral traits* displayed by these same potential role models, which are subject to the indirect bias; and (3) the *preference traits* of the unencultured individual, which determines preference for a given indicator trait and preferred values thereof.

The value of indirectly biased transmission is likely to increase as cultural behavior becomes more complex so that the relationship between different kinds of behaviors and success is obscured. It may be easier for individuals simply to select a trait that seems highly correlated with success and emulate the entire behavioral repertoire—or at least as much as they can—of those individuals who display the trait thought to be most correlated with success. As a rule, one can assume that preference traits select for extreme values of the indicator trait though that is not a necessary condition of the model.

A simple illustration may help in understanding how these various traits and processes interact.[2] Suppose an unencultured individual seeking to adopt an indicator trait has a choice between two potential role models, one of which displays the indicator trait favored by his/her preferences and one that does not.

---

[2]Much of the discussion relating to indirect bias is based on research Gary Macey and I have been conducting on a computer simulation model of indirect bias in which traits are discrete (i.e., qualitative rather than quantitative). This model examines the interactive effects of indirect bias when three traits are considered: indicator, preference, and a third behavioral trait. In this sense, the model is more complex than the original analytical model of indirect bias (Boyd and Richerson 1985:249-266), which examined only the interaction between the indicator and preference traits. Models for the more complex version of indirect bias in which the three traits are quantitative are currently being developed by Macey, Peter Richerson, Robert Boyd, Alan Kaiser, and myself.

In the absence of any bias, each model would have the same enculturative weight, which we will assume is equal to 1.00; preferences of unenculturated individuals alter these enculturative weights. In light of this, suppose, further, that the strength of the direct bias on the indicator trait is 0.50. This is taken to mean that the model with the preferred indicator trait has a potential model weight of 1.5 (which is the unbiased weight, 1.00, plus the weight of the bias, 0.5, = 1.5). Alternatively, the model lacking the preferred indicator trait has a potential model weight of 0.5 (which is the unbiased weight, 1, minus the weight of the bias, 0.5, = 0.5). In short, these biases mean that the model with the preferred indicator trait carries three times the enculturative weight of the potential model lacking the preferred trait (i.e., 1.5/.5 = 3). Thus when confronted by two models, one possessing the desired indicator trait and one lacking it, the unenculturated individual with this direct bias is three times as likely to adopt the indicator trait dictated by his/her preferences as its nonpreferred alternative.

Suppose further that the strength of indirect bias is also 0.5. This means that, as in direct bias, the individual with the preferred indicator is three times as likely to be used as a model as the individual lacking the preferred indicator trait. In this case, however, the traits to be obtained from the preferred model do not include the indicator (obtained previously by direct bias) but consist of other traits that happen to be in the behavioral repertoire of that model and which the unenculturated individual needs to obtain. To save time and effort, the unenculturated individual assumes that models that display the correct indicator traits are likely to have the correct forms of other traits as well.

It should be noted that in this model two kinds of traits are indirectly biased: (1) preference traits, which govern the value placed on different indicator traits; and (2) behavioral traits (other than indicator traits), which dictate different courses of action that affect fitness directly—methods of seed procurement, for example. The unenculturated individual comes equipped with preference traits but, through indirect bias, subsequently modifies them to match the preference trait of the "correct" model (i.e., the one displaying the indicator trait dictated by the original preference of the unenculturated individual). Acting through this indirect bias loop, the preference trait may set up the conditions for its own modification. Behavioral traits are also acquired through indirect bias. Through the indirect bias loop the indicator trait and the adaptive trait may become highly correlated. If the correlation between the indicator trait and the optimal behavioral traits is high enough, indirect bias creates an easy way for unenculturated individuals to maximize their fitness by gaining complex information that would be difficult, costly, or impossible to obtain through direct bias or individual learning.

Apart from its utility as a cheap method for obtaining complex information, indirect bias has at least two interesting effects. First, as just noted, it causes directly biased indicator traits and indirectly biased indicator preference and behavioral traits to become correlated as a consequence of the transmission process. That is, indirect bias causes traits to be transmitted as blocks rather than individually. All other things being equal, the stronger the indirect bias, the higher this correlation will be. Second, indirect bias acting on the preference trait can cause a preference trait and its preferred indicator trait to become increasingly exaggerated over time. This is most likely when, over the population as a whole, the indicator trait has some correlation with the preference trait. Then individuals displaying an exaggerated value of an indicator trait might also have exaggerated preferences favoring that indicator trait. In such a case, an unenculturated individual with only a mild initial preference for a given indicator might through direct bias adopt a more exaggerated value for the indicator trait and through indirect bias obtain an exaggerated preference for that same indicator. Behavioral traits may be carried along over repeated cycles of imitation by this process and, thus, take on more exaggerated forms.

It can be shown that the force of indirect bias on preference and nonindicator behavioral traits can be stronger than the force of a direct bias of equal weight on the indicator trait when the following conditions obtain (Boyd and Richerson 1985:254)

$$abs[\text{Corr}(Z_I, Z_{IB})] > \{\text{Var}(Z_p)/\text{Var}(Z_{IB})\}^{1/2} \tag{8.10}$$

where

> $abs(\text{Corr}(Z_I, Z_{IB}))$ is the absolute value of the correlation in the population between individual estimates of the values of the indicator trait and individual estimates of the indirectly biased trait
>
> $\text{Var}(Z_I)$ is the population variance of individual estimates of the value of the indicator trait
>
> $\text{Var}(Z_{IB})$ is the population variance of individual estimates of the value of the indirectly biased trait

In other words, even when the strengths of direct bias and indirect bias are equal, the force of indirect bias acting on preference traits and nonindicator behavioral traits will be greater than the force of direct bias acting on the indicator trait if the correlation between individual estimates of the indicator trait and the indirectly biased trait is high or if the population variance of individual estimates of the indirectly biased trait is large relative to the population variance of individual estimates of the indicator trait. When these conditions exist, the more subtle indirect effects of cultural transmission will actually be stronger than the more obvious direct ones.

The Evolution of Ethnic Markers

Boyd and Richerson (1987) have recently shown how indirect bias acting through purely symbolic (i.e., nonfunctional) indicator traits can lead to more effective adaptation than direct bias acting on functional traits. In the example, there is migration between two populations that occupy separate habitats in which different behaviors are favored. Migration between the habitats exposes unenculturated individuals in both habitats to models with the "wrong" behavior. At the outset, these unenculturated individuals observe the rates of success associated with the different behaviors to which they are exposed and use direct bias to settle on an appropriate behavior for themselves. Through this process, an equilibrium is established in which the frequency of "correct" behaviors is determined by the relative strengths of migration (which pulls each population away from optimal behavior) and ability to discriminate behavioral success by direct bias (which pulls each population toward optimal behavior).

Boyd and Richerson (1987) examine what would happen in such a situation if unenculturated individuals initially discriminated between potential models on the basis of some purely symbolic trait that, by chance, takes on slightly different values in the two populations. In that case, the unenculturated individual receives a symbolic trait by parental transmission and adopts a behavioral trait (by indirect bias) from the model that most closely matches the previously acquired symbolic trait (i.e., the one preferred by the unenculturated individual). After this, these "protoenculturated" individuals again use direct bias to evaluate rates of success observed in other individuals to modify their own symbolic and adaptive behavior.

Under these circumstances, the initial discrimination between models on the basis of the symbolic indicator trait has the effect of reducing (by indirect bias) the behavioral mixture between populations so that each one has a higher frequency of the "correct" behavior than it does in the absence of symbolic discrimination. The second phase of direct bias acting on observed success subsequently increases the frequency of both the "correct" behavioral trait and the "correct" symbolic trait. In this way a coevolutionary process is established in which the two populations become increasingly differentiated with respect to both the symbolic trait and the behavioral trait, *and* the symbolic traits and behavioral traits become highly correlated with each other. At equilibrium, each population has higher values of the correct behavior than it would in the absence of symbolic discrimination and indirect bias. Each is likewise characterized by extreme (and opposite) values of the symbolic trait that are wholly inexplicable in terms of the intrinsic value of the symbolic trait itself.

This is one example of a case in which cultural transmission promotes adaptation even though some of the cultural behavior involved (i.e., symbolic behavior) is utterly without adaptive value or is even maladaptive (taken in isolation). Further, the stronger this sort of process is, the more likely it is that populations will adopt extreme behaviors: In some cases these may be adaptive, in some cases they may not.[3]

Interestingly, the strength of this process varies directly with amount of migration between populations and other factors (Boyd and Richerson, personal communication, 1988). As the amount of migration between two adaptively different populations increases, the correlation between the adaptive and symbolic traits *and* the value of the symbolic traits both increase. This means that when two populations of unequal size interact, the smaller (which is proportionally more affected by migration) ought to exhibit both more exaggerated symbolic behavior and a higher correlation between adaptive and symbolic traits. It further follows from the model that when two populations of equal size come into contact, the greater their initial symbolic differentiation, the more likely it is that they will come to occupy different adaptive specializations. In this case, greater symbolic variation effectively decreases the mixing effect of migration and, thus, increases the effect of indirect bias. Finally, it also follows from the model that when a series of groups interact across an ecological boundary, the greatest symbolic differentiation between groups and highest correlation between adaptive and symbolic traits within groups should occur at the ecological boundary itself. Again, this has to do with the effect of migration on the correlation between symbolic and adaptive traits, which is greatest at the ecological boundary. My colleague Aram Yengoyan has collected substantial data on symbolic differentiation between adjacent Australian hunter-gatherer groups that tend to confirm the last hypothesis (personal communication, 1989).

Sexual Selection

What is particularly interesting about indirectly biased transmission is its formal similarity to the process of sexual selection in biology. As Fisher (1958) believed – and others have more recently shown (e.g., Lande 1981) – if females of a species prefer a specific trait in the males of that species, given the proper conditions there is the possibility that the trait and the preference for it will become linked in a feedback process. Females produce sons who exhibit above average expressions of the trait and at the same time females who prefer such above average expressions. This system can "run away" to ever more extreme values of preferences and display. A number of biological examples come immediately to mind, the classic case of the peacock tail, for example. Indirect bias works in the same way, in the sense that preference for the indicator trait

---

[3]Working with a more complicated computer simulation, Gary Macey and I have shown that these results pertain over a wider range of conditions than Boyd and Richerson (1987) were forced to assume in their analytical treatment of indirect bias.

can itself become an indirectly biased trait; thus to prefer the indicator trait is to acquire a modified value of the preference. If those who display extreme values of the indicator trait tend to prefer somewhat more extreme values themselves, a similar positive feedback runaway dynamic can occur. It is likely that most prestige systems work in this way.

It is noteworthy that through this runaway process strong indirect bias can easily lead to marked cultural variation between groups because the trajectory of runaway depends on initial conditions that are largely a matter of chance. Thus, like frequency-dependent bias, it can act to promote group selection. More important, the runaway process will very likely lead to behaviors in which the indicators of prestige become exaggerated far beyond levels that would be appropriate were genetic fitness alone involved. Indeed, the value of such exaggerated behaviors in those cases becomes principally symbolic, serving as a proxy measure for cultural fitness. Lastly, indirect bias is likely to blur any simple distinction between style and function (cf. Dunnell 1978) because with indirect bias, it is unclear which is which. It will be commonplace that prestige is a self-fulfilling prophecy, itself leading to success, even though the criteria of prestige are arbitrary and culture specific.

EMPIRICAL SUPPORT

The discussion and examples given here are largely theoretical. Even so, the potential value of a neo-Darwinian theory of culture for understanding human behavior seems clear. It seems far more probable, for instance, that many oddities of culture—especially those that have preoccupied the explanatory efforts of neofunctionalists (the potlatch, sacred cows, Aztec sacrifice, and so on) can be better understood as consequences of frequency-dependent and runaway indirect bias than as essential functions of homeostatic economic systems. As Darwin (1871) originally proposed, sexual selection and its cultural analogs provide a theory of nonadaptive or maladaptive symbolic variations. For arguments that hinge upon group selection, on the other hand, indirect bias and frequency-dependent bias provide a credible defense against the standard sociobiological criticism that such behaviors are unlikely in any species, including humans. At the same time, cultural transmission theory offers an opportunity to move beyond sociobiological arguments that seek to explain all forms of personal sacrifice as concealed genetic selfishness. Sociobiological hypotheses are useful as benchmarks but sociobiology has great trouble with a number of important human behaviors, including cooperation, and its explanatory shortcomings are becoming increasingly apparent (cf. Dunnell 1980:64; see Orans 1975; Murphy 1970 for parallel criticisms of neofunctional interpretations).

On the other hand, it is presently difficult to mount a convincing argument in support of cultural inheritance theory on the basis of the empirical evidence, partly because these theories have only recently been developed and partly because the data available are insufficiently detailed to permit analysis through enculturative theory. Ethnographic accounts, for example, typically fail to provide evidence regarding temporal change and variability that figure prominently in models of cultural transmission. Archaeological data are better on that count, but they often suffer from lack of control over spatial variability and the details of process, which are equally important in theories of cultural transmission. Despite these handicaps, it will be useful to illustrate the potential value of these theories with respect to two empirical cases involving hunter-gatherers, one ethnographic, the other archaeological.

Cultural Inheritance and Ethnography: The Aché Revisited

It is thinkable that a process of cultural transmission resembling indirect bias may account for the unusual (and apparently suboptimal) emphasis the Aché place on hunting (see Chapter 7). To see this, suppose that among the Aché, young males use prestige as a basis for evaluating potential role models and that prestige is measured by hunting success. It is reasonable to believe that in such a case, by using such a "quick-and-dirty" measure as a "gloss" for what it is to be an Aché male, young Aché males might easily and in short order sort through the behavioral variability to which they are exposed and in this relatively painless manner decide upon the behaviors they should use as adult Aché males. Certainly this alternative would seem quite attractive when compared with the risk and tedium of learning or endless individual tests required by direct bias. In short, if Aché male behavior is at all complicated (which seems likely), young Aché males might well optimize their rate of enculturation by maximizing the time they spend watching and emulating high-prestige males and minimizing the time they spend experimenting with alternative behaviors observed among larger sets of males or in attempting to learn on their own.

Note, however, that as a result of indirect bias, some of the behaviors acquired in this way by young Aché males would have nothing to do with hunting at all (e.g., body adornment, demeanor toward women). Others would be related to hunting only indirectly, hunting magic, for example. Some of these traits might include attitudes toward the importance of hunting relative to other activities, for example, gathering and child care. Though only indirectly related to hunting, such attitudes (preferences) should in theory be related to hunting success because individuals would use them as a basis for deciding when to start and stop hunting (e.g., Hawkes et al. 1985).

In such a case, indirect bias might well increase the level of hunting skill among the Aché. However, it would also have an number of other unanticipated effects. First, it would cause seemingly unrelated behaviors (e.g., hunting behavior, body adornment, and demeanor toward women) to become correlated within the population in the sense that individuals who follow a particular mode of hunting would also adorn their bodies in a particular way and behave toward women in a particular way (i.e., the one followed by the high-prestige hunter model). Second, and perhaps more important, through time we would expect attitudes toward the relationship between hunting success and prestige to become increasingly exaggerated. This results from the feedback effect indirect bias has on the preference trait: Young Aché males with a moderate preference for successful male hunters adopt both the behavioral skills of those hunters and their attitude toward hunting. If successful adult Aché hunters value hunting success more highly than the average Aché (which seems plausible), the result of the process would be to increase the valuation of hunting success within the population of Aché males as whole. If the better Aché hunters hunted more often than the average, it would cause the amount of time spent hunting to increase as well. Further, if Aché females followed the same logic when selecting mates (i.e., learned from their parents to value hunting success in males), so that their sons and daughters were enculturated by males who valued hunting success in greater degree than the average Aché, the evolutionary result would be to increase Aché valuation of hunting success in both sexes. Such a process may well account for the prestige the Aché accord successful hunters and the resulting male neglect of potentially more productive activities such as gathering. This would also seem to be a case in which the runaway process has resulted in an individual decision logic that produces group rather than individual benefits via the obligatory sharing of a high prestige commodity. Considering only the Aché case, this hypothesis is, at best, modestly supported relative to its alternatives. More convincing is that the Aché complex, with its fairly rigid sexual division of labor and male prestige system centered on hunting, is so common among hunter-gatherers. The Aché illustrate a seemingly universal tendency for prestige-associated traits to be exaggerated beyond the bounds of functionality in any of the usual senses.

Cultural Inheritance and Archaeology:
The European Upper Paleolithic Transition

The archaeological record furnishes evidence of at least one important evolutionary event that has long resisted explanation and yet fits quite neatly with the neo-Darwinian processes described here: the European Upper Paleolithic transition. The analysis that follows is a sketch rather than an in-depth treatment of the subject. Its purpose is to suggest some ways in which a model of cultural transmission might clarify some of the problems associated with this phenomenon.

Although the details remain unclear, it is widely accepted that the appearance roughly 40,000 years ago of the first anatomically modern (Cro-Magnon) man (*Homo sapiens sapiens*) in Europe was attended by a suite of other important social, technical, and economic innovations previously lacking in human behavior. Collectively these are held to characterize the Upper Paleolithic transition. Most parties agree that major elements of this phenomenon included as relevant conditions or important consequences:

Population

A large and increasingly larger population (R. White 1982:176; Binford 1982:179; Flannery 1969).

Technology

Emerging technical complexity as expressed in the initial development of a bone tool technology (R. White 1982:176; Binford 1982:177) and an advanced lithic technology dominated by specialized flake tools (i.e., blades; cf. Mellars 1973).

The appearance of complexly organized economic behaviors as evident in increased intersite assemblage variation. This presumably reflects seasonal and functional differentiation within logistically organized systems that in turn implies long-term planning and, with it, the need for curated technologies (see Chapter 3). It has been suggested, for example, that organized hunting of migrating herd animals to stockpile stores of meat may have entered the behavioral repertoire of hominids for the first time during the Upper Paleolithic (Binford 1982:178; see Chapter 3).

Interregional Contact

The initial appearance of long-distance trade or travel (R. White 1982:176) and widespread population movement and displacement as a consequence of population growth and climatic change (cf. Jochim 1983).

Ethnicity

The formation of seasonally aggregate social groups consisting of multiple smaller groups perhaps akin to the band (Conkey 1980; R. White 1982:176).

There is evidence of interregional assemblage variation suggesting stylistic, that is, cultural, variability (R. White 1982:174; Binford 1982:179-181; Conkey 1980).

Art and Symbol

The initial appearance of personal adornment, symbols, and art, as exemplified in the highly stylized Venus figures, delicately flaked and essentially nonfunctional bifacial objects (e.g., Solutrean blades), and naturalistic—yet stylized—sculpture and parietal art (cf. Conkey 1978).

Discussion

Why these changes should have occurred more or less all at once has puzzled many students of the Paleolithic. One popular suggestion is that they reflect the increased intellectual capacities of modern man (*Homo sapiens sapiens*). Thus, Neanderthals (*Homo sapiens neanderthalensis*) neither planned, nor spoke, nor made art because they could not (Conkey 1978). Yet this seems to beg the question: Why did modern man evolve at this time with precisely these qualities? An alternative hypothesis is that art, style, and symbols evolved as means of communication within the large social groups that evidently joined together seasonally at certain sites; growing economic complexity may have necessitated such behaviors (Conkey 1978, 1980; Jochim 1983; Gamble 1983). In this view, Neanderthals did not speak because they had nothing to say. The problem here, however, is why communication, the purpose of which is to share information and which requires that meanings be clear, should have evolved via such cryptic forms as symbols and stylized art, where meaning is vague. If I read him correctly, Sackett (1985) has leveled the same criticism at Wiessner's interpretation regarding the communicative value of subtle formal variation in Bushman arrow points.

In sum, it would seem that none of the explanations regarding the Upper Paleolithic presently advanced provides a convincing argument as to why phenomena so different as art, symbol, technology, and ethnicity should have all evolved more or less simultaneously. Binford, however, hints at the answer when he argues that essentially the Upper Paleolithic transition marks the origins of culture (Binford 1972, 1973, 1982). If we interpret this to mean the origins of culture in the sense of the frequency-dependent and, especially, indirect bias mechanisms reviewed previously, then a very good case can be made that this is precisely what happened.

Recall that the conditions favoring the development and use of frequency-dependent and indirect biases in cultural transmission include increasing specialization and complexity in technology and behavior and increasing contact between areas that differ with respect to optimal behaviors. Mixing between adaptively differentiated populations means that unenculturated individuals will be exposed to role models whose behaviors are suboptimal for their own situation (i.e., that of the unenculturated individual). In theory, direct bias can reduce this problem, but as technology become more complex, direct bias becomes increasingly costly because it requires that more and more alternative techniques be tested against each other over increasingly longer times. Elementary statistics suggests this will be rather difficult for small-scale societies to manage. The task is made even more difficult when tactics and strategies involve multiple complex behaviors that are interactively related. In this case, there is a synergism between the component behaviors such that their individual effects cannot be evaluated apart from each other. In such situations, direct bias requires that individuals test each complex of behaviors against all possible other combinations of behaviors—a chore that quickly becomes prohibitive as the number of possible component behaviors increases.

Direct bias is equally ineffective when there is considerable time lag between a behavior and its consequences. Adaptive strategies involving seasonality have this property in the sense that what is being done at any moment is largely contingent on a long-term plan the consequences of which are never fully evident at one point in time and thus not open to objective evaluation through direct bias. Some strategies, such as marriage and mating systems, have such long-term consequences that their effects are not fully felt for many generations. Here again direct bias would be wholly ineffective. In these kinds of cases, frequency-dependent bias and indirect bias will become increasingly attractive. Indirect bias, in particular, makes it possible to adopt behaviors as linked complexes, thus taking advantage of the interactive effects of related behaviors (frequency-dependent bias can have much the same effect, but it tends to discourage adaptive differentiation that would be disadvantageous to Upper Paleolithic groups attempting to find and fill new adaptive niches).

With the forgoing in mind, a strong case can be made that the Upper Paleolithic marks the initial appearance of frequency-dependent and indirect bias. The relevant points are as follows: First, late Pleistocene population growth and climatic change would have certainly created all necessary incentives for local technoeconomic specialization and increased sophistication in procurement tactics (cf. Binford 1982; Flannery 1969). It is conceivable that vocalized language evolved at this time as a direct response to the need to communicate some of this complicated behavioral information. As local adaptive specializations grew increasingly distinct, contact between regions posed an increasingly serious problem because it exposed unenculturated individuals to behaviors (hunting techniques, for example) that might be maladaptive if used in the wrong kind of habitat. At the same time, as movement between areas increased in frequency, immigration became increasingly difficult because success in an old environment no longer guaranteed success in a new one.

It would seem likely that indirect bias and frequency-dependent bias would be rewarded and evolve under conditions such as those described. If so, we would expect several things to be true. First, the development of style ought to occur initially in technology. The origins of regional styles in lithic assemblages and the first evidence for exaggerated aesthetic expression in technology (e.g., Solutrean blades) are perhaps understandable in these terms. Likewise, as a part of this, one would expect stylization to be most pronounced in curated tools because their benefits are long term rather than short term and thus not subject to evaluation by direct bias (Binford [1973] predicts the same result on different grounds). Second, one would expect a variety of magico-religious trappings connected with economy and reproduction to evolve as the result of indirect bias. This would cause certain proxy measures of adaptive success to run away, that is, become increasingly exaggerated. The various forms of "nonutilitarian" Upper Paleolithic art forms (e.g., Venus figurines, cave art, etc.) are consistent with this expectation. Third, one would expect the development of ethnicity, formal social groupings, and group ritual behaviors. These follow as consequences of both frequency-dependent and indirect biases, which would result in conformism and altruistic behaviors. Support for this notion is provided by several lines of evidence cited earlier, which point to the appearance of ethnically marked groups during the Upper Paleolithic.

The preceding explanation is distinctive in its portrayal of art, ethnicity, and ritual as equivalent consequences of a single process. This is in marked contrast to the standard form of structural-functional interpretation, for example, in which here ethnicity would arise in response to population growth and climatic deterioration and art and ritual would subsequently develop to support solidarity with these newly constituted ethnic groups. Note further that our explanation is inherently evolutionary and materialistic in that it explains the Upper Paleolithic transition on the basis of material conditions, specifically population growth and climatic change that elicit a variety of adaptive innovations that cumulatively result in technical sophistication and specialization. Unlike previous attempts, however, this explanation does not seek to render ethnicity, ritual, and art as somehow functioning to resolve these problems directly. Rather, they are viewed as unintended consequences of biases in cultural transmission that are in turn the consequence of the growing demand for complex and sophisticated technologies to solve untenable balances between populations and resources. In short, this model holds art, symbol, ethnicity, and style as equivalent results of a more basic process, specifically the origin of sophisticated forms of cultural transmission. Further, this account is fully consistent with Boasian relativism, in the sense that the rationale of Upper

Paleolithic symbolism is both arbitrary and culture specific—and at the same time wholly in keeping with the general Darwinian principles of evolution.

SUMMARY AND IMPLICATIONS

In Chapter 7 it was noted that evolutionary ecologists are prone to dismiss explanations of behavior in which cultural preference and style are important variables. There it was argued that to take such a position would make sense only if it is assumed that cultural preferences and symbolic behavior were not subject to evolutionary processes (cf. Dunnell 1978, 1980; Kirch 1980). In that case, symbolic behavior and style would either represent random variation or "noise" or would simply "track" genetic fitness, that is, cultural preferences would evolve to match genetically correct courses of action, as a way of rationalizing one's actions, for example. In the former case, when preferences are simply noise, no "evolutionary" model of style would be possible: Simple stochastic models would suffice. In the latter case, where style and preferences track inclusive genetic fitness, the only model that would be needed would be the genetic one.

This chapter takes a different view and, following the lead of Boyd and Richerson, develops a model in which preferences and symbolic variation are subject to evolutionary processes and in which the forces that serve genetic fitness can be either enhanced or subverted by cultural preference. That enhanced genetic fitness may result from cultural transmission (e.g., during the Upper Paleolithic transition) makes it possible to explain how and why cultural transmission evolved in the first place and why it has persisted since then. To produce this result, however, it must be assumed that cultural transmission differs in both structure and consequence from genetic transmission. If that is so, then it follows that behaviors that are the result of cultural transmission often fail to take the form one would expect on the basis of genetic fitness. This means that cultural transmission may sometimes lead to behaviors that are genuinely maladaptive to individuals or groups of close relatives. This model of cultural transmission makes it easier to explain a variety of cultural phenomena that anthropologists have always regarded as fundamentally important but that evolutionary ecologists have dismissed as implausible (e.g., altruism and group selection) or unimportant (e.g., symbolic behavior).

Evolutionary ecologists know that behavioral variation in any species is constrainted by its adaptation. Because the human adaptive complex includes culture, its properties must be taken into account, along with more general Darwinian rules, if one is to understand human behavior. This line of reasoning suggests that symbols, style, and cultural preference ought to be reexamined as part of a larger attempt to account for human behavior in Darwinian terms. In this view, in many instances style may not be merely epiphenomenal, as evolutionary ecologists assume, but actually a driving force underlying culture change. A number of testable implications follow from this view. In particular, evolutionary models of cultural transmission suggest that changes in style ought to correspond rather directly to technoenvironmental culture change or periods of initial contact between cultures. At such times, indirect bias is likely to be more effective than alternative "rational" means (i.e., direct bias and learning) normally used to weigh the benefits of complicated behavioral alternatives. When that is so, symbolic variation ought to become more well defined, and symbolic and adaptive traits should be more highly correlated with each other.

This brings to mind the celebrated debate between Ford and Spaulding regarding the "reality" of artifact types. Ford (1954), it will be recalled, argued that types were imposed by the archaeologist on what was actually a gradual sequence of change. Types (defined as combinations of two or more traits) were unreal because this change occurred at the more elementary level of individual traits—the modes of Rouse (1960). In Ford's view, culture was transmitted trait by trait. Accordingly, the juxtaposition of specific traits embodied in a given artifact was of no special significance, being largely a matter of chance dictated by the frequencies of alternative trait "templates" shared by members of the same culture. Such a notion was fundamentally at odds with the idea that combinations of traits (types) reflect cultural reality, in which context artifacts differing by a single trait generally do not constitute separate entities. Ford saw types as necessary to archaeological analysis but argued that to assume that they were real obscured the process of culture change.

Spaulding (1953), it will also be recalled, took an opposing position. He argued that types, that is, combinations of traits, could be real in the sense of being behaviorally meaningful and that this could be demonstrated where combinations of traits were consistently (i.e., nonrandomly) associated with each other. Such nonrandom association suggested that artisans were making decisions between alternative blocks of traits rather than between alternative traits individually. In effect, Spaulding was arguing for an understanding of types that is consistent with the model of indirect bias outlined here, in which groups of traits are adopted together and, as a consequence, are correlated with each other.

Spaulding did not argue, however, that all combinations of traits were types, only some. The obvious question is why at certain times traits are correlated and why at other times they are not. One answer is suggested here by models of cultural transmission: Technoenvironmental change or culture contact may make it difficult to choose between alternative courses of action on the basis of objective tests of performance or individual learning. Then, indirect bias acting through some symbolic indicator trait thought to be correlated to success may prove to be the best means of acquiring effective behaviors. In this way, the complex of traits directively correlated through indirect bias might then crystallize as a recognizable "style." Subsequently, one would expect direct bias and learning to reexert themselves as greater familiarity is gained with the new technology and individuals have the opportunity to test minor variations in technology against each other. Over time, thus, the correlations between traits would gradually be expected to diminish: Types will cease to be types (Deetz [1965] predicts this result as a consequence of cultural cataclysm, but it is possible to construe his argument in much the same terms presented here). Hewlett and Cavalli-Sforza (1986) suggests that this sort of cycle (indirect bias followed by individual learning and direct bias) may apply to the recent introduction and spread of the cross-bow among the Aka Pygmy of Africa.

In many cases, indirect bias is likely to remain a potent behavioral force, however. Symbols of male and female prestige, for instance, can always be expected to be important in the sense that individuals evaluating prospective spouses must always work on information that is uncertain and imperfect; symbolic indicators of success may then provide the only reasonable means for making choices. This is likely to be especially true for thinly spread, exogamous hunter and gatherers. In this context, the power of such symbols will be further reinforced within the local group because men and women displaying the "right stuff" are more successful in gaining mates than the average individual. Because this is so, the symbols of prestige are seen to bring success in the eyes of younger males and females searching for worthy role models that can be used as a basis for acquiring appropriate adaptive behaviors. In such a case, the symbols marking prestige, however, may themselves vary over time. As individual symbols become increasingly common, they provide increasingly less information useful in evaluating between models. This is because the force of biased transmission depends on population variability; as a symbol becomes more popular within a population, the symbolic variability of that population decreases. It would then be likely that such a symbol would either be replaced by another more informative one or develop in more exaggerated form. It is interesting to note in regard to this discussion that among the Aka Pygmy, where parents account for about 80% of all cultural transmission, the skills most closely connected with prestige (e.g., elephant hunting, singing, and dancing) or mysterious activities such as healing are not acquired from parents but from prestigious individuals, evidently by a process similar to indirect bias (Hewlett and Cavalli-Sforza 1986:929).[4]

---

[4]Following Cavalli-Sforza and Feldman (1981), Hewlett and Cavalli-Sforza (1986) infer that the effect of this "horizontal" transmission process is conservative (*horizontal* here refers to cultural transmission via lines that are other than parental or *vertical*). That is because in Cavalli-Sforza and Feldman's model of cultural transmission, horizontal transmission results in cultural blending (see previous discussion, this chapter) that minimizes the impact of innovations. When it is assumed that biases (direct or indirect) are involved in horizontal transmission, the result is the opposite:

In light of this discussion, it seems no longer useful to argue that symbolic behavior and cultural preference are either phenotypical—and thus intractable from the perspective of evolutionary theory, or reducible to simple inclusive genetic fitness. Symbolic variation and preference require models of their own and are very likely to provide useful insights into important adaptive processes. One particular advantage of this approach is that archaeological data in particular are rich in evidence pertaining to trait correlation over time within populations of artifacts and assemblages. For the most part, this variation has been understood as useful primarily as a basis for defining types that can then be put to use in building chronology or in interpreting the functional or social activities to which they are thought to be related. In this view, it is the type embodied as an artifact or trait complex that is important, that is, it is the whole rather than the constitution of the whole that matters. The kind of model proposed here reverses that logic in that the result is not meant to be a naming of types but an analysis of the way in which traits vary and co-vary with each other as the result of the processes of cultural transmission. The taxonomic approach developed by Whallon (1971), in which groups of artifacts are successively divided on the basis of what amount to indicator traits, would seem particularly well suited to this kind of analysis because, as he notes, it more closely matches the decision-making processes involved in artifact production and in doing so the process identified here as indirect bias. The same approach would be equally appropriate in studying the effects of cultural transmission on more complex entities, for example, ethnic groups.

Lastly, models of cultural transmission examined here have one further advantage: They do not assume that populations are either in equilibrium or at locally adaptive optima. The effects of cultural transmission are often most apparent during periods of change or when processes such as intergroup migration pull local groups away from behaviors that are locally optimal. In this perspective, for example, types are seen to be constantly in the process of forming and then falling apart or developing in more extreme form. The same may well be true of larger, more complex cultural entities and adaptive strategies. In contrast to the models of evolutionary ecology, in which equilibrium and adaptation are often assumed in order to simplify analysis, models of cultural transmission emphasize rather than ignore change and the possibility of disequilibrium. This is an important advantage: Change, after all, is what evolutionary models ought to be about.

Access to a greater number of potential models increases the chance that a favorable innovation will be observed and adopted.

Chapter 9

Hunter-Gatherers: Problems in Theory

Hunter-gatherers are problems in theory. Because that is so, the future of hunter-gatherer research will rest in large part on the extent to which it is grounded in a clear and concise body of theory. Not just any body of theory will do: To qualify it must contain, at minimum, both a general theory and a number of limited theories that illustrate the operation of the general theory in the presence of special circumstances. Such a framework is basic to all productive scientific investigation because facts never speak for themselves. For every "obvious" fact (e.g., the definition of "hunter-gatherer"), there is a theory that defines where that fact starts and stops, what its variation consists of, and what causes that variation. Until the theory exists, the fact as a scientific phenomenon (i.e., as useful data) does not.

THEORIES ABOUT CONSEQUENCES

For the greater part of the history of hunter-gatherer research, the theories in question have been general ones. Early British and American anthropology viewed hunter-gatherers through the lens of progressive social evolutionary theory and, in doing so, established the tradition that hunter-gatherer behavior is outside evolutionary explanation but understandable in terms of general theories regarding the role of environment and ecology. Neofunctionalism continued that tradition and reunited hunter- gatherers with other kinds of societies by shifting the perspective of anthropological general theory away from evolutionary processes and toward the study of adaptation.

Contemporary hunter-gatherer research acknowledges its theory dependency but has chosen to focus on limited theories rather than general ones. The special value currently claimed for theories of limited sets is an historical response to the criticism that the new archaeology was good in theory (at the general level) but bad in practice (at the limited level; e.g., Taylor 1972; Flannery 1968, 1972). The principal thrust of "bridging theory" and the so-called "generation of middle-range research" can be seen as a conscious effort to make good on the loftier theoretical goals of the new archaeology. Many individuals now suggest that this more modest kind of limited theory building provides the archaeologist sufficient guidance for research—certainly enough to insulate the archaeologist from disputes about general theory that seem excessively esoteric when the real question most of them face is understanding the processes of site formation. Unfortunately, that is not so.

The investigative framework commonly termed the *scientific method* demands that operational theories, that is, theories of limited sets, be derived from theories of general sets (Binford 1977a). Accordingly, before embarking upon programs of research to develop bridging theories, middle-range theories, midrange theories (or whatever we choose to call them), it is reasonable to ask in what way they articulate with a workable and explicit framework of general theory capable of sustaining ancillary theories of limited sets. The relationship between general and limited theory need not be clearly spelled out from the start, that being an important part of normal science and paradigm articulation. Nevertheless, that there necessarily exists a relationship between limited theory and general theory must always be understood. In my opinion, the new archaeology had no general theory capable of supporting a body of limited theory about hunter-gatherers, and for the most part contemporary hunter-gatherer research is similarly deprived. This explains my preoccupation with general evolutionary theory.

The most pressing problems in contemporary hunter-gatherer archaeology have little to do with the development of theories of limited sets—less at least than generally believed. The greatest source of confusions and controversies that currently pervade hunter-gatherer archaeology is not at the middle-range level. Contemporary middle range research is neither unimportant nor unproductive. All the same, the basic issue confronting hunter-gatherer research, archaeological and ethnographic, is the same as that which has faced all of anthropology historically: What is the nature of culture? That is an issue of general theory.

To paraphrase Yogi Berra, "It's *deja vu* all over again." The major source of contention between the new and old archaeology centered on the same issue: The definition of culture, what it is and what it does. Right or wrong, the new archaeology identified the old archaeology with a general theory in which culture is norms that guide behavior (Binford 1962, 1968a; e.g., Ford 1954;

Taylor 1948:110) and itself with the theory of Leslie White (1959:9) in which culture is an extra-somatic means of adaptation (Binford 1962:94, 1968b:323). In so doing, the new archaeology committed itself to a non-Darwinian conceptual framework in which the consequences of culture process take precedence over the processes themselves. The eventual ascendancy of the new archaeology over the old archaeology explains in historical terms why, following White, the current generation of American archaeologists interprets culture as adaptive behavior in non-Darwinian terms.

This was undoubtedly beneficial in the short term. It encouraged the formulation of countless productive research programs that have in a scant two decades generated a wealth of priceless information about paleoenvironments and prehistoric human ecology. It had the further effect, quite intentional, of bringing archaeology into the broader fold of anthropology where at least three highly visible schools of thought—cultural ecology (e.g., Steward 1938), neo-functionalism (e.g., Rappaport 1968), and (early) cultural materialism (e.g., Harris 1968a)—argued vigorously for a functional model of culture conceived in adaptive terms compatible with the ideas set forth by many new archaeologists.

But although its new general theory brought archaeology closer to social anthropology, that theory widened the gap between archaeology and the natural sciences (with whom, one might add, some archaeologists felt more comfortable than they did with social anthropology). As Dunnell (1980) notes, as the new archaeology grew, it did so in ways incompatible with the natural sciences because it is exceedingly difficult to reconcile a model of culture as adaptive consequences with neo-Darwinian evolutionary theory, which is principally concerned with processes. As Taylor (1972:32) most cogently observed, from the standpoint of evolutionary theory as understood in the natural sciences, White's adaptive definition seemed to confuse what culture *is* with what culture *does*, that is, it conflated the subject matter (culture process) with its putative consequences (adaptation). When new archaeologists spoke about culture process, what they really had in mind was culture consequences, adaptation in particular. It is symptomatic of the depth of archaeological misunderstanding on this point that Binford, arguably the most penetrating archaeological thinker of our time, misattributes to Darwin his own preference for a neofunctionalist model of homeostatic cultural consequences that is analogous to that of inertia in physics.

> I am essentially a Darwinist. I believe that cultural systems change under conditions of natural selection, that they are pushed and pulled in different directions, and that the way in which change occurs is a function of how people actually solve problems. . . . I think that the most practical principle for us to adopt in theory building is an analog to the principle of inertia. A system will remain stable until acted upon by forces external to its organization as a system. (Binford 1983a:221)

Darwinian theory, of course, has never made any claim for the inevitability or universality of any particular kind of adaptive outcome, equilibrium, nonequilibrium, or otherwise. Binford's position here seems more in keeping with that of Spencer, who assigned primacy to consequences (see Chapter 1) and as part of this made very specific claims about equilibrium.

> Every change is towards a balance of forces; and of necessity can never cease until a balance of forces is reached . . . every aggregate having compound movements tends continually towards a moving equilibrium; since any unequilibrated force to which such an aggregate is subject, if not of a kind to overthrow it altogether, must continue modifying its state until an equilibrium is brought about. (Spencer 1898:519)

In short, it is scarcely worth debating whether archaeology has ever operated under a definable paradigm (if by that we mean a general theory) or whether "new archaeology" offered anything different in the way of general theory than "old archaeology." The vanguard of the new archaeology, and the generation of archaeologists they inspired, operated under and were and are capable of speaking explicitly about an adaptationist paradigm that differed in fundamental ways from the "normative, culture historical" paradigm embraced by Nelson, Kidder, Taylor, Ford, and a host of others (e.g., Binford 1962; cf. Sackett 1986:632-633).

The problem with contemporary hunter-gatherer archaeology is not that it lacks a general theory of culture but that the theory rests on generalizations about consequences. It is unsurprising that the theory has never been formalized as a theory of process. It is problematic whether theories that begin with assumptions about consequences can ever be so formalized. Specifically, to argue that culture is an extrasomatic means of adaptation poisons an evolutionary inquiry from the start by placing cart before the horse and positing consequence as cause—assuming, as it were, one's conclusions (Bettinger 1980). To draw a biological analogy, it would be a gross (and obvious) distortion to argue that genes are somatic means of adaptation. Quite the contrary, biological adaptation is a kind of large-scale result that may (but need not) follow the interaction between genetic inheritance and natural selection.

The new archaeology was not unique in this regard. It shared its preference for theories about consequences with nearly every non-Darwinian interpretation of human behavior widely applied to hunter-gatherers from the nineteenth century on. The earliest of these, progressive social evolution, was most certainly predicated on assumptions about consequences. As we saw in Chapter 1, these theories were driven by a philosophy positing gradual but inevitable cultural progress (Spencer 1868a; Burrow 1966:219). In one of the more explicitly articulated versions, Spencer argued that two processes, natural selection and inheritance of acquired traits, were causally related to progress— but only because he could manipulate both to produce the consequences he wanted (cf. Peel 1972:xxi-xxii; Burrow 1966:115, 203, 222-223). Keenly aware of this, Marx correctly rejected Spencer's version of culture process as perverse and self-serving (cf. Harris 1968a:223-224): Only an upper-class theorist could claim that starvation, disease, and overwork were agents of progress.

When neofunctionalism supplanted progressive social evolution as a general theory in hunter-gatherer studies, it replaced the concept of progress with the concept of adaptation without changing the basic approach to explanation. Neofunctionalism, like progressive social evolutionary theory, builds from its assumptions about consequences and tailors its processes to fit those assumptions. As did the new archaeologists (e.g., Binford) who played key roles in this change in direction of hunter-gatherer studies, neofunctionalists envision homeostatsis as the natural and predictable end product of cultural process and reduce the explanation of behavior and ideas to homeostatic terms.

The "early" theory and early and recent research programs of technoenvironmental cultural materialism can also been seen as emphasizing consequence by their insistence that culture be examined from the perspective of etics and function (Harris 1968a, 1974a, 1977). The motives and ideas of individuals, and ultimately culture itself, are forced into a framework in which an inferred adaptive outcome (consequence) dictates the form processes must take. In the more recent version of cultural materialist theory, Harris (1979) assigns ideas and culture (i.e., structure and superstructure) greater potency as explanations for behaviors that may be maladaptive in the short term. However, Harris believes, as do many hunter-gatherer theorists, that nonoptimal behaviors are momentary evolutionary aberrations and that over the long term ideas and culture (i.e., the cultural process) vary in ways that facilitate the biophysical adaptive drives he proposes to use as general theory (1979:71). As noted in Chapter 7, in this sense, the theory of cultural materialism amounts to a statistical generalization about consequences: A behavioral trait is probably adaptive because behavioral traits are more likely to be adaptive than not. Why this should be so is not explained by means of arguments about process.

Marxist, including structural Marxists, are equally committed to an approach that assigns priority to assumptions about consequences. Marxist theories differ from those of traditional progressive social evolution, neofunctionalism, and cultural materialism only with respect to the kind of the consequence that is postulated. Where the latter tend to see social consensus, equilibrium, or adaptation as natural states or conditions, Marxism sees upheaval, contradiction, and social conflict. Either way, the emphasis is on outcomes (i.e., consequences), arising, evidently, from a deep-seated conviction that it is easier to observe and generalize correctly about the grand design of cultural evolution and the essential nature of the human experience than it is to understand the forces by which these are effected.

It is unclear why anthropology should differ so fundamentally from the natural sciences in preferring theories that assume that large-scale cultural consequences are regularly patterned and that their meaning is self-evident. There are many objections to this approach, perhaps the most fundamental being that it is often hard to know what one has observed in the absence of a processual model of causation (cf. Eaves, Eysenck, and Martin 1989:60). The history of medicine, for example, is full of cases in which elaborate theories were devised about diseases on the basis of what seemed at the time to be their most salient features but which later turned out to be only their superficial symptoms.

It is indicative of the philosophical differences between anthropology and the natural sciences that they entertain markedly different ideas about the meaning of generality as it applies to theories. Adhering to the definition generally agreed upon by philosophers of science, natural scientists take general theories to be those that deal with the qualitatively broadest possible range of subject matter. A theory about two kinds of data is more general than an alternative that speaks only to one kind or that is a special case of another. On the other hand, when anthropologists refer to generality as a characteristic of theory they almost always mean the evolutionary scale of the societies to which it applies. This evidently arises from the assumption that the qualitative differences between societies pertain to an evolutionary stage. From this it follows that the more evolutionarily advanced the phenomenon, the more "general" (i.e., more complex) the level of the theory addressing it: Theories about the origins of civilization are more general than those about unevolved hunter-gatherers. In short, anthropological general theory is evolutionary theory and always attends to the origin of complex (i.e., evolved) societies (e.g., Hallpike 1986:17; cf. Dunnell 1980:73). This recalls once again the tradition established by progressive social evolutionists in which interest in social evolution draws attention away from primitive societies, hunter-gatherers in particular (see Chapter 1). Looked at another way, anthropological theories of the highest order and greatest generality tend to deal with the most limited subject matters, the formation of pristine civilizations, for example. There is, in fact, almost an inverse relationship between generality of anthropological theories and breadth of their subject matter.

In large part, the traditional preference anthropologists display toward theories that proceed from assumptions about consequences are a function of history. As we saw in Chapter 1, anthropology developed as an applied science. Because they were working on problems relevant to social policy, early social scientists had to get their answers right; from the beginning they had to know what the ideal (most evolved) condition of mankind was in order to design social programs that would foster progress toward that condition. Not laboring under that imperative, natural scientists such as Darwin were free to contemplate microlevel processes without worrying about what they implied about the destiny of Britain, mankind, and the universe.

The source of these peculiarities of anthropological history, however, is irrelevant to the point we are trying to make. What matters is that all anthropological theories that proceed from generalizations about consequences to inferences about process are fundamentally flawed. They deny any possibility of developing a truly evolutionary theory of *cultural process* in which *ideas and the motives of individuals* – the most distinctive part of the thing we call culture – have any active part, or in which selection can play a definable role akin to that which it has in the natural sciences. Instead, they are required to envision processes in superorganic teleological terms. The conceptualization and explication of processes is subverted, and the explanation of consequences (i.e., why something is or why it happened) suffers accordingly.

Because in Darwinian theory evolutionary outcomes (consequences) are purely opportunistic, ungoverned by any grand design, the locus and action of reproduction and selection must be specified exactly to produce any expectation about consequence at all. Non-Darwinian theories characteristically lack this detailed attention to process. It is true, of course, that many non-Darwinian anthropological theories are chock-full of references to standard Darwinian processes, especially reproduction and natural selection. As in Social Darwinism, however, their use is largely allegorical and generally takes the form of crude analogies or heuristic devices. Functional models of culture, homeostatic (e.g., neofunctionalism) or not (e.g., Marxism), employ the concept of reproduction not as an independent process as in biology but as one that is system serving. Marxists, for example, speak of two distinct kinds of reproduction: one biological, the other functional. Biological reproduction, referring to subsistence and child bearing, is regarded as more or less fixed in cost and carries no special implications regarding evolutionary processes. The other kind of Marxist reproduction does have important evolutionary implications and refers to behaviors the function or effect of which is to reinforce the system: By participating in a system, one reproduces it. Neofunctionalism, and to a lesser extent the research program and early theory of technoenvironmental cultural determinism, adopt much the same kind of logic regarding reproduction though they differ from Marxist theory with respect to the degree to which systems are successfully reproduced. As the example of Binford indicates, when reproduction is conceived in these terms, the result is inertial: A system faithfully reproduces itself unless conditions change. By definition, therefore, the end product of this kind of cultural reproduction is nothing more than the original system, perhaps changed in some way but nonetheless maintaining its superorganic "essence." In this way it is possible for the system gradually to transform itself through cumulative subsystem change. In Marxism, for instance, inherent contradictions (i.e., conflict or positive feedback loops) between various elements of the social formation bring about this transformation.

Selection is unavoidably problematic in such models. Because these theories are transformational, the system itself is always reproduced, so in one sense it cannot be the locus of selection unless we take selection to mean group selection but this does not seem to be implied by any of the non-Darwinian theories under review. It is certainly not a part of Marxist explanation nor a important part of progressive social evolution, having a role only in Social Darwinism and there only a minor one. Cultural materialism and neofunctionalists draw heavily on the idea of group selection when talking theory but not when accounting for actual cases. For instance, when Vayda and Rappaport (1968) speak of the selective effects of the Plains environment on the various eastern and western tribes that entered the Plains following the introduction of the horse, it is not implied that well-adapted tribes outcompeted poorly adapted ones but rather that these tribal systems transformed themselves from within: Old behaviors that needed to change changed—and those that did not did not. So neofunctional reproduction occurs at the level of the system, whereas neofunctional selection acts on a level below that of the individual, that is, on certain nonadaptive behaviors of individuals. This implies a very complex evolutionary interaction that requires detailed models that are lacking in neofunctionalist theory.

There is an inescapable relationship between the degree of specificity in one's models of process and the level at which one expects interesting behaviors to occur. Theories of culture that lack analytically discrete models of cultural reproduction and selection that involve individuals must concern themselves with the behaviors that might characterize whole cultural superorganisms, for example, systems and the transformation of those systems. This is why non-Darwinian models are predisposed to methodological and philosophical collectivism and to models of superorganic transformation rather than selection (cf. Dunnell 1980).

In sum, cultural theories that lack true models of selection and reproduction and reduce reproduction to the needs of the system (i.e., the system reproduces what it needs) can never be reconciled with neo-Darwinian theories. Without formal models in which the units of reproduction are specified, the locus, and hence action, of selection cannot be defined in any useful way (e.g., Harris 1979:60-62; cf. Foin and Davis 1984). Evolution refers to the differential persistence of variability (Dunnell 1980) and without explicit models of reproduction and selection, such persistence has no point of reference.

Whatever middle-range theorists would like to think, middle- range theory cannot divorce itself from these problems. Quite the contrary, the fundamental flaws of neofunctionalist and cultural materialist general theory are passed along intact to the middle-range theories about hunter-gatherer adaptation that are derived from them. They are merely more deeply concealed.

THEORIES ABOUT PROCESSES

We have made the strongest case we can that Darwinian models of culture are inherently preferable to non-Darwinian theories of culture. The former permit detailed modeling of important evolutionary processes (most important, selection and reproduction) for which the latter provide no intelligible account except in terms of a kind of "bottom line" reasoning in which these forces contribute in unspecified ways to a final cultural outcome or consequence. Theories that begin with assumptions about consequences can never allow processes to act independently.

I will presume my argument is convincing to this point; if not, there is little else I can do to convince the reader. It remains to review the various Darwinian theories available to us in terms of their potential application to the human case. Fortunately there are only two basic choices and, more fortunately still, either one gives us a general theory intelligible to natural scientists and compatible with their general theory. These theories differ primarily in the locus and mode of operation of the opposing forces of selection and reproduction.

Evolutionary Ecology

In evolutionary ecological theory, selection acts on, and reproduction is construed in terms of, genetically reproducing individuals, that is, in purely biological terms—terms subject to the familiar constraints (e.g., food, water, reproduction, shelter, disease, etc.). There is no ambiguity with respect to selection or reproduction. Selection sorts out individuals that differ both genetically and behaviorally. Genetic reproduction in this case conforms to the neo-Darwinian model exactly. Except for a few genetically programmed traits, on the other hand, behavioral variability is the product of individual and social learning via the forces of guided variation and direct bias, which are themselves subject to forces acting on genes. Furthering the biological analogy, both these forces seem applicable to many animals other than humans, nonhuman primates and marine mammals, for example.

Evolutionary ecologists divide themselves or can be divided into "software" and "hard-wiring" schools distinguishable by the proportions in which individual and social learning (software) and genetic programming (hard-wiring) are believed to contribute to behavior. Both schools agree, however, that the utility of various behaviors can be evaluated with respect to genetic fitness. Culture in any of the usual senses in which it is employed in anthropology has a minor place in evolutionary ecological theory—its force, in any case, is negligibly weak. Evolutionary ecologists willingly concede that humans are special in the amount of behavioral programming that is imparted extragenetically within and between generations but contend that this specific programming is so efficiently filtered by individual biases and learning that any initial cultural variability between genetically similar individuals is quickly eliminated. In this way, cultural behavior ceases to be a source of variability upon which selection can act. Most evolutionary ecologists argue that the ability to filter between optimal and nonoptimal behaviors was established by genetic selection in the more remote past; only a few argue that genetic differences in this and similar abilities are capable of explaining behavioral differences between contemporary groups.

Evolutionary ecologists have an impressive body of theory standing behind them, and there are really only two important objections to the way they propose to interpret human behavior, one theoretical, the other methodological. The theoretical objection turns on the issue of how cultural behaviors are transmitted. As just noted, evolutionary ecologists tend to treat cultural transmission (in effect, cultural reproduction) as a relatively weak evolutionary force and to view the larger part of cultural variations as phenotypical. There are good reasons for rejecting this view. These are discussed in detail in Chapter 8 and will be mentioned again in reference to cultural inheritance theory.

The preceding theoretical objection to evolutionary ecology is related to the methodological objection, which is essentially the same one raised earlier against non-Darwinian theories. Owing to the complexity of the problem of studying evolutionary processes in humans, evolutionary ecologists are prone to assume that the groups they study are both adapted and in equilibrium. In what Gould and Lewontin (1979) term the *adaptationist program*, much evolutionary ecological research proceeds from initial assumptions about the general consequences of evolutionary processes and in varying degree subverts the empirical investigation of processes and mechanisms to suit that assumption. The theoretical objection that evolutionary ecology ignores the importance of cultural transmission is related to this methodological objection in the following way: Without an independent model of cultural reproduction (transmission), evolutionary ecologists, like neofunctionalists and cultural materialists, are forced to interpret cultural behavior in purely adaptive terms—as behaviors that promote adaptation. At best, this is a reasonable working hypothesis. At worst, it leads to a program of research in which, as in traditional hunter-gatherer research, one simply assumes that cultural behaviors are adaptive and that one's job is to show that this is so. The dangers in this are obvious: The interactive effects of even the simplest evolutionary processes are complex and without clearly developed models of process, the most sensible assumptions about adaptation often turn out to be wrong.[1]

---

[1]Sex ratios are a case in point. Simple adaptive logic suggests that efficient sexually reproducing populations should have many fewer males than females (only enough to to fertilize all females) yet in most sexually reproducing species there are as many males as females. A simple model explains why this is so (Fisher 1958). Suppose sex of offspring is genetically controlled (which it is). Suppose further that for some reason in a population there are many more females than males. This situation favors individuals who tend to produce males because when males are rarer they individually have more opportunities to mate than more numerous females. This advantage for male-producing

Research guided by optimal foraging theory, the limited theory through which evolutionary ecology has been most often applied to hunter-gatherers, frequently incorporates this unfortunate assumption regarding the adaptive consequences of Darwinian processes. It is certainly worthwhile investigating whether cultural behaviors match the expectations of microeconomic theory, but it should come as no surprise when they do not: Economizing and adaptation are not necessary implications of Darwinian theory.

Cultural Inheritance

Cultural inheritance theory differs fundamentally from evolutionary ecology by assuming that culture is an extrasomatic means of transmitting programs of behavior and that because it is extrasomatic may not lead to behaviors that conform to the expectations arising from models in which reproduction is genetic. In this view, culture is subject to forms of selection that are different from those which act on genes. It is argued that because they depart from normal genetic models and hence from the usual biological expectations about the sources of behavior, cultural reproduction and selection constitute a fundamental evolutionary division between humans (at least modern humans) and other animals, which evidently lack the more sophisticated modes of cultural inheritance.

There are at least two very persuasive arguments that favor the notion that culture is not reducible to the genetic forms of explanation favored by evolutionary ecologists. First, as we saw in Chapter 8, the heritability of behavior is not at all like that of genes: Genetic and cultural inheritance are asymmetric. The genetic model would apply generally if and only if one adopted behaviors from one's genetic parents or closely related kin, which is generally not so. Second, the forces of guided variation and direct bias are less likely to be effective where the suite of alternative behavioral responses is great and the alternatives themselves are complex and where uncertainty regarding outcomes is equally high. These are precisely the situations in which more sophisticated forms of cultural transmission—frequency-dependent transmission and indirect bias—are likely to be effective and where selection acting on behavior is likely to be the greatest. All other things equal, we would expect these forms of transmission to confer distinct evolutionary advantages for individuals with them even though the behavior of those individuals might not always be wholly optimal from the genetic perspective.

That humans are subject to special forces of cultural inheritance unavailable to other species means neither that cultural transmission obeys no objective

----

genotypes persists until the sex ratio becomes even. For the same reason, when there are more males than females, female-producing genotypes will be favored.

logic nor that human behavior cannot be understood and explained in Darwinian terms. The exemplary work of Boyd and Richerson (1985) illustrates the wealth of insights that can be obtained through exploratory quantitative modeling of certain simple cultural processes. Further, cultural inheritance theory does not imply that the cultural inheritance irrevocably separates humans from other animals. In its most general form, Darwinian theory does not specify the mechanism by which behavioral variability is transmitted. Cultural inheritance theory, thus, is a special case of the broader Darwinian framework in which the opposing forces of selection and reproduction produce variety in endless and opportunistic array. To treat culture as transmission allows us to approach humans as special kinds of animals—in short, as cultural animals, ultimately subject to the same kinds of laws that govern all things but also subject to special processes as a consequence of the manner in which their patterns of behavior are obtained. And that, as anyone who has been paying attention knows, is what anthropologists have been saying all along.

References

Alland, A., Jr., 1985, *Human Nature: Darwin's View.* New York: Columbia University Press.

Altick, R. D., 1978, *The Shows of London.* Cambridge: Belknap Press of Harvard University Press.

Althusser, L., 1970, *For Marx.* New York: Vintage Books.

Althusser, L., and Balibar, E., 1970, *Reading Capital.* London: New Left Books.

Asch, M., 1979, The ecological-evolutionary model and the concept of mode of production. In David H. Turner and Gavin A. Smith, eds., *Challenging Anthropology,* pp. 81–99. Toronto: McGraw-Hill, Ryerson Limited.

Asch, N. B., Ford, R. I., and Asch, D. L., 1972, Paleoethnobotany of the Koster Site: The Archaic Horizons. Illinois State Museum, *Reports of Investigations 24,* and Illinois Valley Archaeological Program, *Research Papers 6.*

Axelrod, R., 1984, *The Evolution of Cooperation.* New York: Basic Books.

Axelrod, R., and Hamilton, W. D., 1981, The evolution of cooperation. *Science* 211:1390–1396.

Bailey, H. P., 1960, A method of determining the warmth and temperateness of climate. *Geografiska Annaler* 43(1):1–16.

Balicki, A., 1970, *The Netsilik Eskimo.* New York: Natural History Press.

Bamforth, D., 1986, Technological efficiency and tool curation. *American Antiquity* 51:38–50.

Basgall, M., 1987, Resource intensification among hunter-gatherers: Acorn economics in prehistoric California. *Research in Economic Anthropology* 9:21–52.

Bean, L. J., 1972, *Mukat's People: The Cahuilla Indians of Southern California.* Berkeley: University of California Press.

Begler, E. B., 1978, Sex, status, and authority in egalitarian society. *American Anthropologist,* 80:571–588.

Beidelman, T., 1989, Review of "The Predicament of Culture" by J. Clifford. *Anthropros* 84:263–267.

Belshaw, C. S., 1965, *Traditional Exchange and Modern Markets.* Englewood Cliffs: Prentice Hall, Inc.

Bender, B., 1979, Gatherer-hunter to farmer: A social perspective. *World Archaeology* 10:204–222.

Bender, B., 1981, Gatherer-hunter intensification. In A. Sheridan and G. Bailey, eds., *Economic Archaeology*, pp. 149–157. BAR International Series 96. Oxford.

Bender, B., 1985, The fallacy of "hot" and "cold" societies: A comparison of prehistoric developments in the American Midcontinent and in Brittany, northwest France. In D. Price and J. Brown, eds., *Complexity among Hunter-Gatherers*, pp. 21–57. New York: Academic Press.

Benedict, R., 1959, *Patterns of Culture*. New York: New American Library, Mentor Books.

Berger, A., 1976, Structural and eclectic revisions of Marxist strategy: A cultural materialistic critique. *Current Anthropology* 17(2):290–305.

Bettinger, R. L., 1980, Explanatory/predictive models of hunter-gatherer adaptation. *Advances in Archaeological Method and Theory* 3:189–255. New York: Academic Press.

Bettinger, R. L., 1983, Comment on "Anthropological applications of optimal foraging theory: A critical review," by E. A. Smith. *Current Anthropology* 24:650–641.

Bettinger, R. L., 1987, Archaeological approaches to hunter-gatherers. *Annual Review of Anthropology* 16:121–142.

Bettinger, R. L., 1989, Pinyon House, Two Eagles, and Crater Middens: Three residential sites in Owens Valley, eastern California. *Anthropological Papers of the American Museum of Natural History* 67.

Bettinger, R. L., and Baumhoff, M. A., 1982, The Numic spread: Great Basin cultures in competition. *American Antiquity* 47(3):485–503.

Bettinger, R. L., and Baumhoff, M. A., 1983, Return rates and intensity of resource use in Numic and Prenumic adaptive strategies. *American Antiquity* 48(4):830–834.

Binford, L. R., 1962, Archaeology as anthropology. *American Antiquity* 28:217–225.

Binford, L. R., 1968a, Archaeological perspectives. In S. R. Binford and L. R. Binford, eds., *New Perspectives in Archaeology*, pp. 5–32. Chicago: Aldine.

Binford, L. R., 1968b, Post-Pleistocene adaptations. In S. R. Binford and L. R. Binford, eds., *New Perspectives in Archaeology*, pp. 313–341. Chicago, Aldine.

Binford, L. R., 1972, Contemporary model building: Paradigms and the current state of Paleolithic research. In D. L. Clark, ed., *Models in Archaeology*, pp. 109–166. London: Methuen.

Binford, L. R., 1973, Interassemblage variability—the Mousterian and the "functional" argument. In C. Renfrew, ed., *The Explanation of Culture Change*, pp. 227–254. London: Duckworth.

Binford, L. R., 1977a, General introduction. In L. R. Binford, ed., *For Theory Building in Archaeology*, pp. 1–10. New York: Academic Press.

Binford, L. R., 1977b, Forty-seven trips: A case study in the character of archaeological formation processes. In R. V. S. Wright, ed., *Stone Tools as Cultural Markers: Change, Evolution, and Complexity*, pp. 24–36. Canberra: Australian Institute of Aboriginal Studies.

Binford, L. R., 1978a, *Nunamiut Ethnoarchaelogy*. New York: Academic Press.

Binford, L. R., 1978b, Dimensional analysis of behavior and site structure: Learning from an Eskimo hunting stand. *American Antiquity* 43:330–361.

Binford, L. R., 1979, Organization and formation processes: Looking at curated technologies. *Journal of Anthropological Research* 35:255–273.

Binford, L. R., 1980, Willow smoke and dogs' tails: Hunter-gatherer settlement systems and archaeological site formation. *American Antiquity* 45:4–20.

Binford, L. R., 1981, *Bones: Ancient Men and Modern Myths*. New York: Academic Press.

Binford, L. R., 1982, The archaeology of place. *Journal of Anthropological Archaeology* 1:5–31.

Binford, L. R., 1983a, *In Pursuit of the Past: Decoding the Archaeological Record*. London: Thames and Hudson.

Binford, L. R., 1983b, *Working at Archaeology*. New York: Academic Press.

Binford, L. R., 1985, Human ancestors: Changing views of their behavior. *Journal of Anthropological Archaeology* 4:292, 327.

Birdsell, J. B., 1953, Some environmental and cultural factors influencing the structuring of Australian aboriginal populations. *American Naturalist* 87(834):171–207.

Bloch, M., 1983, *Marxism and Anthropology*. Oxford: Oxford University Press.

Boas, F., 1888, The Central Eskimo. *Report of the Bureau of Ethnology 1884–1885*:399–669. Washington: Smithsonian Institution.

Bohannan, P., 1965, Introduction. In L. H. Morgan, ed., *Houses and House-Life of the American Aborigines*, pp. v–xxi. Chicago: University of Chicago Press.

Borgerhoff-Mulder, M., 1988, Behavioral ecology in traditional societies. *Tree* 3:26–263.

Bowen, T., 1976, Seri prehistory: The archaeology of the central coast of Sonora, Mexico. *Anthropological Papers of the University of Arizona 27*. Tucson.

Bowen, T., 1983, Seri. *Handbook of North American Indians, Volume 10: Southwest*, pp. 230–249. Washington, DC: Smithsonian Institution.

Boyd, R., and Richerson, P. J., 1982, Cultural transmission and the evolution of cooperative behavior. *Human Ecology* 10:325–351.

Boyd, R., and Richerson, P. J., 1983, The cultural transmission of acquired variation: Effects on genetic fitness. *Journal of Theoretical Biology* 100:567–596.

Boyd, R., and Richerson, P. J., 1985, *Culture and Evolutionary Process*. Chicago: University of Chicago Press.

Boyd, R., and Richerson, P. J., 1987, The evolution of ethnic markers. *Cultural Anthropology* 2:65–79.

Boyd. R., and Richerson, P. J., 1988, The evolution of reciprocity in sizable groups. *Journal of Theoretical Biology* 132:337–356.

Bradby, B., 1980, The destruction of the natural economy. In H. Wolpe, ed., *The Articulation of Modes of Production: Essays from Economy and society*, pp. 93–127. London: Routledge and Kegan Paul.

Brosius, J. P., 1988, A separate reality: Comments on Hoffman's *The Punan: Hunters and Gatherers of Borneo*. *Borneo Research Bulletin* 20(2):81–106.

Buettner-Janusch, J., 1957, Boas and Mason: Particularism versus generalization. *American Anthropologist* 59:318–324.

Burling, C. R., 1962, Maximization theories and the study of economic anthropology. *American Anthropologist* 64:802–821.

Burrow, J. W., 1966, *Evolution and Society: A Study in Victorian Social Theory*. Cambridge: Cambridge University Press.

Bye, R. A., Jr., 1972, Ethnobotany of the Southern Paiute Indians in the 1870's: With a note on the early ethnobotanical contributions of Dr. Edward Palmer. In D. D. Fowler, ed., *Great Basin Cultural Ecology: A Symposium*, pp. 87–104. Reno: Desert Research Institute Publication in the Social Sciences 8.

Caldwell, J. R., 1958, Trend and tradition in the prehistory of the eastern United States. *American Anthropological Association Memoirs 88.*

Caldwell, J. R., 1959, The new American archaeology. *Science 129*:303–307.

Campbell, J. M., 1968, Territoriality among ancient hunter-gatherers: Interpetations from ethnography and nature. In B. Meggers, ed., *Anthropological Archaeology in the Americas*, pp. 1–21. Washington, DC: Anthropological Society of Washington.

Carniero, R. L., 1970, A theory of the origin of the state. *Science 169*:733–738.

Cassirer, E., 1951, *Philosophy of the Enlightenment. Princeton: Princeton University Press.*

Cavalli-Sforza, L. L., and Feldman, M. W., 1981, *Cultural Transmission and Evolution: A Quantitative Approach.* Princeton: Princeton University Press.

Chard, C., 1969, *Man in Prehistory.* New York: McGraw-Hill, Inc.

Charnov, E. L., 1976, Optimal foraging: The marginal value theorem. *Theoretical Population Biology 9*:129–136.

Chestnut, V. K., 1902, Plants used by the Indians of Mendicino County, California. *Contributions from the U.S. National Herbarium 12.* Washington, DC: U.S. Government Printing Office.

Childe, V. G., 1935, Changing methods and aims in prehistory: Presidential Address for 1935. *Proceedings of the Prehistoric Society 1*:1–15.

Chinard, G., 1947, Eighteenth century theories on America as a human habitat. *Proceedings of the American Philosophical Society 91*:27–57.

Clark, A. H., 1912, The distribution of animals and its bearing on the peopling of America. *American Anthropologist 14*:23–30.

Clark, J. G. D., 1971, *Excavations at Starr Carr.* Cambridge: Cambridge University Press.

Clark, D. L., 1968, *Analytical Archaeology.* London: Methuen.

Clark, C. W., and Mangel, M., 1984, Foraging and flocking strategies: Information in an uncertain environment. *American Naturalist 123*:626–641.

Codere, H., 1950, Fighting with property. *American Ethnological Society Monographs 18.*

Cohen, M., 1977, *The Food Crisis in Prehistory.* New Haven: Yale University Press.

Cohen, M., and Armelagos, G. J., 1984, *Paleopathology and the Origins of Agriculture.* New York: Academic Press.

Collier, D., and Tschopik, H., 1954, The role of museums in American anthropology. *American Anthropologist 56*:768–779.

Comaroff, J. L., 1984, The closed society and its critics: Historical transformation in African ethnography. *American Ethnologist 11*:571–583.

Conkey, M., 1978, Style and information in cultural evolution: Toward a predictive model for the paleolithic. In C. L. Redman, J. M. Berman, E. V. Curtin, W. T. Langhorne, N. M. Versaggi, and J. C. Wanser, eds., *Social Archaeology: Beyond Subsistence and Dating*, pp. 61–85. New York: Academic Press.

Conkey, M., 1980, The identification of prehistoric hunter-gatherer aggregation sites: The case of Altimira. *Current Anthropology 21*:609–630.

Cordell, L. S., 1984, *The Prehistory of the Southwest.* New York: Academic Press.

Coville, F. V., 1892, The Panamint Indians of California. *American Anthropologist* 5:351–361.

Cowgill, G., 1975, A selection of samplers: Comments on archaeo-statistics. In J. W. Mueller, ed., *Sampling in Archaeology*, pp. 258–274. Tucson: University of Arizona Press.

Curtis, L. P., Jr., 1968, *Anglo-Saxons and Celts*. New York: New York University Press.

Dalton, G., 1961, Economic theory and primitive society. *American Anthropologist* 63:1–25.

Dalton, G., 1969, Theoretical issues in economic anthropology. *Current Anthropology* 10:63–102.

Dalton, G., and Kocke, J., 1983, The work of the Polanyi group: Past, present and future. In S. Ortiz, ed., *Economic Anthropology: Topics and Theories*, pp. 21–50. Monographs in Economic Anthropology I. Society of Economic Anthropology. Lanham, Maryland: University Press of America.

Damas, D., 1969, Introduction. In D. Damas, ed., *Contributions to Anthropology: Ecological Essays*, 1–12. Ottawa: National Museums of Canada Bulletin 230.

Daniel, G., 1950, *A Hundred Years of Archaeology*. London: Duckworth.

Darrah, W. C., 1951, *Powell of the Colorado*. Princeton: Princeton University Press.

Darwin, C., 1871, *The Descent of Man and Selection According to Sex*. London: Murray.

Davis, W. G., 1973, *Social Relations in a Philippine Market*. Berkeley: University of California Press.

Davis, W. G., 1978, Review of "Max Weber's Theory of Concept Formation: History, Laws, and Ideal Types," by T. Burger. *American Anthropologist* 80:121–124.

Dawkins, R., 1976, *The Selfish Gene*. New York: Oxford University Press.

De Laguna, F., 1960, The development of anthropology. In F. De Laguna, ed., *Selected Papers from the American Anthropologist: 1888–1920*, pp. 91–104. Evanston: Row, Peterson, and Company.

Deetz, J., 1965, The dynamics of stylistic change in Arikara ceramics. *Illinois Studies in Anthropology 4*.

Denbow, J. R., 1984, Prehistoric herders and foragers of the Kalahari: The evidence for 1500 years of interaction. In C. Schrire, ed., *Past and Present in Hunter-Gatherer Studies*, pp. 175–193. Orlando: Academic Press.

Dickens, C., 1853, The noble savage. *Household Words* 7(168):337–339. London: Bradberry and Evans.

Dixon, R., 1928, *The Building of Cultures*. New York: Scribner's Sons.

Douglas, M., 1962, The Lele: Resistance to change. In P. Bohannan and G. Dalton, eds., *Markets in Africa*, pp. 211–233. Evanston: Northwestern University Press.

Dragoo, D. W., 1976, Some aspects of eastern North American prehistory. *American Antiquity* 41(1):3–27.

Dunnell, R., 1978, Style and function: A fundamental dichotomy. *American Antiquity* 43:192–202.

Dunnell, R., 1980, Evolutionary theory and archaeology. *Advances in Archaeological Method and Theory* 3:35–99. New York: Academic Press.

Dutcher, B. H., 1893, Pinon gathering among the Panamint Indians. *American Anthropologist* 6:377–380.

Dyson-Hudson, R., and Smith, E. A., 1978, Human territoriality: An ecological reassessment. *American Anthropologist* 80:21–41.

Eaves, L., Eysenck, H., and Martin, N., 1989, *Genes, Culture and Personality*. New York: Academic Press.

Elster, J., 1985, *Making Sense of Marx*. Cambridge: Cambridge University Press.

Emlen, J. M., 1973, *Ecology: An Evolutionary Approach*. Reading, Massachusetts: Addison-Wesley.

Engels, F., 1972, *The Origin of the Family, Private Property, and the State*. New York: Pathfinder Press.

Faris, J. C., 1979, Social evolution, population, and production. In S. Diamond, ed., *Toward a Marxist Anthropology*, pp. 421–453. The Hague: Mouton.

Fisher, R. A., 1958, *The Genetical Theory of Natural Selection*. Revised edition. New York: Dover.

Flannery, K. V., 1967, Review of "An Introduction to American Archaeology, Volume I: North and Middle America," by G. R. Willey. *Scientific American* 217:119–122.

Flannery, K. V., 1968, Archaeological system theory and early Mesoamerica. In B. Meggars, ed., *Anthropological Archaeology in the Americas*, pp. 67–87. Washington, DC: Anthropological Society of Washington.

Flannery, K. V., 1969, Origins and effects of early domestication in Iran and Near East. In P. J. Ucko and G. W. Dimbleby, eds., *The Domestication and Exploitation of Plants and Animals*, pp. 73–100. Chicago: Aldine.

Flannery, K. V., 1972, The cultural evolution of civilizations. *Annual Review of Ecology and Systematics* 3:399–426.

Flannery, K. V., 1973, Archaeology with a capital "S." In C. L. Redman, ed., *Research and Theory in Current Archaeology*, pp. 47–53. New York: Wiley and Sons.

Flannery, K. V., 1982, The golden Marshalltown: A parable for the archaeology of the 1980's. *American Anthropologist* 84:265–278.

Foin, T. C., and Davis, W. G., 1984, Ritual and self-regulation of the Tsembaga Mariing ecosystem in the New Guinea highlands. *Human Ecology* 12:385–412.

Ford, J. A., 1954, On the concept of types. *American Anthropologist* 56:42–53.

Forde, C. D., 1934, *Habitat, Economy, and Society*. New York: Harcourt, Brace, and Company.

Fowler, D. D., and Fowler, C. S., 1971, Anthropology of the Numa: John Wesley Powell's manuscripts on the Numic peoples of Western North America, 1868–1880. *Smithsonian Contributions to Anthropology 14.*

Fried, M., 1967, *The Evolution of Political Society: An Essay in Political Anthropology*. New York: Random House.

Friedman, J., 1974, Marxism, structuralism, and vulgar materialism. *Man* 9:444–469.

Friedman, J., 1975, Tribes, states, and transformations. In M. Bloch, ed., *Marxist Analyses and Social Anthropology*, pp. 161–202. New York: John Wiley and Sons.

Friedman, J., 1979, Hegelian ecology: Between Rousseau and the World Spirit. In P. C. Burnham and R. F. Ellen, eds., *Social and Ecological Systems*, pp. 253–270. New York: Academic Press.

Funk, R. E., 1976, Recent contributions to Hudson Valley prehistory. *New York State Museum Memoir 22.*

Funk, R. E., 1978, Post-Pleistocene adaptations. In *Handbook of North American Indians 15: Northeast*, pp. 16–27. Washington, DC: Smithsonian Institution.

Funk, R. E., 1983, The northeastern United States. In J. D. Jennings, ed., *Ancient North Americans*, pp. 303–371. San Francisco: W. H. Freeman.

Gamble, C., 1981, Social control and the economy. In A. Sheridan and G. Bailey, eds., *Economic Archaeology*, pp. 215–229. BAR International Series 96. Oxford.

Gamble, C., 1983, Culture and society in the Upper Paleolithic of Europe. In *Hunter-Gatherer Economy in Prehistory: A European Perspective*, pp. 201–211. Cambridge: Cambridge University Press.

Gilman, A., 1984, Explaining the Upper Paleolithic transition. In M. Spriggs, ed., *Marxist Perspectives in Archaeology*, pp. 115–126. London: Cambridge University Press.

Glacken, C. J., 1967, *Traces on the Rhodian shore*. Berkeley: University of California Press.

Godelier, M., 1972, *Rationality and Irrationality in Economics*. London: New Left Books.

Godelier, M., 1973, *Marxist Perspectives in Anthropology*. London: Cambridge University Press.

Godelier, M., 1975, Modes of production, kinship, and demographic structures. In M. Bloch, ed., *Marxist Analyses and Social Anthropology*, pp. 3–27. New York: John Wiley and Sons.

Godelier, M., 1977, *Horizon, trajets marxistes en anthropologie*. Paris: Maspero.

Godelier, M., 1982, The problem of the "reproduction" of socioeconomic systems. In I. Rossi, ed., *Structural Sociology*, pp. 259–291. New York: Columbia University Press.

Godelier, M., 1984, To be a Marxist in anthropology. In J. Maquet and N. Daniels, eds., *On Marxist Perspectives in Anthropology: Essays in Honor of Harry Hoijer*, pp. 35–57. Malibu, California: Undenae (for the University of California, Los Angeles, Department of Anthropology).

Goodyear, A. C., Raab, L. M., and Klinger, T. C., 1978, The status of archaeological research design in cultural resource management. *American Antiquity* 43:159–173.

Goldschmidt, W., 1974, Subsistence activities among the Hupa. In R. Beals and J. Hester, Jr., eds., *Indian Land Use and Occupancy in California, Volume I*, pp. 52–55. New York: Garland Publishing.

Gordon, R. J., 1984, The !Kung in the Kalahari exchange: An ethnohistorical perspective. In C. Schrire, ed., *Past and Present in Hunter-gatherer Studies*, pp. 195–224. Orlando: Academic Press.

Gould, R. A., 1969, Subsistence behavior among the Western Desert Aborigines. *Oceania* 39:53–74.

Gould, R. A., ed., 1978, *Explorations in Ethnoarchaeology*. Albuquerque: University of New Mexico Press.

Gould, S. J., and Lewontin, R. C., 1979, The Spandrels of San Marco and the Panglossian paradigm: A critique of the adaptationist programme. *Proceedings of the Royal Society of London* B205:581–598.

Grayson, D. K., 1986, Eoliths, archaeological ambigutiy, and the generation of "middle-range" research. In D. J. Meltzer and D. D. Fowler, eds., *American Archaeology: Past and Future*, pp. 77–133. Washington, DC: Smithsonian Institution Press.

Grayson, D. K., 1988, Danger Cave, Last Supper Cave, and Hanging Rock Shelter: The faunas. *Anthropological Papers of the American Museum of Natural History* 66(1).

Griffin, J. B., 1983, The Midlands. In J. D. Jennings, ed., *Ancient North Americans*, pp. 243–301. San Francisco: W. H. Freeman.

Gudeman, S., 1986, *Economics as Culture*. London: Routledge and Kegan Paul.

Hallowell, A. I., 1960, The beginnings of anthropology in America. In F. De Laguna, ed., *Selected Papers from the American Anthropologist: 1888–1920*, pp. 1–90. Evanston: Row, Peterson, and Company.

Hallpike, C. R., 1986, *The Principles of Social Evolution*. Oxford: Clarendon Press.

Hamilton, W. D., 1963, The evolution of altruistic behavior. *American Naturalist* 97:354–356.

Hamilton, W. D., 1964, The genetical theory of altruistic behavior I, II. *Journal of Theoretical Biology* 7:1–52.

Hamilton, W. D., 1986, Biological constraints of social evolution: Kinship, recognition, reciprocity. Sloan Seminar Lecture. University of California, Davis.

Hardin, R., 1982, *Collective Action*. Baltimore: Johns Hopkins University Press.

Harris, M., 1966, The cultural ecology of India's sacred cattle. *Current Anthropology* 7:51–59.

Harris, M., 1968a, *The Rise of Anthropological Theory*. New York: Crowell.

Harris, M., 1968b, Comments. In S. R. Binford and L. R. Binford eds., *New Perspectives in Archaeology*, pp. 360–361. Chicago: Aldine.

Harris, M., 1971, *Culture, Man and Nature: Introduction to General Anthropology*. New York: Crowell.

Harris, M., 1974a, *Cows, Pigs, Wars, and Witches: The Riddles of Culture*. New York: Random House.

Harris, M., 1974b, Why a perfect knowledge of all the rules one must know to act like a native cannot lead to the knowledge of how natives act. *Journal of Anthropological Research* 30:242–251.

Harris, M., 1977, *Cannibals and Kings: The Origins of Cultures*. New York: Random House.

Harris, M., 1979, *Cultural Materialism*. New York: Random House.

Hassan, F., 1981, *Demographic Archaeology*. New York: Academic Press.

Hawkes, K., and O'Connell, J. F., 1981, Affluent hunters? Some comments in light of the Alyawara case. *American Anthropologist* 83:622–626.

Hawkes, K., Hill, K., and O'Connell, J. F., 1982, Why hunters gather: Optimal foraging and the Ache of eastern Paraguay. *American Ethnologist* 9:379–398.

Hawkes, K., O'Connell, J. F., Hill, K., and Charnov, E. L., 1985, How much is enough? Hunters and limited needs. *Ethnology and Sociobiology* 6:3–15.

Heizer, R. F., 1958, Prehistoric central California: A problem in historical-developmental classification. *University of California Archaeological Survey Reports* 41:19–26.

Hellman, G., 1968, *Bankers, Bones, and Beetles: The First Century of the American Museum of Natural History*. Garden City: Natural History Press.

Hempel, C. G., 1965, *Aspects of Scientific Explanation*. New York: Free Press.

Hewlett, B. S., and Cavalli-Sforza, L. L., 1986, Cultural transmission among Aka pygmies. *American Anthropologist* 88:922–934.

Hill, J. N., 1968, Broken K Pueblo: Patterns of form and function. In S. R. Binford and L. R. Binford, eds., *New Perspectives in Archaeology*, pp. 103–142. Chicago: Aldine.

Hill, J. N., 1970, Broken K Pueblo: Prehistoric Social Organization in the American Southwest. *University of Arizona Anthropological Papers 18.*

Hill, K., Kaplan, H., Hawkes, K., and Magdelena Hurtado, A. M., 1987, Foraging decisions among Ache hunter-gatherers: New data and implications for optimal foraging models. *Ethology and Sociobiology* 8:1–36.

Hindess, B., and Hirst, P. Q., 1975, *Pre-capitalist Modes of Production.* London: Routledge and Kegan Paul.

Hinsley, C. M., Jr., 1981, *Savages and Scientists: The Smithsonian Institution and the Development of American Anthropology, 1846–1910.* Washington, DC: Smithsonian Institution Press.

Hobbes, T., 1962, *Leviathan.* New York: Collier (reprint of 1651 edition).

Hobsbawm, E. J., 1964, Introduction. In *Pre-capitalist Economic Formations, by Karl Marx,* pp. 1–65. New York: International Publishers.

Hodder, I., ed., 1982a, *Symbolic and Structural Archaeology.* London: Cambridge University Press.

Hodder, I., 1982b, *Symbols in Action: Ethnoarchaeological Studies of Material Culture.* London: Cambridge University Press.

Hodder, I., 1983, *The Present Past: An Introduction to Anthropology for Archaeologists.* London: Batsford; New York: Pica Press.

Hodder, I., 1986, *Reading the Past: Current Approaches to Interpretation in Archaeology.* London: Cambridge University Press.

Hoffman, C. L., 1984, Punan foragers in the trading networks of Southeast Asia. In C. Schrire, ed., *Past and Present in Hunter-Gatherer Studies,* pp. 123–149. Orlando: Academic Press.

Hofstadter, R., 1944, *Social Darwinism in American Thought.* Boston: Beacon Press.

Hudson, K., 1981, *A Social History of Archaeology.* London: Macmillan Press.

Huntington, E., 1945, *Mainsprings of Civilization.* New York: Wiley and Sons.

Huntington, E., 1963, *The Human Habitat.* New York: Norton (original 1927)

Isaac, G. L., 1968, Traces of Pleistocene hunters: An East African example. In R. B. Lee and I. Devore, eds., *Man the Hunter,* pp. 253–261. Chicago: Aldine.

Isaac, G. L., 1978, The food sharing behavior of protohuman hominids. *Scientific American* 238(4):90–108.

Isaac, G. L., and Crader, D., 1981, To what extent were early hominids carnivorous? An archaeological perspective. In R. S. O. Harding and G. Teleki, eds., *Omnivorous Primates: Gathering and Hunting in Human Evolution,* pp. 37–103. New York: Columbia University Press.

Jefferson, T., 1787, *Notes on the State of Virginia.* London: John Stockdale.

Jennings, J. D., 1957, Danger Cave. *Society for American Archaeology Memoir 14.*

Jennings, J. D., 1968, *Prehistory of North America.* New York: McGraw-Hill.

Jennings, J. D., 1978, Prehistory of Utah and the Eastern Great Basin. *University of Utah Anthropological Papers 98.*

Jochim, M., 1983, Paleolithic cave art in ecological perspective. In G. Bailey, ed., *Hunter-Gatherer Economy in Prehistory: A European Perspective,* pp. 212–219. Cambridge: Cambridge University Press.

Jones, G. T., Grayson, D. K., and Beck, C., 1983, Artifact class richness and sample size in archaeological surface assemblages. In R. C. Dunnell and D. K. Grayson, *Lulu Linear Punctated: Essays in Honor of George Irving Quimby*, pp. 55–73. Anthropological Papers of the Museum of Anthropology, University of Michigan.

Kaplan, H., and Hill, K., 1985, Food sharing among Ache foragers: Tests of explanatory hypotheses. *Current Anthropology* 16:223–246.

Kaskija, L., 1988, Carl Hoffman and the Punan of Borneo. *Borneo Research Bulletin* 20(2):121–129.

Keenan, J., 1977, The concept of the mode of production in hunter-gatherer societies. *African Studies* 36(1):57–69.

Keene, A. S., 1979, Economic optimization models and the study of hunter-gatherer subsistence settlement systems. In C. Renfrew and K. Cooke, eds., *Transformations: Mathematical Approaches to Culture Change*, pp. 369–404. New York: Academic Press.

Keene, A., 1981, *Prehistoric Foraging in a Temperate Forest: A Linear Programming Model*. New York: Academic Press.

Kennedy, J. G., 1978, *Herbert Spencer*. Boston: Twayne.

Kidder, A. V., 1927, Southwestern archaeological conference. *Science* 66:486–491.

Kimball, E. P., 1968, *Sociology and Education: An Analysis of the Theories of Spencer and Ward*. New York: Columbia University Press. AMS Press (original 1932).

Kirch, P. V., 1980, The archaeological study of adaptation: Theoretical and methodological issues. *Advances in Archaeological Theory and Method* 3:101–156. New York: Academic Press.

Kluckholn, C., 1940, The conceptual structure in Middle American studies. In A. M. Tozzer, ed., *The Maya and Their Neighbors*, pp. 41–51. New York: Appleton-Century.

Kluckhohn, C., 1944, *Navaho Witchcraft*. Boston: Beacon Press.

Kramer, C., ed., 1979, *Ethnoarchaeology: Implications of Ethnography for Archaeology*. New York: Columbia.

Kroeber, A. L., 1939, Cultural and natural areas of native North America. *University of California Publications in American Archaeology and Ethnology 38*.

Kuhn, T. S., 1962, *The Structure of Scientific Revolutions*. Chicago: University of Chicago Press.

Kus, S., 1984, The spirit and its burden: Archaeology and symbolic activity. In M. Spriggs, ed., *Marxist Perspectives in Archaeology*, pp. 101–107. London: Cambridge University Press.

Lack, D., 1954, *The Natural Regulation of Animal Numbers*. Cambridge: Cambridge University Press.

Lande, R., 1981, Models of speciation by sexual selection on polygenetic traits. *Proceedings of the National Academy of Sciences* 78:3721–3725.

Lathrap, D., 1968, The "hunting" economies of the tropical forest zone of South America: An attempt at historical perspective. In R. B. Lee and I. Devore, eds., *Man the Hunter*, pp. 23–29. Chicago: Aldine.

Lee, R. B., 1968, What hunters do for a living, or how to make out on scarce resources. In R. B. Lee and I. Devore, eds., *Man the Hunter*, pp. 30–48. Chicago: Aldine.

Lee, R. B., 1969, !Kung Bushman subsistence: An input-output analysis. In D. Damas, ed., *Contributions to Anthropology: Ecological Essays*, pp. 73–94. Ottawa: National Museums of Canada Bulletin 230.

Lee, R. B., and Devore, I., eds., 1968, *Man the Hunter*. Chicago: Aldine.

Longacre, W. A., 1968, Some aspects of prehistoric society in east-central Arizona. In S. R. Binford and L. R. Binford, eds., *New Perspectives in Archaeology*, pp. 89–102. Chicago: Aldine.

Longacre, W. A., 1970, Archaeology as anthropology: A case study. *University of Arizona Anthropological Papers 17.*

Lovejoy, A. O., 1964, *The Great Chain of Being*. Cambridge: Harvard University Press.

Lubbock, Sir J., 1872, *Prehistoric Times as Illustrated by Ancient Remains and the Manners and Customs of Modern Savages*. New York: Appleton and Company.

Lumsden, C., and Wilson, E. O., 1981, *Genes, Mind, and Culture*. Cambridge: Harvard University Press.

Lyman, R. L., 1895, Bone frequencies: Differential transport, in situ destruction, and the MGUI. *Journal of Archaeological Science 12:*221–236.

MacArthur, R. H., and Pianka, E. R., 1966, On optimal use of a patchy environment. *American Naturalist 100:*603–609.

MacNeish, R. S., 1964, Ancient Mesoamerican civilization. *Science 143:*531–537.

Maine, H. S., 1861, *Ancient Law*. London: Murray.

Madsen, D. B., and Kirkman, J. E., 1988, Hunting hoppers. *American Antiquity 53:*593–604.

Malthus, T. R., 1803, *An Essay on the Principle of Population*. London: Johnson.

Marx, K., 1967, *Capital 1*. Edited by Frederich Engels. New York: International Publishers (original 1887).

Marx, K., 1977, *Karl Marx: Selected Writings*. Edited by D. McLellan. Oxford: Oxford University Press.

Marx, K., and Engels, F., 1967, *The Communist Manifesto*. Middlesex: Penguin.

Marx, K., and Engels, F., 1970, *The German Ideology*. New York: International Publishers.

Mason, O. T., 1894, Technogeography, or the relation of the earth to the industries of mankind. *American Anthropologist 7:*137–161.

Mason, O. T., 1895, Influence of environment upon human industries or arts. *Smithsonian Institution Annual Report, 1893:*639–665.

Mason, O. T., 1905, Environment. In F. W. Hodge, ed., *Handbook of American Indians*, pp. 427–430. *Bureau of American Ethnology Bulletin 30.*

Maynard Smith, J., 1982, *Evolution and the Theory of Games*. Cambridge: Cambridge University Press.

Maynard Smith, J., and Price, G. R., 1973, The logic of animal conflict. *Nature 246:*15–18.

Mayr, E., 1987, Punctuated equilibrium and macroevolution. Ecology Seminar Lecture. University of California, Davis.

McGee, W. J., 1898, The Seri Indians. *Seventeenth Annual Report of the Bureau of American Ethnology, 1895–96:*1–344.

McGee, W. J., 1899, The trend of human progress. *American Anthroplogist 1:*401–447.

McKern, W. C., 1939, The Midwestern Taxonomic Method as an aid to archaeological study. *American Antiquity 4:*301–313.

Mead, M., 1960, Introduction. In R. Bunzel, ed., *The Golden Age of American Anthropology*, pp. 1–12. New York: Braziller.

Meadows, P., 1952, John Wesley Powell: Frontiersman of science. *University of Nebraska Studies, New Series 10.*

Meggers, B., 1971, *Amazonia: Man and Culture in a Counterfeit Paradise*. Chicago: Aldine.

Meillassoux, C., 1972, From production to reproduction. *Economy and Society* 1:93–105. bet refg2 pd

Meillassoux, C., 1973, On the mode of production of the hunting band. In P. Alexandre, ed., *French Perspectives in African Studies*, pp. 187–203. London: Oxford University Press.

Mellars, P. A., 1973, The character of the Middle-Upper Paleolithic transition in south-west France. In C. Renfrew, ed., *The Explanation of Culture Change: Models in Prehistory*, pp. 255–276. London: Duckworth.

Meltzer, D. J., 1983, The antiquity of man and the development of American archaeology. *Advances in Archaeological Method and Theory* 6:1–51. New York: Academic Press.

Meltzer, D. J., 1990, Review of "Social Theory and Archaeology" by M. Shanks and C. Tilley. *American Antiquity* 55(1):186–187.

Merton, R. K., 1968, *Social Theory and Social Structure* (3rd edition). New York: Free Press.

Metcalfe, D., and Jones, K. T., 1988, A reconsideration of animal body-part utility indices. *American Antiquity* 53:486–504.

Moore, O. K., 1965, Divination: A new perspective. *American Anthropologist* 59:69–74.

Morgan, L. H., 1876, Montezuma's dinner. *North American Review* 122:265–308.

Morgan, L. H., 1877, *Ancient Society*. New York: World Publishing.

Morgan, L. H., 1881, Houses and house life of the American Aborigines. *Contributions to North American Ethnology 4.* Washington, DC: Government Printing Office.

Moseley, K. P., and Wallerstein, I., 1978, Precapitalist social structures. *Annual Review of Sociology* 4:259–290.

Murdock, G. P., 1949, *Social Structure*. New York: Macmillan.

Murphy, R. F., 1970, Basin ethnography and ecological theory. In *Languages and Cultures of Western North America: Essays in Honor of Sven Liljeblad*, pp. 152–171. Pocatello: Idaho State University Press.

National Academy Sciences, 1968, *Recommended Dietary Allowances*. Washington, DC: National Academy of Sciences. Seventh revised edition.

O'Connell, J. F., and Hawkes, K., 1981, Alyawara plant use and optimal foraging theory. In B. Winterhalder and E. A. Smith, eds., *Hunter-Gatherer Foraging Strategies*, pp. 99–125. Chicago: University of Chicago Press.

O'Connell, J. F., and Hawkes, K., 1984, Food choice and foraging sites among the Alyawara. *Journal of Anthropological Research* 40:504–435.

O'Connell, J. F., Jones, K. T., and Simms, S., 1982, Some thoughts on prehistoric archaeology in the Great Basin. In D. B. Madsen and J. F. O'Connell, eds., *Man and Environment in the Great Basin*, pp. 227–240. Washington, DC: Society for American Archaeology Papers 2.

Odum, E. P., 1959, *Fundamentals of Ecology*. Philadelphia and London: Saunders.

O'Laughlin, B., 1975, Marxist approaches in anthropology. *Annual Review of Anthropology* 4:341–370.

Ollason, J. G., 1980, Learning to forage—optimally? *Theoretical Population Biology* 18:44–56.

Orans, M., 1975, Domesticating the functional dragon: An analysis of Piddocke's potlatch. *American Anthropologist* 77:312–328.

Orians, G. H., and Pearson, N. E., 1979, On the theory of central place foraging. In D. J. Horn, G. R. Stairs, and R. D. Mitchell, eds., *Analysis of Ecological Systems*, pp. 155–177. Columbus: Ohio State University.

Orlove, B., 1980, Ecological anthropology. *Annual Review of Anthropology* 9:235–273.

Palmer, E., 1871, Food products of the North American Indians. *Report of the Commissioner of Agriculture for 1870:*404–428.

Palmer, E., 1874, Die vegetabilischen Nahrungsmittel der Indianer in Nordamerika von Dr. Edward Palmer. *Monatschrifter Vereines Befoerderung Gartnerei* 27:22–28, 76–84, 133–136, 154–175, 236–240.

Palmer, E., 1878, Plants used by the Indians of the United States. *American Naturalist* 12:593–606, 646–655.

Parkington, J. E., 1984, Soaqua and Bushmen: Hunters and robbers. In C. Schrire, *Past and Present in Hunter-Gatherer Studies*, pp. 151–174. Orlando: Academic Press.

Pasquinelli, C., 1983, The history of a relationship: Contemporary cultural anthropology and Marxism in France and Italy. *Dialectical Anthropology* 7(3):195–207.

Pearce, R. H., 1988, *Savagism and Civilization.* Berkeley: University of California Press.

Peel, J. D. Y., 1972, *Herbert Spencer on Social Evolution: Selected Writings.* Chicago: University of Chicago Press.

Peoples, J., 1982, Individual or group advantages? A reinterpretation of the Maring ritual cycle. *Current Anthropology* 23:291–310.

Piddocke, S., 1965, The potlatch system of the southern Kwakiutl: A new perspective. *Southwestern Journal of Anthropology* 21:244–264.

Plog, S., 1978, Social interaction and stylistic similarity. *Advances in Archaelogical Method and Theory* 1:143–182. New York: Academic Press.

Polanyi, K., 1957, The economy as instituted process. In K. Polanyi, C. Arensburg, and H. Pearson, eds., *Trade and Market in the Early Empires*, pp. 243–270. New York: Free Press.

Powell, J. W., 1883, Human evolution. *Transactions of the Anthropological Society of Washington* 2:176–208.

Powell, J. W., 1885, From savagery to barbarism. *Transactions of the Anthropological Society of Washington* 3:173–196.

Powell, J. W., 1888a, From barbarism to civilization. *American Anthropologist* 1:97–123.

Powell, J. W., 1888b, Competition as a factor in human evolution. *American Anthropologist* 1:297–323.

Powell, J. W., 1891, Indian linguistic families of America north of Mexico. *Annual Report of the Bureau of Ethnology* 7:1–142.

Powell, J. W., 1898, Administrative Report. *Annual Report of the Bureau of American Ethnology* 17:xxvii–xciii.

Raab, L. M., and Goodyear, A. C., 1984, Middle-range theory in archaeology: A critical review of origins and applications. *American Antiquity* 49:255–268.

Rappaport, R. A., 1968, *Pigs for the Ancestors.* New Haven: Yale University Press.

Rappaport, R. A., 1970, Sanctity and adaptation. *Io* 7:46–71.

Rappaport, R. A., 1977, Ecology, adaptation and the ills of functionalism. *Michigan Discussions in Anthropology* 2:138–190.

Rappaport, R. A., 1984, *Pigs for the Ancestors*. New Haven: Yale University Press. Enlarged edition.

Rathje, W. L., 1972, Praise the gods and pass the metates: A hypothesis of the development of lowland rainforest civilizations in Mesoamerica. In M. Leone, ed., *Contemporary Archaeology*, pp. 365–392. Carbondale: Southern Illinois University Press.

Reidhead, V. A., 1979, Linear programming models in archaeology. *Annual Reviews in Anthropology* 8:543–578.

Reidhead, V. A., 1980, Economics of subsistence change. In T. K. Earle and A. L. Christensen, eds., *Modeling of Prehistoric Subsistence Economies*, pp. 141–186. New York: Academic Press.

Rey, P. P., 1979, Class contradiction in lineage societies. *Critique of Anthropology* 41–60.

Roll, E., 1953, *A History of Economic Thought*. Faber and Faber.

Roper, D. C., 1979, The method and theory of site catchment analysis: A review. *Advances in Archaeological Method and Theory* 2:119–140. New York: Academic Press.

Rosenberg, A., 1980, *Sociobiology and the Preemption of Social Science*. Baltimore: Johns Hopkins University Press.

Rouse, I., 1960, The classification of artifacts in archaeology. *American Antiquity* 25:313–323.

Rudner, R. S., 1966, *Philosophy of the Social Sciences*. Englewood Cliffs, New Jersey: Prentice-Hall.

Rutz, H. J., 1977, Individual decisions and functional systems: Economic rationality and environmental adaptation. *American Ethnologist* 4(1):156–174.

Sackett, J. R., 1985, Style and ethnicity in the Kalahari: A reply to Wiessner. *American Antiquity* 50:154–159.

Sackett, J. R., 1986, Style, function, and assemblage variability: A reply to Binford. *American Antiquity* 51:628–634.

Sahlins, M. D., 1963, Poor man, rich man, big-man, chief: Political types in Melanesia and Polynesia. *Comparitive Studies in Society and History* 5(3):285–303.

Sahlins, M. D., 1968, Notes on the original affluent society. In R. B. Lee and I. Devore, eds., *Man the Hunter*, pp. 85–89. Chicago: Aldine.

Sahlins, M. D., 1972, *Stone-Age Economics*. Chicago: Aldine.

Sahlins, M. D., 1976, *Culture and Practical Reason*. Chicago: University of Chicago Press.

Salmon, M. H., 1976, "Deductive" versus "inductive" archaeology. *American Antiquity* 41:376–381.

Salmon, M. H., 1978, What can systems theory do for archaeology? *American Antiquity* 43(2):174–183.

Salwen, B., 1975, Post-glacial environments and culture change in the Hudson River Basin. *Man in the Northeast* 10:43–70.

Sapir, E., 1912, Language and environment. *American Anthropologist* 14:226–242.

Schiffer, M. B., 1972, Archaeological context and systemic context. *American Antiquity* 37:156–165.

Schiffer, M. B., 1976, *Behavioral Archaeology*. New York: Academic Press.

Schiffer, M. B., and Rathje, W. L., 1973, Efficient exploitation of the archaeological record: Penetrating problems. In C. L. Redman, ed., *Research and Theory in Current Archaeology*, pp. 169–179. New York: Wiley and Sons.

Schoener, T. W., 1974, The compression hypothesis and temporal resource partitioning. *Proceedings of the National Academy of Sciences* 71:4169–4172.

Schrire, C., 1984, Wild surmises on savage thoughts. In C. Schrire, ed., *Past and Present in Hunter-Gatherer Studies*, pp. 1–25. New York: Academic Press.

Sellato, J. L., 1988, The nomads of Borneo: Hoffman and "devolution." *Borneo Research Bulletin* 20(2):106–120.

Semple, E. C., 1911, *Influences of Geographic Environment: On the Basis of Ratzel's System of Anthropogeography*. New York: Holt.

Service, E. R., 1962, *Primitive Social Organization: An Evolutionary Perspective*. New York: Random House.

Shanks, M., and Tilley, C., 1987, *Social Theory and Archaeology*. Cambridge: Polity Press.

Simms, S., 1984, *Aboriginal Great Basin Foraging Strategies: An Evolutionary Analysis*. Doctoral dissertation, Department of Anthropology, University of Utah.

Siskind, J., 1978, Kinship and mode of production. *American Anthropologist* 80:860–872.

Smith, A., 1776, *An Inquiry into the Nature and Causes of the Wealth of Nations*. London: Strahan and Cadell.

Smith, E. A., 1980, *Evolutionary Ecology and the Analysis of Human Foraging Behavior: An Inuit Example from the East Coast of Hudson Bay*. Doctoral dissertation, Cornell University.

Smith, E. A., 1981, The application of optimal foraging theory to the analysis of hunter-gatherer group size. In B. Winterhalder and E. A. Smith, eds., *Hunter-Gatherer Foraging Strategies*, pp. 35–65. Chicago: University of Chicago Press.

Smith, E. A., 1983, Anthropological applications of optimal foraging theory. *Current Anthropology* 24:625–651.

Sollas, W. J., 1915, *Ancient Hunters and Their Modern Representatives*. London: Macmillan. Second edition.

Spaulding, A. C., 1953, Statistical techniques for the discovery of artifact types. *American Antiquity* 18:305–313.

Spaulding, A. C., 1968, Explanation in archaeology. In S. R. Binford and L. R. Binford, eds., *New Perspectives in Archaeology*, pp. 33–39. Chicago: Aldine.

Speck, F. G., 1915, The family hunting band as the basis of Algonkian social organization. *American Anthropologist* 17:289–305.

Spencer, H., 1852, A theory of population deduced from the general law of animal fertility. *Westminster Review* (New Series) Volume 1 (April, Article IV):468–501.

Spencer, H., 1865, *Social Statics*. New York: Appleton. (Original 1850)

Spencer, H., 1868a, *Progress: Its Law and Cause*. Essays I:1–60. London: Williams and Norgate (Original *Westminster Review*, April 1857).

Spencer, H., 1868b, *The Social Organism*. Essays I:384–428. London: Williams and Norgate (Original *Westminster Review*, January 1860).

Spencer, H., 1868c, *Over-legislation*. Essays II:48–106. London: Williams and Norgate (Original *Westminster Review*, July 1853).

Spencer, H., 1870, *Illustrations of Universal Progress*. New York: Appleton.

Spencer, H., 1876, *The Principles of Sociology I*. London: Williams and Norgate.

Spencer, H., 1882, *Principles of Sociology II*. London: Williams and Norgate.

Spencer, H., 1896, *Principles of Sociology III*. London: Williams and Norgate.

Spencer, H., 1898, *Principles of Biology I*. New York: Appleton. Revised and enlarged edition. (Original 1866)

Spencer, H., 1910a, *First Principles*. New York: Appleton. 6th edition. (Original 1864)

Spencer, H., 1910b, *The Study of Sociology*. New York: Appleton. (Original 1873)

Stanner, W. E. H., 1965, Religion, totemism, and symbolism. In R. M. Berndt and C. H. Berndt, eds., *Aboriginal Man in Australia: Essays of Honour of Emeritus Professor A. P. Elkin*, pp. 207–237. Sydney: Angus and Roberston.

Stephens, D. W., and Charnov, E. L., 1982, Optimal foraging: Some simple stochastic models. *Behavioral Ecology and Sociobiology* 10:251–263.

Steward, J. H., 1936, The economic and social basis of primitive bands. In R. Lowie, ed., *Essays in Honor of A. L. Kroeber*, pp. 331–350. Berkeley: University of California Press.

Steward, J. H., 1937, Ecological aspects of southwestern society. *Anthropos* 32:85–104.

Steward, J. H., 1938, Basin-plateau aboriginal sociopolitical groups. *Bureau of American Ethnology Bulletin 120*.

Steward, J. H., 1955, *Theory of Culture Change*. Urbana: University of Illinois Press.

Steward, J. H., and Setzler, F. M., 1938, Function and configuration in archaeology. *American Antiquity* 4:4–10.

Street, B. V., 1975, *The Savage in Literature*. London: Routledge and Kegan Paul.

Struever, S., 1968, Woodland subsistence-settlement systems in the lower Illinois Valley. In S. R. Binford and L. R. Binford, *New Perspectives in Archaeology*, pp. 285–312. Chicago: Aldine.

Taylor, W. W., 1948, A Study of Archaeology. *American Anthropological Association Memoir 69*.

Taylor, W. W., 1972, Old wine and new skins. In M. Leone, ed., *Contemporary Archaeology: A Guide to Theory and Contributions*, pp. 28–33. Carbondale: Southern Illinois University Press.

Terray, E., 1969, *Le Marxisme devant les societes 'primitives.'* Paris: Maspero.

Terray, E., 1972, *Marxism and "Primitive" Societies*. New York: Monthly Review Press.

Thomas, D. H., 1972, Western Shoshone ecology: Settlement patterns and beyond. In D. D. Fowler, ed., *Great Basin Cultural Ecology: A Symposium*, pp. 135–153. Reno: Desert Research Institute Publications in the Social Sciences.

Thomas, D. H., 1979, *Archaeology*. New York: Holt, Rinehart, and Winston.

Thomas, D. H., 1983a, On Steward's models of Shoshonean sociopolitical organization: A great bias in the Basin? In E. Tooker, ed., *The Development of Political Organization in Native North America*, pp. 59–68. 1979 Proceedings of the American Ethnological Society.

Thomas, D. H., 1983b, The Archaeology of Monitor Valley I: Epistemology. *Anthropological Papers of the American Museum of Natural History* 58(1).

Thomas, D. H., 1983c, The Archaeology of Monitor Valley II: Gatecliff Shelter. *Anthropological Papers of the American Museum of Natural History* 59(1).

Thomas, D. H., 1986, Contemporary hunter-gatherer archaeology in America. In D. J. Meltzer and D. D. Fowler, eds., *American Archaeology: Past and Present*, pp. 237–276. Washington, DC: Smithsonian Institution Press.

Thomas, D. H., and Meyer, D., 1983, Behavioral faunal analysis of selected horizons. *Anthropological Papers of the American Museum of Natural History* 59(1):353–391.

Torrence, R., 1983, Time budgeting and hunter-gatherer technology. In G. Bailey, ed., *Hunter-Gatherer Economy in Prehistory: A European Perspective*, pp. 11–22. Cambridge: Cambridge University Press.

Trivers, R., 1971, The evolution of reciprocal altruism. *Quarterly Review of Biology* 46:35–57.

Turnbull, C. M., 1968, The importance of flux in two hunting societies. In R. B. Lee and I. Devore, eds., *Man the Hunter*, pp. 132–137. Chicago: Aldine.

Tylor, E. B., 1871, *Primitive Culture: Researches into the Development of Mythology, Philosophy, Religion, Language, Art, and Custom*. London: J. Murray.

USDA, 1963, *Composition of Foods. Agriculture Handbook 8*. Washington, DC: United States Department of Agriculture.

Vayda, A. P., 1968, Foreword. In *Pigs for the Ancestors* by R. A. Rappaport, pp. ix–xiii. New Haven: Yale University Press.

Vayda, A. P., and Rappaport, R. A., 1968, Ecology, cultural and non-cultural. In J. A. Clifton, ed., *Introduction to Cultural Anthropology*, pp. 477–497. Boston: Houghton.

Vita-Finzi, C., and Higgs, E. S., 1970, Prehistoric economy in the Mount Carmel area of Palestine: Site catchment analysis. *Proceedings of the Prehistoric Society* 36:1–37.

Ward, L., 1903, *Pure Sociology*. New York: Macmillan.

Washburn, S. L., and Lancaster, C. S., 1968, The evolution of hunting. In R. B. Lee and I. Devore, eds., *Man the Hunter*, pp. 293–303. Chicago: Aldine.

Weber, M., 1948, *The Theory of Social and Economic Organization*. Translated by A. M. Henderson and T. Parsons. New York: Free Press.

Welling, J., 1888, The law of Malthus. *American Anthropologist* 1:1–23.

Whallon, R., Jr., 1971, A computer program for monothetic subdivisive classification in archaeology. *Michigan University of Museum of Anthropology Technical Reports 1*.

Wheeler, M., 1954, *Archaeology from the Earth*. Baltimore: Penguin.

White, L., 1949, *The Science of Culture*. New York: Grove Press.

White, L., 1959, *The Evolution of Culture*. New York: McGraw-Hill.

White, R., 1982, Rethinking the Middle/Upper Paleolithic transition. *Current Anthropology* 23:169–192.

Wilke, P. J., Bettinger, R. L., King, T. F., and O'Connell, J. F., 1972, Harvest selection and domestication in seed plants. *Antiquity* 46:203–209.

Willey, G. R., and Phillips, P., 1958, *Method and Theory in American Archaeology*. Chicago: University of Chicago Press.

Willey, G. R., and Sabloff, J. A., 1980, *A History of American Archaeology*. New York: Freeman.

Williams, G., 1966, *Adaptation and Natural Selection: A Critique of Some Current Evolutionary Thought*. Princeton: Princeton University Press.

Wilmsen, E. N., 1983, The ecology of illusion: Anthropological foraging in the Kalahari. *Review in Anthropology* 10(1):9–20.

Winterhalder, B., 1977, *Foraging Strategy Adaptations of the Boreal Forest Cree: An Evaluation of Theory and Models from Evolutionary Ecology*. Doctoral dissertation, Cornell University.

Winterhalder, B., 1980, Canadian fur bearer cycles and Cree-Ojibwa hunting and trapping practices. *American Naturalist* 115:870–879.

Winterhalder, B., 1981, Optimal foraging strategies and hunter-gatherer research in anthropology. In B. Winterhalder and E. A. Smith, eds., *Hunter-Gatherer Foraging Strategies: Ethnographic and Archaeological Analyses*, pp. 13–35. Chicago: University of Chicago Press.

Winterhalder, B., 1983, Opportunity-cost foraging models for stationary and mobile predators. *American Naturalist* 122:73–84.

Winterhalder, B., 1984, Reconsidering the ecosystem concept. *Reviews in Anthropology* 11: 301–313.

Winterhalder, B., 1986a, Diet choice, risk, and food sharing in a stochastic environment. *Journal of Anthropological Archaeology* 5:369–392.

Winterhalder, B., 1986b, Optimal foraging: Simulation studies of diet choice in a stochastic environment. *Journal of Ethnobiology* 6:205–223.

Winterhalder, B., Baillargeon, W., Cappelletto, F., Daniel, Jr., I. R., and Prescott, C., 1989, The population ecology of hunter-gatherers and their prey. *Journal of Anthropological Archaeology* 7:289–328.

Winters, H. D., 1968, Value systems and trade cycles of the late Archaic in the Midwest. In S. R. and L. R. Binford, eds., *New Perspectives in Archaeology*, pp. 175–221. Chicago: Aldine.

Winters, H. D., 1974, Introduction to the new edition. In W. S. Webb, *Indian Knoll*. Knoxville: University of Tennessee Press.

Wissler, C., 1914, Material cultures of the North American Indians. *American Anthropologist* 16:447–505.

Wissler, C., 1926, *The Relation of Nature of Man in Aboriginal America*. New York: Oxford University Press.

Wobst, M. H., 1974, Boundary conditions for paleolithic systems: A simulation approach. *American Antiquity* 39(2):147–178.

Wolpe, H., 1980, Introduction. In H. Wolpe, ed., *The Articulation of Modes of Production*, pp. 1–43. London: Routledge and Kegan Paul.

Woodburn, J., 1968, Stability and flexibility in Hadza residential groupings. In R. B. Lee and I. Devore, eds., *Man the Hunter*, pp. 103–110. Chicago: Aldine.

Wynne-Edwards, V. C., 1962, *Animal Dispersion in Relation to Social Behavior*. Edinburgh: Oliver and Boyd.

Yellen, J., 1977, *Archaeological Approaches to the Present: Models for Reconstructing the Past*. New York: Academic Press.

Yengoyan, A., 1968, Demographic and ecological influences on aboriginal Australian marriage sections. In R. Lee and I. Devore, eds., *Man the Hunter*, pp. 185–199. Chicago: Aldine.

Yengoyan, A., 1979, Economy, society, and myth in aboriginal Australia. *Annual Review of Anthropology* 8:393–415.

Yengoyan, A., 1985, Digging for symbols: The archaeology of everyday material life. *Proceedings of the Prehistoric Society* 51:329–334.

Index

243

explain the replacement of native *Juncus kraussii* by *Typha orientalis* in Western Australian salt marshes. *Australian Journal of Ecology*, **15**, 57–72.

Zelazny, J. and Feierabend, J. S. (eds.) (1988). *Increasing our Wetland Resources*. Proceedings of a conference in Washington, DC October 4–7, 1987. National Wildlife Federation–Corporate Conservation Council

Zhulidov, A. V., Headley, J. V., Roberts, R. D., Nikanorov, A. M. and Ischenko, A. A. (1997). *Atlas of Russian Wetlands*, ed. M. J. Branned, translated by Y. V. Flingeffman and O. V. Zhulidov. Environment Canada, National Hydrology Research Institute, Saskatoon, Saskatchewan.

Zobel, M. (1988). Autogenic succession in boreal mires – a review. *Folia Geobot. Phytotax. Praha*, **23**, 417–45.

Index